# LEXICON URTHUS

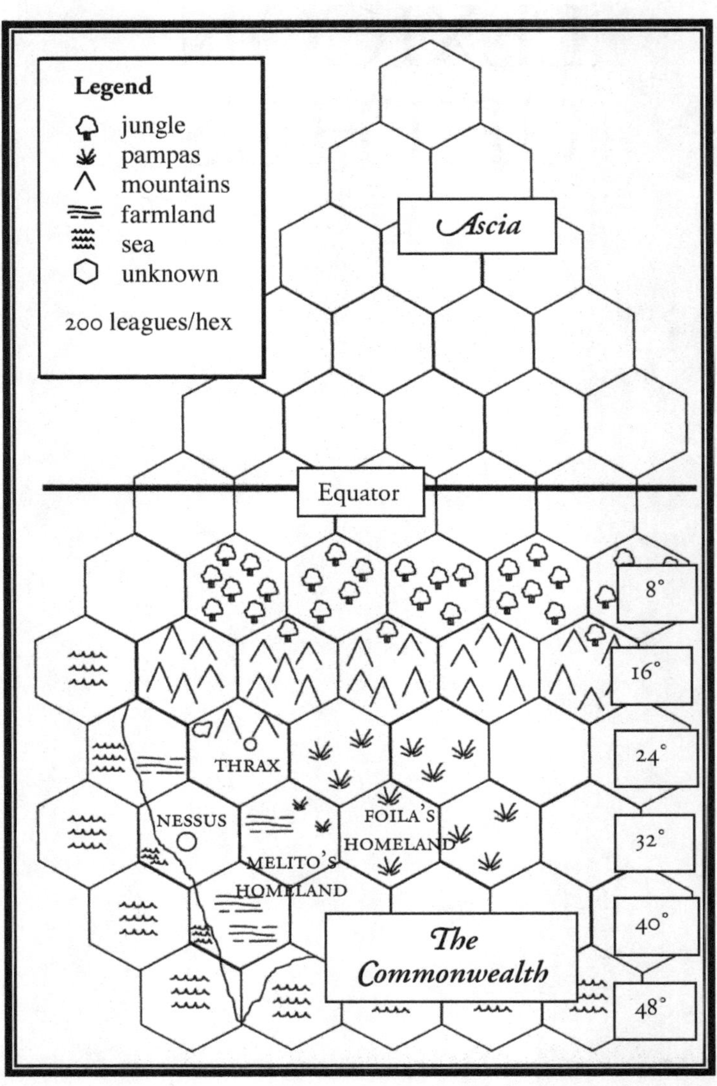

Legend
jungle
pampas
mountains
farmland
sea
unknown
200 leagues/hex
Ascia
Equator
8°
16°
24°
32°
40°
48°
THRAX
NESSUS
FOILA'S HOMELAND
MELITO'S HOMELAND
The Commonwealth

# LEXICON URTHUS

## A DICTIONARY FOR THE URTH CYCLE

SECOND EDITION

MICHAEL ANDRE-DRIUSSI

WITH A FOREWORD BY
GENE WOLFE

SIRIUS FICTION
ALBANY, CALIFORNIA

Second edition 2008; corrected 2014.

Hardcover ISBN: 978-0-9642795-0-6
Paperback ISBN: 978-0-9642795-1-3

Cover design by Nola Burger.

Map on page 412 by Mary Jo Cowart.

Printed in the United States of America.

10 9 8 7 6 5 4 3 2 1

Sirius Fiction
P.O. Box 6248
Albany, CA 94706

If *The Book of the New Sun* is "The Book of Gold," then *The Castle of the Otter* must be a Book of Silver, the work of John Clute and others constituting a Book of Copper, making this lexicon a Book of Iron, or Lead and Sweat. We find ourselves back in the oubliette.

This little book is dedicated to that Magician who, in the autumnal afternoon of November 1st, 1991, before an audience of several dozen spectators and more than a few luminaries, turned me into an imp.

I would like to say "I got better" but fear that it would be a lie.

# CONTENTS

# LIST OF SPECIAL ARTICLES AND TABLES

## LEXICOGRAPHER'S INTRODUCTION

I am pleased to present the corrected and expanded edition of the Lexicon. It incorporates materials from several chapbooks (*Additions, Errata, &cetera* [1995], *Additions, Errata, &cetera: Volume II* [1996], *Additions, Errata, &cetera: Volume III* [1998], *Synopsis of the Narrative of Severian* [1998]).

There is also new material. In the "Lexicographer's Introduction" of AE&1, I wrote:

> Other readers will feel that there are not enough characters included, i.e., the text is too short . . . I never had the intention to comb them all from the text and put each through at least two main searches (saints and mythology); such a labor would create a character list (3).

For this edition I did just such combing and processing, and I hope that it is fairly complete. There are around twenty-eight named gods, around 215 named characters, and around 90 unnamed characters (from "algophilist" to "waitress"). This totals around 330 entries. The first edition had around 110 named characters.

In the first edition, as you will see in the pages to follow, Gene Wolfe invited readers to contribute. Many of them did: by letters at first, and then by email as that technology became available. This gave rise to the first AE& chapbook.

At about the same time, Ranjit Bhatnagar started his online resource, Urth List.[1] This became a central meeting place for

[1] located at http://www.urth.net/

Wolfe fans, further expanding the population and fueling the activity. Many of us owe Ranjit a lot for setting up the Urth List and keeping it running: thank you, Ranjit! The List has proven to be a germinating place of books: Robert Borski's *Solar Labyrinth* (2004) and *The Long and the Short of It* (2006) were both spurred by conversations on the Urth List, and even an off-topic book on John Crowley's fiction (*Snake's-hands* [2003]) sprang from associations made there.

The List was not the only internet site devoted to Wolfe's fiction. Paul Duggan's Gene Wolfe Web Page[2] provides general news and links to all sorts of relevant items. Ultan's Library,[3] an online journal of Gene Wolfe studies by Jonathan Laidlow and Nigel Price, offers articles and reviews. Geoff Cohen's online resource showed great promise, with a work-in-progress character list and a chapter-by-chapter annotation for *The Shadow of the Torturer,* but it was abandoned and eventually vanished.

All this activity and easy communication meant that, where before I had drudged alone, now there was a mighty group whom I led like a chiliarch, or a vigntner, at least. Contributors to the chapbooks are Neal Baker, Nathan Bardsley, Robert Borski, Jeremy Crampton, Paul Duggan, Charles Dye, Doug Eigsti, Ted Gerney, David Langford, David Lebling, James B. Jordan, Don Keller, Mike Marano, Peeter Piegaze, Mark Pitcavage, Darrell Schweitzer, Lester Sharpless, Michael Swanwick, Adam Thornton, Alice K. Turner, Peter Westlake, Curt Wiederhoeft, and Jeff Wilson.

---

[2] located at http://mysite.verizon.net/~vze2tmhh/wolfe.html

[3] located at http://www.ultan.org.uk/index.html

The new material for inclusion was proofread by Roy C. Lackey, Adam Stephanides, and Alice K. Turner. Naturally there are bound to be new mistakes, all mine.

I must single out Roy C. Lackey for special thanks. He put in a tremendous amount of work with me on the very difficult calendar section. He also worked on the question of exultant heights, details of duality and duplicity (the two busts of Severian under "abscititious," the gender of the COOK OF THE INN OF LOST LOVES) and many other elements too embedded to list here. Though he chooses to remain unpublished, he is a first-rate Wolfe scholar whose grasp of the texts is exemplary, and I always value his keen insights.

— Michael Andre-Driussi

*Colossal Statue of Mount Athos*

Original caption: "as designed by Dinocrates, architect to Alexander the Great, who formed a project of cutting the mount [Mount Athos] into the image of a man sitting, who in one hand was to hold a basin which was to be a reservoir for the water that issued from the top of the mountain, from whence in its passage to the sea it was to run through a city part whereof was to be built in his lap. Alexander thought this design worthy of his greatness but never attempted to put it in execution. Printed for John Bowles at the Black Horse in Cornhill, 1741." A likely inspiration for Mount Typhon.

# FOREWORD (GENE WOLFE, 1994)

In *The Castle of the Otter* I tried to provide a brief glossary for *The Shadow of the Torturer,* listing some unusual words in the order in which they occurred in the book. Several readers have complained about that format, saying with varying degrees of politeness and vehemence that they would have preferred to have the words in alphabetical order; many more have asked for similar glossaries for *The Claw of the Conciliator, The Sword of the Lictor, The Citadel of the Autarch,* and *The Urth of the New Sun.* A few have even gone so far as to suggest a single alphabetical volume covering the whole series.

That is what Michael Andre-Driussi gives us here, with far more dogged determination and painstaking scholarship than I could ever have brought to bear on the project. His part of this text — that is to say, everything except the bit you're reading — lists all the individual words that may have puzzled or (as I hope) delighted you, and explains them.

My part here, at least as I have defined it, is to answer the questions I've been asked about the words used in these books in general:

"Why did you use so many funny words?" Because I thought them the best ones for the story I was trying to tell. We who write fiction try to make each character speak in character; Severian, for example, should talk like a thoughtful man whose education has been in a practical discipline. In just the same way, a book should speak like the sort of book it is — and it is, by a delightful paradox, the sort of book that its language makes it.

"Why are there words in your books that I can't find in my dictionary?" Because your dictionary doesn't contain all the words of even the English language. Many people seem to think that an unabridged dictionary is one that lists every word. No publisher of dictionaries would make that claim. To abridge a thing is to shorten it. (Severian's area of expertise, as it happens.) Lexicographers begin by composing and publishing an unabridged dictionary, then cut it down to create a collegiate dictionary, one or more desk dictionaries, and so on. Here I can't resist adding that Samuel Johnson, who was very nearly the first lexicographer and surely one of the greatest, defined a lexicographer as *a writer of dictionaries; a harmless drudge, that busies himself in tracing the original, and detailing the signification of words.*

The very learned lexicographers responsible for *The Oxford English Dictionary* try to include every English word in theirs, but would be the first to admit that their goal is unattainable though their dictionary runs to dozens of unwieldy volumes. If this talk of dictionary-making interests you, I suggest you go on to Johnson's when you've finished this one. After that, you can dip into *The Oxford English Dictionary,* to see what Johnson started. Either should tell you that *abridge* comes from the Latin *ad brevis,* "toward shortness."

"Why is it I felt I understood so many of your obscure words, when I don't know what they mean?" In the first place, you know a great many Latin and Greek roots that you're not conscious of knowing. Take *theogony,* which means the origin of the gods, as this book will explain. You undoubtedly know the word *theology,* which has taught you that *theo* pertains to divinity (Greek *theos,* god). You also know *gonad* as the name of the male reproductive gland (Greek *gonos,* "that which is begotten.") Since you're intelligent enough to see jokes for what they are — half irrelevancy and half clue — you quickly and almost unconsciously make a guess that hits the mark or at least comes very close.

In the second place, I have tried to employ these seldom-seen words in a context in which they *would* be employed by a writer like Severian. There is an enormous difference between meeting an unusual word that has been trotted out to show off, and meeting it in a meaningful context. Some years ago, I read an account of an American who knew no German and a German who knew no English building a boat together. The American would say, "Bring me a flat board," and the German would bring him a board of the proper size. They were actually doing something, you see; and the German understood what it was they were doing. Because they were working together (exactly as a writer and a reader must) the unintelligible request was heard as "I need something," and the German had little difficulty guessing what was needed.

Why bother, in that case, to learn English? Or German? Why do you need a book like this one? In the narrowest sense, you don't. You can get through the whole *Book of the New Sun* without it; and it's more than likely that you already have. But knowing is better and broader and deeper than even the best guessing, and knowing is more fun. Think how much the American would have liked to know German, and how much the German would have liked to know English.

"Didn't you make up most of the funny words?" I tried not to make up any, but there are several I misspelled, and a few more that the typesetter misspelled. This book will point them out and give you the words they should have been.

"Where did you find so many obscure words?" Anywhere I could, to tell the truth. In *Roget's International Thesaurus,* to begin with. Do you know that wonderful moment in *The Bored of the Rings* when the thesaurus rises from the pool roaring, "Maim! Mutilate, mangle, crush. See HARM"? In *The New York Times Everyday Reader's Dictionary of Misunderstood, Misused, Mispronounced Words; Allen's Synonyms and Antonyms;* and *Mrs. Byrne's Dictionary of Unusual, Obscure, and Preposterous Words.*

And (of course) in *The Compact Oxford English Dictionary,* in

*A Glossary of the Construction, Decoration and Use of Arms and Armor in All Countries and in All Times* (usually called *Stone,* from the name of its author); and in the big unabridged dictionary that my father's master left behind when he went away to fight the First World War without his apprentice. In other places as well — where I could find them, as I said.

If you'd like to follow in my footsteps, here's a secret technique: Get a good English-Latin dictionary, of which there are many, and *Woodhouse's English-Greek Dictionary.* When you need a rare or unusual word, look up the nearest equivalent in English, then check the Latin and Greek roots in an unabridged dictionary.

Lastly, a question you haven't asked. Is everything in this book right? No, it's not. The problem is that although mistakes have been made, neither Michael Andre-Driussi nor I know where they are. He has already found and fixed dozens if not hundreds, and I have found a few myself — and asked him to fix them.

But no book like this can be written and published without a few errors creeping in. If you find one, please write to Michael and tell him. He will be happy to get your letter, happy that you have bought his book, happy that you have read it with attention, and happy that you cared enough to write a letter in the hope of improving it. And if you're wrong, he'll be even happier.

We both will.

— Gene Wolfe

## ACKNOWLEDGMENTS (1994)

This harmless drudge would like to thank those Professionals who helped him navigate the dark and torturous Library of Nessus in search of words wild and wooly, to wit: John Brunner, who graciously volunteered to read an earlier draft and pointed out several vexing errors; Greer Gilman, who found the very hardest words after I had all but given up; Lois Tilton and Jennifer Stevenson for tidbits here and there; Debbie Notkin and other Change of Hobbits for *Mrs. Byrne's* as well as a crash-course in how to read Greek dictionaries; and Gene Wolfe himself, who helped a great deal as well as being a good sport about it.

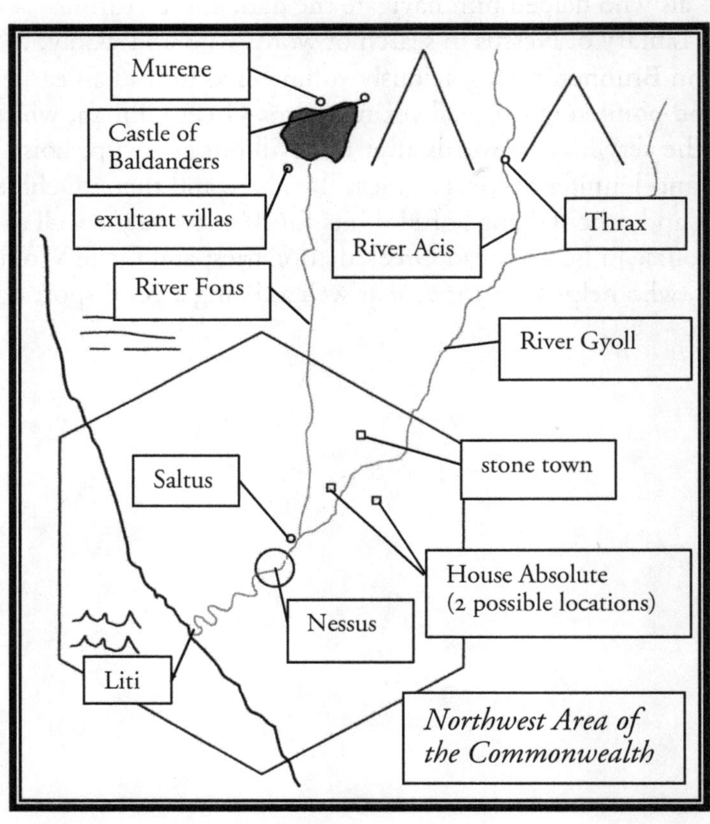
Murene
Castle of Baldanders
exultant villas
River Acis
Thrax
River Fons
River Gyoll
stone town
Saltus
House Absolute
(2 possible locations)
Nessus
Liti
*Northwest Area of the Commonwealth*

a brief

Lexicon for Gene Wolfe's

*The Book of the New Sun,*

*The Urth of the New Sun*, and

*Empires of Foliage and Flower* as

well as Shorter Stories, including

glosses on Biblical Allusions,

Ships of Sail and Oar,

Kabbalistic Notions,

Archaic English Words,

Diverse Arms and Armor,

Extinct and Exotic Animals,

Latin Terms military and civic,

in addition to Myths and Legends

from China, Greece, Arabia, Oceania,

Rome, India, Persia, and South America.

## A NOTE ON CITATIONS

I = *The Shadow of the Torturer* (first edition)
II = *The Claw of the Conciliator* (first edition)
III = *The Sword of the Lictor* (first edition)
IV = *The Citadel of the Autarch* (first edition)
V = *The Urth of the New Sun* (first edition)

CD = *Castle of Days*
EFF = *Empires of Foliage and Flower*
ES = *Endangered Species*
IA = *Innocents Aboard*
PE = *Plan[e]t Engineering*
SS = *Starwater Strains*
ST = *Strange Travelers*

OED = *Oxford English Dictionary*

For purists who question the use of "v" as an abbreviation for The Urth of the New Sun (which suggests that Urth is the fifth book in the series, rather than a stand-alone sequel), the following rationale is offered: the "v" is not for "volume five," but for "Urth," harkening to that time when the Latin "V" was used as both a consonant and a vowel.

The "Urth Cycle" is a term of my own invention [1994] for all the Urth related material.

**abacination** “Where are their abacinations, that shall leave them blind?” (I, chap. 30, 258). To blind by placing hot irons, or metal plates, in front of the eyes. See HETHOR.

**Abaddon** “All of us know they exist, many being mere endless plains of rock, others spheres of ice or cindery hills where lava rivers flow, as is alleged of Abaddon” (III, chap. 12, 101). Possibly the planet Mercury (see SOLAR SYSTEM TABLE), but a more hellish, other-dimensional place seems implied. Two candidates for such a region are the “subspace” universe from which the mirror creatures of specula are drawn (different from the “hyperspace” of Yesod), and the noisy (yet lava-free) interior of the worldship Yesod. See YESOD: THE MECHANICS OF HYPERSPACE.
*Literature:* used in Revelations as the name of “the angel of the bottomless pit” from a Greek word for “destroyer,” and applied by Milton to the abyss of hell itself.

**Abaia** “It is a thing from Erebus, from Abaia, a fit companion for me” (I, chap. 12, 118). A lord of the Other People, Abaia is one of the great monsters of Urth, a malignant, aquatic being that manipulates the ASCIANS into war in the hope of enslaving the entire population of Urth. Abaia is a “warm” monster with a host of undine concubines, in contrast to the icy EREBUS. Abaia is the size of a mountain (II, chap. 8, 70), and perhaps he is glimpsed

among the giants in Severian's undine-sent dream (I, chap. 15, 140). See ARIOCH; SCYLLA.
*Myth:* (Melanesian) a giant magic eel inhabiting the waters of a lake in the South Pacific, Abaia became angry when an old woman caught fish in his lake, so he sent a deluge. Only an old woman who had eaten of the magic fish escaped.

**Abban** a monstrously fat man in an apron, he is the owner of the Inn of Lost Loves, located in Nessus near the Sanguinary Field (I, chap. 25, 219). He employs Ouen, Trudo, the cook of the Inn of Lost Loves, and the kitchen girl.
*Onomastics:* "white" (Latin); "abbot" (Irish).
*History:* there are two Saints Abban: the 5th-century Irish founder of Kill-Abban Abbey in Leinster, nephew of Saint Ibar; and the 6th-century nephew of Saint Kevin. (See IBAR.)

**Abdiesus** Archon of Thrax (I, chap. 13, 123). An exultant, his face is coarse, with a hook nose and large eyes rimmed with dark flesh; his robe is perfumed with musk (I, chap. 13, 123). (See PERFUME.)
*Onomastics:* "servant of Jesus"? (Arabic).
*History:* Saint Abdiesus, or "Hebedjesus" (A.D. 341–380), was one of the vast multitude of Persians martyred under King Shapur II.

**ablegate** Severian sees a person at the RIDOTTO in the costume of an ablegate (III, chap. 4, 42), so the office must exist in the Commonwealth, if only in legend. Perhaps the autarch takes the place of the papal see as the source of authority.
*History:* an envoy of the papal see who brings a newly appointed cardinal his insignia of office.

**Abraxas** "Abraxas perceives all of time as an eternal instant" (II, chap. 31, 289).
*History:* Gnostic god identified with both Mithra and Jehovah, called "Our Father" and "Lord of Hosts" in the early Christian era. Like Mithra, Abraxas represented "the 365 Aeons," 365,000 years allotted to the present world's life span (based upon the Hindu idea that one god year equals 1,000 man-years). Mithra and Abraxas were gods of numerology, and the numeric value of their names each totaled 365. Orthodox Christianity came to view Abraxas as a demon; at the same time, he was assimilated to the Gnostic "Lord of this World" whose attributes were both divine and demonic. As the creator of the material universe, he was declared a devil by way of the Gnostic opinion that all matter was evil. Through the Medieval Period, Abraxas was a favorite deity of several heretical sects. He is usually depicted with the torso and arms of a man, the head of a cock, and serpents for legs. See GNOSTICISM.

**abscititious** [presumably "ab-skih-TIH-shus"] "I've seen his portrait and his bust. They're in the Hypogeum Abscititious, where the Autarch put them when she married again" (V, chap. 44, 314).
*Latin: abscido,* "to tear off, wrench away"; transferred into "to divide or separate."
*Commentary:* there are two types of Severian's portrait and bust discussed in the text. One type is realistic, showing him with scarred cheek (314), and the other type is idealistic, showing him the way Valeria thought he might look upon his return from Yesod, the scar on his cheek erased (V, chap. 43, 303). Or there is only one set and Valeria is lying about the idealistic one.

**Abundantius** the chief sorcerer in the arboreal village (III, chap. 21, 170).
*History:* unreliable sources call Saint Abundantius (died 304?) a deacon in Rome, who, along with a priest Abundius, a senator Marcian, and the latter's son John, was beheaded during the persecution of Diocletian.

**acarya** "I have talked with the heptarch and with various acaryas" (IV, chap. 31, 253).
*History:* ("one who knows the rules") a Hindu religious teacher, or any illustrious or learned person in India.

**accretive** "Our destination was one of those accretive structures seen in the older parts of the city . . . in which the accumulation and interconnection of what were originally separate buildings produce a confusion of jutting wings and architectural styles" (I, chap. 9, 87).
*History:* growing by accretion; increase by external addition or accumulation.

**achico** a South American missile consisting of three balls connected by a strong cord, which is thrown to bring down an enemy's horse or a hunted animal by becoming entangled around its legs (II, chap. 14, 118). "Bolas" is a more general term for this weapon. (A similar weapon is the somai, a two-balled South American bolas.)

**achroma** "I saw they were of a hue for which I can find no name but that stands to achroma as gold to yellow, or silver to white" (IV, chap. 21, 166).

*History:* gray.

**Acies Castle** [uh-KEY-us] the castle situated at the first cataract of the Acis River, overlooking Thrax (III, chap. 1, 9). It is the chief administrative building of the city, where court is in session every two weeks, "from the first appearance of the new moon to the full" (III, chap. 1, 10). It is not the residence of the archon, who lives in a palace near the river.
*Latin:* "the sword point."

**Acis River** [UH-kiss] a tributary to Gyoll, the Acis River has at least two cataracts, the first being at Thrax (III, chap. 1, 7).
*Myth:* (Greek) Acis was the son of Faunus and a Naiad. The cyclops Polyphemus loved the goddess Galatea, but she spurned him for Acis. Enraged, Polyphemus hurtled a mountain at Acis and killed him. Galatea endowed Acis with the honors of his grandfather, a river-god, and thus Acis was changed into a river.

**acosmist** "Just as summer-killed meat draws flies, so the court draws spurious sages, philosophists, and acosmists" (III, chap. 38, 295).
*History:* one who denies the existence of the universe or its distinctness from God.

**Adamnian Steps** "I think the Adamnian Steps will be to our right" (I, chap. 19, 170). A landmark in the Botanic Garden area of Nessus. The head of the stairs is marked by statues of the eponyms. The steps are of white stone and are sometimes very gradual, other times as abrupt as a ladder. The sides are lined with venders selling apes, confections, and other items. The steps wind

back and forth across a long hillside and are flanked by brutal busts.
*History:* there is a saint Adomnan (a.k.a. Adamnan, Adam, Eunan), A.D. 627–704, abbot of Iona. He wrote up "the Law of Adomnan" (Cain Adomnain) which protected women by exempting them from combat and insisting that women, boys, and clergy be treated by all as non-combatants. These rules came to be accepted throughout Ireland circa A.D. 727. This is interesting because on the Adamnian Steps, Agia is leading Severian toward combat.

**Adonai** "a phoebad put forward as an ultimate truth the ancient sophistry of the existence of three Adonai, that of the city (or of the people), that of the poets, and that of the philosophers" (III, chap. 38, 295).
*History:* one of the names given in the Old Testament to the deity; a name of the supreme being.

**aelurodon** [ee-LURE-o-don] "Beasts — aelurodons, lumbering spelaeae, and slinking shapes to which I could put no name . . . moved among the dead" (II, chap. 31, 292). Severian glimpses these creatures during the resurrection of the stone town, so they may be native to Apu-Punchau's time in the Age of Myth or come from an even earlier period.
*History:* a wolf-like panther, common ancestor of both canines and felines, that reached a peak of geographic expansion in the Miocene epoch.

**aeronaut** a person who serves in the autarch's aerial force, in the air-galleys and flyers (IV, chap. 24, 197).

**aes** [EE-S] in the Commonwealth, a small provincial coin of brass, bronze, or copper (I, chap. 16, 151). A single aes buys an egg. See MEASUREMENT TABLES.
*History:* a Roman coin of bronze or copper.

**agamite** "But as we were setting up our theater yesterday, a highly placed servant from the House Absolute — an agamite, I think, and they are always close to the ear of authority — came asking if our troupe was the one in which you performed" (II, chap. 26, 247).
*History:* a sexless being.

**agathodaemon** "That there is no agathodaemon or afterlife. That the mind is extinguished in death as in sleep, yet more so" (I, chap. 8, 79).
*Myth:* a good divinity or minor spirit.

**Age of Myth** the earliest named period of post-history (V, chap. 41, 294). See HISTORY OF URTH.

**Agia** twin sister of Agilus, with whom she runs a used clothing shop in Nessus (I, chap. 18, 161). She is of average height, full-figured, and narrow-waisted (III, chap. 15, 117). She has "an upturned nose and strangely tilted eyes" (I, chap. 17, 157). Her skin is pale gold and her rich brown hair goes halfway down her back. She says she is twenty-three years old (I, chap. 26, 227). Agilus is her lover, but after he is executed by Severian, Agia pursues him relentlessly, enlisting Hethor to help her.

> "If I had withheld my body I could have done nothing with him, but I did all the queer little things he wished me to do, and made him believe I love him. Now he will do anything I ask" (III, chap. 15, 119).

(Based on Hethor's terms "scopolagna" and "poppet," perhaps she acts like a doll for him.) The eternal adversary, Agia eventually kills and replaces Vodalus. See FAMILY TREES.
*Onomastics:* "holy (feminine)" (Greek).
*History:* "Agia" is another name for Saint Austregildis, who was the mother of Saint Loup of Sens. Agia (died 714), the wife of Saint Hydulphus of Hainault (she entered the nunnery of Mons while he joined the monks of Lobbes), is especially venerated by the Beguines of Belgium.

**Agilus** twin brother of Agia (I, chap. 18, 161). He covets *Terminus Est,* and conspires with Agia to kill Severian by using trickery at the Sanguinary Field. His plans go awry, however, and while trying to escape he kills several spectators. He is captured, quickly sentenced, and executed.
*History:* Saint Agilus (A.D. 580–650) was a Frankish nobleman, a monk under Saint Columbanus, and later abbot of Rebais near Paris.

**agnation** "But when our Autarch came for us and we woke to life, we found no agnation in all that we had studied" (V, chap. 42, 300). Valeria found no connection between her book-studies and real life.

*History:* meaning "relation," from *agnate,* related on or descended from the father or male side; from a common source, kin. Figuratively, kinship by descent.

**agouti** a meat served at the torturers' feast (I, chap. 11, 105); "I recalled the agoutis served at our masking banquets, with their fur of spiced coconut and their eyes of preserved fruits" (II, chap. 11, 98).
*History: Dasyprocta agouti* is a short-eared animal the size and appearance of a hare, common in the West Indies and adjacent parts of South America.

**alcalde** "There's going to be a fair, you know. The alcalde announced it" (II, chap. 1, 10).
*History:* a magistrate of a town; a sheriff or justice. (Origin: Spain and Portugal.)

**Alcmund** a Vodalarius named in passing (II, chap. 11, 93).
*History:* there are two Saints Alcmund. One (died 781) was the seventh bishop of Hexham. The other (died 800) had many years of exile among the Picts of Scotland, and was martyred.

**Alcyone** name of Captain Hadelin's ship on Urth in reign of Typhon (V, chap. 30, 213). Members of the crew include COOK OF THE ALCYONE, MATE OF THE ALCYONE, and SAILOR, BRAWNY.
*Myth:* (Greek) Alcyone (or Halcyone) was the daughter of Aeolus (keeper of winds). When her husband Ceyx died in a shipwreck, Alcyone threw herself into the sea, and the gods changed the two of them into the halcyon birds, fabled animals identified with the kingfisher. While the halcyons are breeding, Aeolus holds back

his winds and the seas are calm. Thus the halcyon became a symbol of tranquility, and the term "halcyon days" a period of prosperity. Another myth has Alcyone as one of the Pleiades, and beloved of Poseidon.
*Commentary:* a fitting name in light of the episode where Severian saves the ship from destruction by calming the storm (raised by his unconscious anger).

**alfange** "an ancient alfange, for years past an ornament" (II, chap. 17, 145).
*History:* the Spanish form of the Persian word *khanjar,* a knife or dagger.

**Algedonic Quarter** meaning "pain and pleasure district," the semi-ruinous section of Nessus in which the Citadel is located (I, chap. 8, 84).
*Commentary:* the name probably alludes to the presence of both the Matachin Tower of the torturers and the Echopraxia brothel within the area.

**algophilist** "She came near to making an algophilist of me" (II, chap. 23, 207), as Severian writes regarding Jolenta. Meaning "a person who has a morbid pleasure in the pain either of oneself or of others; a masochist or a sadist." On the night before the execution of Agilus, Severian encounters a group of five torture enthusiasts (I, chap. 30, 256), three men and two women:

- A tall fat man, an exultant bastard, aged fifty or more. Severian sees him and the two women close to the scaffold at the execution (I, chap. 31, 264). When Agilus is beheaded this man seems to have a sexual climax (265).

- A thin woman of twenty or so, with hungry eyes and a lamia aspect.
- A short and slight man, with the high bumpy forehead of an intellectual (this man gives Severian an asimi). He might be BEUZEC.
- A woman with gray hair straggling over her face, who gives Severian a handkerchief to dip in the blood.
- A smaller, grayer man who later turns out to be HETHOR.

**alouatte** "We can try to hide behind the trunks like alouattes" (II, chap. II, 91).
*History:* the Howling Monkey of South America.

**alraune** "They'd fight like alraunes if either of you tried to have anything to do with them. They're sacred and forbidden, the Daughters of War" (IV, chap. 22, 176).
*Myth:* (Germanic) female demon.

**alticamelus** [ALL-tee-ka-MEE-lus] "Or inquire at the alticamelus around the corner on Velleity" (I, chap. 23, 205).
*History:* a prehistoric camel resembling a giraffe, here used as a sign for a tavern.

**Alto** given as a very common name in the Commonwealth of Severian's youth, along with Bolcan (II, chap. 15, 130).
*History:* Saint Alto (died 760?), believed to be Irish, appeared in Germany in 743 as a hermit.

**alzabo** an animal (probably extraterrestrial in origin) that assumes the personality of the prey it has devoured (I, chap. 35, 293). It is red in color, roughly the size of a destrier, with jaws

"large enough to bite a man's head as a man bites an apple," and claws larger and coarser than those of a bear. On Urth its habitat is the snow swept tablelands.
*Arabic:* an archaic transliteration of "al-dhi'b," meaning wolf, jackal, or a star in Canis.
*Legend:* Pliny's description of the hyena (*Natural History,* book VIII) tells of an animal that can simulate human speech as well as remember a person's name in order to call him out of doors and eat him. Furthermore, Pliny writes that this animal alone digs up graves in search of corpses.
*Commentary:* the alzabo may very well be the "ghoul-bear" of the planet Sainte Anne in Wolfe's *The Fifth Head of Cerberus.*

**amadou** "I lifted them from each drawer to see if there was not a steel, igniter, or syringe of amadou beneath them" (IV, chap. 36, 294).
*History:* a German tinder, prepared from a species of fungus that grows on trees, employed as both a match and a styptic. The origin of the term is uncertain: some sources (including *Chambers* and *Collins*) trace it through French (*Collins* takes it further back to Latin *amator,* "lover," the rationale being that the tinder readily ignites). The OED notes French *amadouer* "to allure," but also gives Old Norse *mata* (Danish *made*) "to feed." Thanks to John Brunner for pointing out this complication.

**Amand, Saint** mentioned by Abban, innkeeper of the Inn of Lost Loves, "May moderation and St. Amand bless you, sieur" (I, chap. 25, 222).
*History:* a French monk (A.D. 584–679), famous for missionary work and founding numerous monasteries in Belgium.

*Commentary:* this is the only instance within the Urth Cycle of a saint being invoked as a saint (that is, Katharine is called Holy Katharine, not Saint Katharine; the patron saints of the guilds are called simply "patrons"; and even the eponyms, whose busts line the Twisted Way, might be logically construed as being de-emphasized saints).

**amaranthine** "The giantesses lift arms like the trunks of sycamores, each finger tipped with an amaranthine talon" (II, chap. 8, 72). A color, being "a dark reddish-purple." See HYPOGEUM AMARANTHINE.
*History:* of or pertaining to amarant(h), a supposedly everlasting flower; or by extension fadeless, immortal, undying.

**amphisbaena** Severian's name for a CONSTELLATION (III, chap. 14, 101). See also UROBOROS.
*Myth:* a fabled serpent of the ancients, with a head at each end, and able to move in either direction.
*History:* a Gnostic symbol.

**amphitryon** the name of a tribe of the Commonwealth's extreme north (III, chap. 2, 18). As the name means "harassing on either side" in Greek, perhaps the tribe inhabits the region of Orithyia, which is hotly fought over by both Ascia and the Commonwealth.
*Myth:* Amphitryon was the king of Thebes and foster father of Heracles.
*History:* a host, an entertainer to dinner.

**amschaspand** “As though an amschaspand had touched them with his radiant wand, the fog swirled and parted to let a beam of green moonlight fall” (1, chap. 1, 14). A term for an intermediary being between the Increate and Man, an angelic being. The Urth word for Hierogrammate.
*Myth:* a Zoroastrian archangel. There are only six of them (or seven, in some sources where Vohu Manah is included) and they attend upon Ahura Mazda in Persian mythology: Vohu Manah (also Bahman), the recording angel; Asha, angel of truth; Kshathra Vairya, personifying might, majesty, dominion, and power; Armaiti, devotion; Haurvatat, integrity; Ameretat, immortality; and Sraosha, obedience. Asha seems the closest parallel to Tzadkiel.

**anacreontic** “Some days passed before I could rid my thoughts of Thecla of certain impressions belonging to the false Thecla who had initiated me into the anacreontic diversions and fruitions of men and women” (1, chap. 10, 95).
*History:* convivial and amatory, after the manner of the Greek poet Anacreon.

**anacrisis** “His expression was the one I have seen our clients wear when Master Gurloes showed them the instruments to be used in their anacrisis” (1, chap. 21, 190).
*History:* preliminary hearing, or interrogation accompanied by torture.

**anagnost** “I saw two cataphracts, an anagnost reading prayers, Master Gurloes, and a young woman” (1, chap. 12, 111).

*History:* a reader, a prelector; one employed to read aloud; the reader of the lessons in church.

**analeptic** "The analeptic alzabo is prepared from a gland at the base of the animal's skull. Do you understand me?" (II, chap. 10, 90).
*History:* restorative, comforting.

**anchorite** "A sentence, or a phrase, some say even a single word, that can be wrung from the lips of a certain statue, or read in the firmament, or that an anchorite on a world across the seas teaches his disciples?" (I, chap. 32, 271).
*History:* a person who has withdrawn or secluded himself from the world; a recluse, a holy hermit.

**ancilla** "Hardly well mannered for you to introduce yourself in such a way, Pega. You were her ancilla" (V, chap. 44, 312). See SOUBRETTE.
*History:* a maidservant, a handmaid.

**android** "Sidero was an android, then, an automaton in human form such as my friend Jonas had once been" (V, chap. 8, 58). The mechanical men of the star-sailing ships, often referred to as "sailors," which see. The androids trace their evolution from the earliest space suits. Some of them, like Sidero, are hollow and large enough that they may be worn like a suit of armor. Others, like Jonas, are human sized. It may be that the hollow ones are non-commissioned officers, and the smaller ones are commissioned officers. Named characters include Hadid, Hierro, Sidero, and Zelazo.

*History:* the term, meaning "man-like," first appeared in English in 1727, in reference to the attempts of the alchemist Albertus Magnus to create a homunculus, or artificial man. It was commonly used in science fiction until the 1940s. Tangled and confused with the term *robot,* android has come to usually denote an artificial man of organic substance. But like the application of "robot" to such creatures (e.g., the original robots of *R.U.R.*), there is also a tradition of using "android" to describe mechanical men.
*Commentary:* "robot" is too modern a term, and its Czech roots have no place in the cultural tapestry of Urth, in contrast to the Greek roots of "android." See ROBOT.

**androsphinx** statues erected in the ages before Typhon to memorialize the thinking machines (III, chap. 6, 54).
*Myth:* a fantastic creature having the body of a lion with human head and hands, symbolizing the union of intellectual and physical powers.

**angelus** a prayer, mentioned for the amount of time required to say it, presumably around a minute and a half (I, chap. 23, 202). See TEMPORAL under MEASUREMENT TABLES.
*History:* a devotional prayer said by Roman Catholics at morning, noon, and sunset, at the sound of a bell rung for that purpose.

**Anian** in Typhon's era, one of the best wood carvers of Gurgustii (V, chap. 30, 209). He and Ceallach make a staff for the Conciliator (V, chap. 33, 236).

*History:* Saint Anian ("Sanch Anian" in the Occitan dialect of French), a disciple of Benoit d'Aniane, in A.D. 825 founded a monastery in what is now Saint Chinian of Southern France.

**animal associations** many characters in Severian's narrative have specific animals associated with them.
- Burgundofara: red roe.
- Cumaean: reptile.
- Dorcas: gazelle.
- Fechin: red monkey.
- Gunnie: cow/blue bird.
- Hildegrin: arctother/badger.
- Inire: monkey/ibis.
- Old Autarch: ox.
- Severian: wolf.
- Dr. Talos: fox.
- Thea: dove.

**anpiel** a member of the Autarch's elite aerial forces (IV, chap. 20, 163). Anpiels have the bodies of slender young women with rainbow-colored wings, and in combat they fight naked, with a pistol (of stellar technology) in each hand. Each squadron is led by a seraph.
*Myth:* from rabbinic lore, an angel in charge of the protection of birds, who resides in the Sixth Heaven.

**Anskar** Hallvard's uncle, murdered by his own brother Gundalf (IV, chap. 7, 54).
*Onomastics:* "spear of God."

*History:* Saint Anskar (A.D. 800–865), native of Denmark, named first archbishop of Hamburg.

**antechamber** a prison for those accused of less serious crimes committed within the precincts of the House Absolute (II, chap. 16, 139).
*History:* a waiting room or outer office, but it implies the existence of a chamber, or inner office. While the prison is certainly a "waiting" room, it is also in rather close proximity to a genuine chamber: the Presence Chamber.

**antepilani** "The men who followed him on foot were antepilani of the heavy infantry, big shouldered and narrow waisted, with sun-bronzed, expressionless faces" (IV, chap. 1, 12).
*History:* Roman front-line (hastati) and second-line (principes). The third-line soldiers were known as triarii or pilani (hence the name).

**anthroposophy** "[Baldanders] had accelerated the growth of this poor boy in so far as was possible to his anthroposophic knowledge" (III, chap. 35, 280). Seemingly a synthesis of all sciences relating to the human body, a "magical" knowledge which enables Baldanders to create homunculi, accelerate growth, and even modify his own body.
*Greek:* "the wisdom of man."
*History:* a spiritualistic movement split from Theosophy. Rudolf Steiner (A.D. 1861–1925) originated the term, though it was used in a different sense in the 17th century by Rosicrucian Thomas Vaughn as *anthroposophica theomagica.* Steiner's anthroposophy is

an attempt to create a spiritual science whereby man can come into harmony with himself, and the universe.

**Antrustione** in the Commonwealth, a foreigner voluntarily serving the autarch (IV, chap. 35, 288).
*History:* a voluntary follower of the Old Frankish princes at the period of the national migrations.

**Apeiron** "the male's seed penetrates the female body to produce (if it be the will of Apeiron) a new human being" (IV, chap. 19, 147). A god of procreation or a similar aspect of the INCREATE.
*Myth:* the unlimited, indeterminate, and indefinite ground, origin, or primal principle of all matter, postulated especially by Anaximander, the ancient Greek philosopher.

**Apheta** a Hierogrammate larva (V, chap. 19, 138), she is Severian's lover, also his mother, in a sense (V, chap. 20, 145).
*History:* "The giver of life in a nativity" from the astrological term for a planet which starts a human being in his career (OED).
*Onomastics:* a Greek word meaning "starting place," attached to several places, including a street in Argos where suitors for the hands of the Danaids were to start their foot race; the starting point in Sparta for the race in which Odysseus won Penelope as a bride; and the place in Magnesia from which the *Argo* sailed on the expedition for the Golden Fleece. (There is also a hint of "apheta" as meaning "without speech" in the way that the character has no vocal cords but shapes ambient sound into words.)

**Aphrodisius** a lover of Thecla (IV, chap. 2, 21).
*Onomastics:* the word *aphrodisi* means "sexual desire" (Greek).
*History:* Saint Aphrodisius (5th century) was martyred by Arian Vandals in northern Africa.

**apocatastasis** "Yet I am as I am, your own race having made us so before the apocatastasis," as Tzadkiel says to Severian (V, chap. 21, 151). Here it seems to refer to the birth of Briah, the universe Severian was born into.
*History:* restoration, re-establishment, renovation; return to a previous condition.

**apostis** a part of a ship (V, chap. 27, 194).
*History:* the hulls of classical galleys were very narrow (for speed) and the thole pins against which the oars bore were held in a balcony-like affair, called the apostis, which extended from the side of the ship, running the length of the hull.

**apotropaic** designed to avert or avoid evil. See HOUSE ABSOLUTE.
*History:* literally "turning away," descriptive of any protective device, such as garlic worn to fend off vampires or the Eye of Horus to avert the evil eye.

**Appian** "The Autarch Appian permitted her to leave our House Absolute at once" (ES, 215). Penultimate autarch of Urth, the "old" autarch, the second autarch to take the test and fail (the first being Ymar). See also MARUTHAS.
*History:* Via Appia ("Appian Way") is the oldest and best preserved of all Roman roads, commenced by Appius Claudius, the

censor, in 312 B.C. There are also two Saints Appian: one a martyr at Caesarea in Palestine during the persecution of Galerius and Maximian (died 306), the other a Benedictine monk who evangelized the Adriatic area (died c. 800). All three Appians may be said to have paved the way for others. Curiously, the word *appianus* can refer to a cheap green pigment (see VIRIDIAN). Finally there is the word "apian" [AY-pee-uhn], an adjective meaning "of or related to bees," which seems significant since the old autarch seems to have served in his youth in the House Absolute under the honey steward Paeon.

**apport** the categorical name for a creature created or captured by the sails of a ship that travels between the stars (V, chap. 2, 13). See ZAK.
*History:* motion or production of an object by a spiritualist medium without apparent physical agency, or the object so produced.

**Apu-Punchau** a legendary figure who guided civilization in the Age of Myth as a forerunner of the Conciliator, he is the vivimancer of the stone town and his face is the same as that of the funeral bronze in Severian's MAUSOLEUM (II, chap. 31, 287). See HISTORY OF URTH.
*Myth:* meaning "Head of the Day," Apu-Punchau is another name for Inti, the Inca Sun god. Inti is portrayed as a human with a bright face surrounded by sun rays. It was believed that he crossed the sky, dove into the sea, and swam under the earth, reappearing again in the east, refreshed from his dip.

**aquastor** "We are aquastors, beings created and sustained by the power of imagination and the concentration of thought" (IV, chap. 31, 251). The scientific term for most (if not all) of the eidolons encountered in the Urth Cycle. As Wolfe notes, "I think, therefore he is."
*Latin:* "aqua" means water, so *aquastor* might be construed as a being created from water, but a corruption of "quaesitor" (investigator, inquirer) seems closer to the mark.

**Aratron** the name used by the Hierodules for the planet Saturn (IV, chap. 31, 247). See SOLAR SYSTEM TABLE.
*Myth:* Aratron is the alchemist who rules Saturn and leads 17,640,000 spirits in the occult tradition of the Seven Olympic Spirits. He teaches alchemy, magic, and medicine and is able to make a person invisible.

**arbalest** a weapon of Urth-level technology that fires pyrotechnic quarrels (II, chap. 7, 60). The more advanced models, like the ones used by Agia's henchmen, are autoloading.
*History:* a type of crossbow. Medieval Chinese repeater-crossbows could hold up to ten quarrels, but these were probably mounted.

**archimage** "They say the Autarch wants some people to remain in each [botanical garden] to accent the reality of the scene, and so his archimage, Father Inire, has invested them with a conjuration" (I, chap. 19, 178).
*History:* the high priest of the Persian fire worshippers, or a great sorcerer or wizard.

**architrave** the main beam that rests upon the capital (or top) of a column; the epistyle (I, chap. 9, 88).

**archon** the chief magistrate of a town or city, appointed by the Autarch (I, chap. 33, 281).
*History:* such a rank was used in ancient Athens.
*Myth:* "Archon" can also be used as a name for a power subordinate to the Deity, held by some of the Gnostics to have created the world. See DEMIURGE.

**arciones** the peaks of a war-saddle, before and behind the rider; here the pommel is meant (IV, chap. 19, 153).

**arctother** a creature used for bloodsports in the Bear Tower of the Citadel (I, chap. 1, 14). The Atrium of Time has statues of arctothers along one wall (I, chap. 4, 43).
*History:* a generic term for a very large bear of prehistoric times, from Greek *arcto* (bear) and *ther* (wild beast). The best candidate seems to be the Giant Short-Faced Bear *(Arctodus simus)*, the largest mammal carnivore to exist in North America. It lived from 800,000 to 12,500 years ago and was up to fifty percent larger than the largest living bears.

**arctother-man** a jiber on the ship of Tzadkiel, his hands have been modified into bear claws (V, chap. 14, 101). Severian kills him in close combat. See also URSINE-MAN.

**Arioch** a third great monster in league with ABAIA and EREBUS (IV, chap. 1, 9). See SCYLLA.

*Literature:* ("lion-like") the name given in the Book of Daniel (2:14) for the captain of Nebuchadnezzar and also used in Milton's *Paradise Lost* for a fallen angel. A demon of vengeance, a follower of Satan, sometimes depicted as bat-winged.

**armiger** in the Commonwealth, a social class below exultant and above optimate; a fighting class similar to that of the samurai who served the daimyos of feudal Japan (I, chap. 1, 20). ("Samurai" literally means "those who serve," and it is interesting to note that the letter of safe conduct which Mannea gives Severian is addressed "To Those Who Serve" [IV, chap. 15, 117].) Titles include waldgrave and wildgrave. Armigers in the text include Cyriaca's husband, Lomer, Racho, Racho's armiger companion, Simulatio (possibly), and Waldgrave.
*History:* armor-bearer, squire (of a knight); one entitled to armorial bearings.

**Armiger's Daughter, The** Foila's story, the adventure of a young woman selecting a husband among three suitors (IV, chap. 13). The first suitor seems too insensitive and forceful, and the second too cunning, but the third is trusting enough to embark on a mysterious journey as a partner.

**armigette** a female armiger; a woman of the petty nobility of the Commonwealth (I, chap. 12, 112). Armigettes in the text include Cyriaca, Ia, Nicarete, Valeria, and probably Foila.

**armoire** "I had found a red rag in the armoire, moistened it at the laver, and begun to wipe away the dust" (V, chap. 3, 21).
*History:* a cupboard, an ambry.

**arquebus** "the Ascian arquebuses on its roof sent gouts of violet energy crashing among them" (IV, chap. 20, 163). An Ascian energy rifle of stellar-level technology, it would seem to be as large and difficult to handle as its namesake.
*History:* the early type of portable gun, varying in size from a small cannon to a musket, which on account of its weight was, when used in the field, supported by a tripod or a forked rest.

**arsinoither** [ar-SIN-o-theer] an elephantine creature used in Bear Tower bloodsports (IV, chap. 18, 141), and, when equipped with a howdah, used on the front lines of Orithyia as carriers of the Daughters of War (IV, chap. 22, 176).
*History: Arsinoitherium* was a gigantic herbivore with four horns: two diverging horns on the nose and a smaller pair over the eyes. It grazed in Africa during the Oligocene Period (34 to 26 million years ago).

**artellos** a typo (see CD, 241), which should read "martellos" (I, chap. 16, 150).

**ascetic** a person not inclined to earthly pleasures (I, chap. 6, 67).

**Ascia** ["uh-SHAY-uh" (CD, 241)] the Commonwealth term for the nation of the northern hemisphere against whom it is at war. Ascia is ruled by the GROUP OF SEVENTEEN, but they in turn are controlled by ABAIA, ARIOCH, EREBUS, and SCYLLA. The name is said to be a backformation from *Ascian.*

**Ascian commander** the second Ascian Severian talks with, whom he describes as a man "only slightly taller than the rest; the intelligence in his face was the kind one sometimes sees in cunning madmen" (IV, chap. 20, 160).

**Ascians** the invaders of the Commonwealth from the north (I, chap. 3, 36). The Ascians of Urth are human, and although they look strange enough with their cropped hair, bulging eyes, and protruding teeth, their most peculiar aspect is their speech, which is made up only of quotations from AUTHORIZED TEXT, sentences approved by their rulers, the GROUP OF SEVENTEEN. They call this practice "Correct Thought." Little is known about Ascian society: there are farmers, there are beggars, there are cities, and there are "enemies of the populace," internal (thieves, malcontents, etc.) as well as external (armies of the Commonwealth).
*Myth:* the legendary inhabitants of the equatorial area, who twice a year have the sun directly overhead at noon, and then cast no shadow.

**Ash** inhabitant of the LAST HOUSE, last man on an Urth locked in ice (IV, chap. 16, 124). Master Ash was born on another world, a descendant of the refugees of the ice who were taken away by ships, and he seems to be studying the timeline of the final ice age. When Severian forces Master Ash to leave the Last House, the Ragnarok-future timeline (the result of victory for the enemies of the NEW SUN) collapses, and Ash ceases to exist.
*Myth:* the first man in Norse mythology, Ash was carved by the gods from an ash tree. In a similar way the gods made his wife, Embla (vine).

**ashlar** a square hewn stone for building purposes and pavement; also used as a missile in defending fortresses (II, chap. 2, 18).

**asimi** [uh-SEE-me] a silver coin of the Commonwealth (I, chap. 3, 31). An asimi buys "a well made coat suitable for an optimate" (II, Appendix, 300). See MEASUREMENT TABLES.

**aspice ut aspiciar** a motto from the Atrium of Time (I, chap. 4, 44).
*Latin:* "Look at me so that I may be looked upon."

**assize** "I was held till the assize, and then the judge ordered me flogged and made me sign on a carrack" (V, chap. 46, 326).
*History:* a periodic session of a superior court.

**astara** "a rabbit went skipping ahead of me in dread of the whirling astara I did not possess" (III, chap. 27, 222).
*History:* the Hindu boomerang.

**Asterion** name of the male dog in the Hounds constellation in "The Old Woman Whose Rolling Pin Is the Sun" (IA, 44). See CHARA.
*Astronomy:* the northern dog of the constellation Canes Venatici. His name means "starry" from the little stars marking his body.

**Asteroengineering** here are several reasons for putting a black hole into the Sun. Most of them involve asteroengineering, the engineering of stars.

1) Tapping energy directly from the Sun for all the usual uses that civilizations and/or godlings use power for. (Note how Severian's use of the Claw, and later *any* available power source, points to this sort of "energy circuit" scheme. If we take Severian's case as being typical of godlings like Thyme, Typhon, and Abaia, then we can wonder where they get their various energies from. Such musings remind us that Urth lacks volcanoes, which is surprising since natural vulcanism would not likely end while Earth is still habitable. Perhaps another energy source is being tapped to the maximum, feeding some chthonic deity? But if the old sun is an energy grid hook-up, who or what is it feeding? Aside from Yesod, that is: see YESOD: THE MECHANICS OF HYPERSPACE.)

In his article "Solar System Industrialization" (1985), David R. Criswell writes:

> Perhaps an advanced civilization capable of husbanding a star could convert the original stellar core into a suitable black hole. If this could be done for Sol . . . [we can assume] that the Sol-derived black hole would output approximately $1.6 \times 10^{13}$ GW [gigawatts]. The cultured black hole could likely support 13 million times more people than on Earth now if each person used 200 kw of power [the industrially advanced nations today use 20 kw/person] (*Interstellar Migration and the Human Experience,* 63).

2) Interrupting the natural evolution of the Sun so as to both lengthen its lifetime and avoid the disasterous giant phase. This obviously very far-looking engineering strategy is touched upon

in Martyn Fogg's *Terraforming* (1995), as well as the techniques for moving a new star to replace an old sun (457–461).

3) A vengeance weapon with no positive applications. Launched by someone other than Typhon, since it contributes to his ruin and he doesn't seem to know a reason for it. Perhaps one of his rebellious children. If placed by Yesod for their own reasons, it might be more of a "tire boot" on the car for the probationary period of 1000 years within which Urth must evolve or die the slow death.

Finally, there is a theory of how there might already be a black hole in the heart of our star, a condition that would explain why scientists of the mid-20th century could not find the neutrinos that theory dictated would be present.

In his 1977 article "A Potpourri," Jerry Pournelle describes a routine experiment in the 1960s to establish the validity of the notion that proton-proton fusion was going on in the Sun. The neutrino collector was expected to capture about 6 SNU; the results were "a maximum of 1.3 SNU, and possibly none at all. This is astounding. Has the Sun gone out?" (*A Step Farther Out,* 276).

Among the many possibilities presented by Pournelle, one seems especially germane: "there's a black hole of around 1% of the Sun's mass dead center in our star, and the Sun shines because matter falling into the hole gives off energy; there's no fusion in there at all" (277).

**atelier** "What the ziggurat had once been, I never guessed. Perhaps a prison indeed; perhaps a temple, or the atelier of some forgotten art" (IV, chap. 26, 213).
*History:* a workshop; an artist's or sculptor's studio.

**athame** Agia's weapon at the mine, a poisoned blade (II, chap. 7, 60; IV, appendix, 314).
*History:* a Greek name for the warlock sword, used for magical rituals. The blade does not have much of a cutting edge, but it does possess a fairly sharp point, used to trace occult symbols and patterns of power.

**atole** "'Atole,' she said. . . . It tasted like stale bread boiled in milk" (V, chap. 9, 67).
*History:* cornmeal that is cooked and eaten as mush or that is drunk as a thin gruel.

**Atrium of Time** "Is that what you call it? The Atrium of Time? Because of the dials, I suppose." "No, the dials were put there because we call it that" (I, chap. 4, 44). A time-traveling portal to a larger structure, like the ground level of the LAST HOUSE, located in the heart of the Citadel. It has some broken timepieces at the center, and statues of a different animal stand at each wall: barylambdas, arctothers, glyptodons, and smilodons. The surrounding building is inhabited by at least Valeria and her old servant (her old nurse?), but it may also house Catherine or the maid who plays Katharine.
*Commentary:* regarding the animals represented by statues, the barylambda comes from an earlier time (the paleocene, around fifty million years ago) and the others are contemporary to each

other in the pleistocene (1.8 million years ago). While the glyptodon originated in the pliocene (5.5 to 1.8 million years ago), it seems to have survived into the pleistocene.

**atrox** a truly great cat that stalks the pampas of the Commonwealth (II, chap. 29, 248).
*History:* [AY-trox] *Felis atrox,* an ice-age giant lion of North America. At eleven feet long, it is larger than a smilodon, and probably too big to easily climb trees.

**atroxes** "If everyone who came tarried at my inn, why it wouldn't be my inn — I'd have sold it, and be living comfortable in a big stone house with atroxes at the door" (I, chap. 25, 222).
*History:* horrors; painted or sculptured figures to impress the public with a patron's danger and importance (CD, 245). As an example, note that tormented faces are painted on the metal of the Matachin Tower (I, chap. 5, 53).

**aubade** "Oh, no, you mustn't. Not until they play the aubade" (III, chap. 5, 48).
*History:* a musical announcement of dawn; a sunrise song or open-air concert.

**aureate** "These colors, falling upon the throng of monomachists and loungers much as we see the aureate beams of divine favor fall on hierarchs in art, lent them an appearance insubstantial and thaumaturgic" (I, chap. 27, 236).
*History:* golden, gold-colored; brilliant or splendid as gold.

**autarch** the supreme leader of the Commonwealth. The autarchy of the Commonwealth seems to be a non-hereditary position open only to non-exultants: "Most are only common men and women, sailors and artisans, farmwives and wantons. Most of the rest are eccentric second-rate scholars" (IV, chap. 34, 272). This is undoubtedly a factor in the animosity between the Exultants and the Phoenix Throne. The first autarch was Ymar the Almost Just. Other named autarchs include Appian, Maruthas, Maxentius, Paeon (possibly), Severian the Great, and Sulpicius.

Phrases used in praise of the autarch include "whose pores outshine the stars themselves," "whose perspiration is the gold of his subjects," "may he endure to see the New Sun," "whose thoughts are the music of his subjects," and "may his spirit live in a thousand successors."
*History:* ("self-ruler") a ruler subject to no restraints, internal or external.
*Commentary:* Clute assumes that it is forbidden for the autarch to pass the Phoenix Throne on to his or her offspring, but further investigations reveal that dynasties may have been the rule during the Age of the Autarch, rather than the exception.

**autarchia** "Anyway, your autarchia, she was Autarch" (V, chap. 46, 328). Used in the Urth Cycle as the feminine form of autarch, its historical meaning is "perpetual happiness," at least according to *Mrs. Byrne's Dictionary.* (John Brunner, mystified, suggests that Mrs. Byrne meant "eutarchia" from Greek *evtykhia.*)

**Authorized Texts** the Ascian ideology is "Correct Thought" which is based on "Authorized Texts." Ascian language is made up of tag lines from Authorized Text. Following is a collection of Ascian utterances, arranged into broad categories.

BRAVERY

❧ "If their wounds are in their backs, who shall stanch their blood?" (IV, chap. 11, 88).

❧ "United, men and women are stronger; but a brave woman desires children, and not husbands" (IV, chap. 5, 40; IV, chap. 11, 85).

CAUSALITY/DETERMINATION

❧ "Behind everything some further thing is found, forever; thus the tree behind the bird, stone beneath soil, the sun behind Urth. Behind our efforts, let there be found our efforts" (IV, chap. 11, 86).

❧ "For the Armies of the Populace, defeat is the springboard of victory, and victory the ladder to further victory" (IV, chap. 5, 39).

❧ "No failure is permanent failure. But inevitable success may require new plans and greater strength" (IV, chap. 20, 161). Meaning: *We might try something different.*

CHARITY

❧ "It is better to be just than to be kind, but only good judges can be just; let those who cannot be just be kind" (IV, chap. 11, 87). This phrase is used by Ascian beggars.

CITIZENSHIP

- "One is strong, another beautiful, a third a cunning artificer. Which is best? He who serves the populace" (IV, chap. 11, 85).
- "As a good child to its mother, so is the citizen to the Group of Seventeen" (IV, chap. 11, 86).
- "The citizen renders to the populace what is due to the populace. What is due to the populace? Everything" (IV, chap. 11, 87).

CORRECT THOUGHT

- "The light of Correct Thought penetrates every darkness" (IV, chap. 20, 161).
- "Correct Thought is the thought of the populace. The populace cannot betray the populace or the Group of Seventeen" (IV, chap. 5, 42).
- "All endeavors are conducted well or ill precisely in so far as they conform to Correct Thought" (IV, chap. 5, 39).
- "External battles are already won when internal struggles are conducted with Correct Thought" (IV, chap. 5, 39).

EDUCATION

- "All who speak Correct Thought speak well. Where then is the superiority of some students to others? It is in the speaking. Intelligent students speak Correct Thought intelligently. The hearer knows by the intonation of their voices that they understand. By this superior speaking of intelligent students, Correct Thought is passed, like fire, from one to another" (IV, chap. 9, 73).
- "Study of Correct Thought eventually reveals the path of success (IV, chap. 20, 161). Meaning: *We approve of your plan.*

ENEMIES

- "Those who do the will of the populace are friends, though we have never spoken to them. Those who do not do the will of the populace are enemies, though we learned together as children" (IV, chap. 5, 39).
- "Those who fight for the populace fight with a thousand hearts. Those who fight against them with none" (IV, chap. 11, 88).

INTERROGATION

- "Only he who acts against the populace need hide his face" (iv, chap. 29, 232). Meaning: *Tell us who you are, stranger.*
- "Who is the friend of the populace? He who aids the populace. Who is the enemy of the populace?" (IV, chap. 29, 233). Meaning: *Are you friend or foe?*

JUSTICE

- "Where the Group of Seventeen sit, there final justice is done" (IV, chap. 11, 86).
- "Can all petitioners be heard? No, for all cry together. Who, then, shall be heard — is it those who cry loudest? No, for all cry loudly. Those who cry longest shall be heard, and justice shall be done to them" (IV, chap. 11, 86).
- "Let no one oppose the decisions of the Group of Seventeen" (IV, chap. 11, 88).

LOYALTY

- "In times past, loyalty to the cause of the populace was to be found everywhere. The will of the Group of Seventeen was the will of everyone" (IV, chap. 11, 85).

- "I am Loyal to the Group of Seventeen" (IV, chap. 6, 46).

MEN AND WOMEN

- "United, men and women are stronger; but a brave woman desires children, and not husbands" (IV, chap. 5, 40; IV, chap. 11, 85).
- "The roots of the tree are the populace. The leaves fall, but the tree remains" (IV, chap. 5, 40).

PRISON

- "Those who will not serve the populace shall serve the populace" (IV, chap. 11, 88).

PRUDENCE

- "The servants of the Group of Seventeen must not be expended without purpose" (IV, chap. 20, 160).

PUNISHMENT

- "The people meeting in counsel may judge, but no one is to receive more than a hundred blows" (IV, chap. 11, 85).
- "So say the Group of Seventeen: From those who steal, take all they have, for nothing they have is their own" (IV, chap. 11, 69).
- "Those who will not serve the populace shall serve the populace" (IV, chap. 11, 88).
- "If their wounds are in their backs, who shall stanch their blood?" (IV, chap. 11, 88).
- "Where are those who in times past have opposed the decisions of the Group of Seventeen?" (IV, chap. 11, 88).

ROADS

❧ "How are the hands nourished? By the blood. How does the blood reach the hands? By the veins. If the veins are closed, the hands will rot away" (IV, chap. 11, 85–86).

SACRIFICE

❧ "The merit of sacrifice falls on him who without thought of his own convenience offers what he has toward the service of the populace" (IV, chap. 29, 233). Meaning: *You will give us everything for nothing in return.*

SALUTATION

❧ "Glory to the Group of Seventeen" (IV, chap. 5, 38).

❧ "All persons belong to the populace" (IV, chap. 20, 233). Meaning: *Over and out* (a radio signing off phrase).

SENSE AND NONSENSE

❧ "What is foolish speech? It is wind. It has come in at the ears and goes out of the mouth" (IV, chap. 11, 87).

❧ "The cries of the children are the cries of victory. Still, victory must learn wisdom" (IV, chap. 5, 41).

THE STATE

❧ "How shall the state be most vigorous? It shall be most vigorous when it is without conflict. How shall it be without conflict? When it is without disagreement. How shall disagreement be banished? By banishing the four causes of disagreement: lies, foolish talk, boastful talk, and talk which serves only to incite quarrels. How shall the four causes be banished? By speaking only Correct Thought. Then shall the state be without disagreement. Being without disagreement it shall be without conflict. Being without conflict it shall be vigorous, strong, and secure" (IV, chap. 5, 43–44).

WORK

- "All must do their share in the service of the populace. The bullock draws the plow and the dog herds the sheep, but the cat catches mice in the granary. Thus men, women, and even children can serve the populace" (IV, chap. 11, 84).
- "Let no one be idle. If one is idle, let him band together with others who are idle too, and let them look for idle land. Let everyone they meet direct them. It is better to walk a thousand leagues than to sit in the House of Starvation" (IV, chap. 11, 85).
- "Let the work be divided by a wise divider of work. Let the food be divided by a just divider of food. Let the pigs grow fat. Let rats starve" (IV, chap. 11, 85).
- "Let there be clean water for those who toil. Let there be hot food for them and a clean bed. Then they will sing at their work, and their work will be light to them. Then they will sing at the harvest, and the harvest will be heavy" (IV, chap. 11, 86; twice on page 88).

**autochthon** a dark, squat race in the Commonwealth. Some autochthons live in pit villages on the pampas (II, chap. 1, 11). *History:* literally, a human being sprung from the soil he inhabits, hence, the earliest known dwellers in any country.

**Ava** slender, gray-eyed postulant of the Pelerines (IV, chap. 10, 75). She is an optimate's daughter (77), rare among members of the order. Ava grew up in Nessus near the Sanguinary Field. She

saw the duel between Agilus and Severian and she is likely the one who said, "Is he dead?" (1, chap. 27, 239; chapter title). She came to the order just after the cathedral was burned (83), so she has been a postulant for a few months when Severian meets her at Orithyia.
*Onomastics:* "like a bird" (Latin); possibly "life" or "serpent" (Hebrew).
*History:* Saint Ava (died 850?), niece of King Pepin, was cured of blindness by Saint Rainfreidis and became a Benedictine nun and abbess at Dinart, Hainault, France. Another Ava (died 1127) was not a saint but a poet who created a number of simple verses on New Testament themes as well as a metrical life of Saint John the Baptist, written in the assonantal and alliterative style of earlier German poetry.

**avern** an artichoke-like plant of extraterrestrial origin, grown in the Botanical Gardens of Nessus, and used as a lethal weapon by duelists on the Sanguinary Field. Its sharp petals are incredibly poisonous to terrestrial life-forms, and in combat they are plucked from the flower and thrown like daggers (1, chap. 17, 156). Father Inire had them planted forty years after Dorcas's death (1, chap. 22, 198), so they seem to have only been there for a year or two when Severian sees them. Likewise the custom of dueling with them must be quite new. C. N. Manlove points out that "to fight with flowers is to conduct war with an image of peace" (*Science Fiction: Ten Explorations,* 205).
*Myth:* named after Avernus ("the birdless lake" near Puteoli, said to be an entrance to the infernal regions) because no birds can survive around it.

*Commentary:* Dorcas notes of the opening avern flower, "There was something underneath . . . a face like the face poison would have, if poison had a face" (I, chap. 28, 244). This passage recalls a scene from Robert Graves's *I, Claudius,* in which an ancient chest bears the motto "Poison is Queen" and depicts the Face of Poison (which has an uncanny resemblance to Caesar's wife Livia, yet it was constructed a hundred or more years before her birth). While considering how these scenes relate to each other, remember also that Livia was Claudius's grandmother.

**Aybert, Brother** a torturer remembered for his work in preparing meals, possibly the same person as Brother Cook (II, chap. 18, 163). He is a guild member who does not actually do any torturing (see also COOK, BROTHER; CORBINIAN, BROTHER; and PORTER, BROTHER).
*History:* Saint Aybert (A.D. 1060–1140) entered the Benedictine abbey of Crepin. He was its provost and cellarer for twenty-five years.

# B

**bacele** a military unit of fifty or sixty horsemen commanded by lancers (knights or sergeants) in medieval Europe (IV, chap. 19, 150). See MILITARY ORGANIZATION.

**baculus** a staff, a crosier: the pastoral staff of a bishop, shaped like a shepherd's staff (I, chap. 26, 233).

**badelaire** a short, heavy broadsword, curved like a scimitar, with S-shaped quillions (I, chap. 1, 12). A weapon from the 16th century.

**Baiulo Island** an island, presumably on Gyoll in the vicinity of Os (V, chap. 21, 222). The sailor Zama drowned near this isle in Typhon's era.
*Latin:* from *baiulo,* to carry, bear (a load).

**Baldanders** the giant (I, chap. 15, 144). He is so tall that eight-foot-tall merlons are only as high as a railing to him. Although Baldanders seems at first to be the creation of Dr. Talos (an image that echoes down through the ages to surface in Mary Shelley's *Frankenstein*), in fact Talos is Baldanders's creature. Baldanders also made the Natrium slug thrower used by the Shore Folk of Lake Diuturna. His tower is full of ancient devices, among them the mist machine, the belt of weightlessness, and the energy mace.

The lower level of the tower is full of the victims of his hideous experiments. Baldanders is similar to Abaia and the undines (probably by choice and design rather than by birth) and is nearly too large to live on land any longer when Severian meets him. *Literature:* Baldanders comes from *The Adventurous Simplicissimus Teutsch* (1669) by Johann Hans Jakob Cristoffel von Grimmelshausen by way of Borges's *Book of Imaginary Beings* (1957) (CD, 253). According to Borges, the name means "Soon-another" or "At-any-moment-something-else," and the character ultimately derives from Proteus, the old man of the sea. *The Adventurous Simplicissimus* seems to be in part about "Centrum Terrae," an aquatic kingdom 900 miles below the earth's surface, reached through several deep lakes, among them the Mummelsee in Germany. The denizens of this land are a race of water spirits, mortal and having mortal souls. ("Centrum Terrae" entry of *The Dictionary of Imaginary Places* [expanded edition], by Manguel and Guadalupi.)

**baldric** a wide belt worn over one shoulder to support a sword or a bugle (I, chap. 14, 128).

**balmacaan** "Thus I stared at balmacaans and surtouts" (I, chap. 16, 151). A short, rough overcoat.

**balneary** a bath or bathing place; a medicinal spring (V, chap. 25, 179).

**baluchither** [ba-LOO-chih-ther] a gargantuan beast of burden used in the Commonwealth (II, chap. 9, 73).

*History:* from *Baluchitherium,* a very large Oligocene mammal related to the rhinoceros, but lacking a horn, found in central Asia. With a height of eighteen feet at the shoulders, this creature dwarfs even the tallest MAMMOTH (fourteen feet).

**balustrade** a row of balusters (short pillars or columns), surmounted by a rail or coping, forming an ornamental parapet or barrier along the edge of a terrace, balcony, et cetera (II, chap. 23, 203).

**Barbara** patron saint of the matrosses (I, chap. 11, 104).
*Onomastics:* "foreign woman" (Latin).
*History:* one of the most popular saints of the calendar. At Nicomedia under Maximinus Thrax, Barbara was shut up in a tower by her father, who killed her for being a Christian, whereupon he was struck dead by lightning. The legend is clearly spurious, and some doubt whether she ever existed. Nevertheless, she is the patron saint of firework makers, artillerymen, and others.

**Barbatus** of the group Ossipago, Barbatus, and Famulimus, travelling back in time with their flying saucer (III, chap. 33, 262). Barbatus is the male hierodule. Severian thinks Barbatus and Famulimus are descended from a once aquatic race, something like kelpies, but they dispute this (V, chap. 5, 35).
*Myth:* (Roman) a minor god who oversaw the sprouting of a boy's beard.

**Barbea** a prostitute at the House Azure, in Nessus (I, chap. 9, 89). Hence, she is the khaibit of a chatelaine who is a member of the old autarch's inner circle. She is no more than seventeen

years old, and her hair is gold. See also GRACIA, THEA'S KHAIBIT, and THECLA'S KHAIBIT.
*History:* Saint Barbea and her brother Saint Sarbelius were tortured with red-hot irons before being martyred in Edessa under Trajan in A.D. 101.

**barbican** an outer fortification or defense to a city or castle, especially a double tower erected over a gate or bridge; often made strong and lofty and serving as a watchtower (I, chap. 1, 9).

**barbute** a type of helmet used from the mid-14th to the late 15th century. Generally bullet-shaped and forged in one piece (IV, chap. 1, 14).

**barghest** the costume worn by Abdiesus at the ridotto, signifying his resolve to have Cyriaca executed (III, chap. 7, 62).
*Myth:* a German goblin fabled to appear in the form of a large dog, with various horrible characteristics, and to portend imminent death or misfortune.

**Barnoch** a man of Saltus accused of being a spy for Vodalus and sealed up in his own house as punishment (II, chap. 1, 10).
*History:* Saint Barnoch (Barrog) was a 7th century disciple of the great Welsh Saint Cadoc. He has left his name to Barry Island, where he lived as a hermit.

**Barrus** the brother of the child who travels with Thyme in EFF, after whom the child names her own son by Prince Patizithes. A soldier she meets says that the name means "the handsome one" (SS, 259). See PATIZITHES.

*Onomastics:* elephant (from Latin "to carry").
*Literature:* the soldier's comment is an allusion to the Roman poet Horace (65–8 B.C.), who wrote about a vain contemporary, "It's as if you had Barrus' disease, Who wished to be thought of as handsome" *(Satire #6).*

**bartizans** "The guards in the bartizans were not city roundsmen but peltasts in half-armor, bearing transparent shields" (I, chap. 14, 132).
*History:* turrets or small towers that cling to a wall or other structure (in this case, a bridge) and have no foundations of their own.

**barylambda** [bar-ee-LAMB-da] the Atrium of Time has barylambda statues (I, chap. 4, 43).
*History:* large, primitive herbivores. About the size of a pony, with five-toed limbs and a large powerful tail, almost dinosaurian in appearance. Ruminated in North America during the Paleocene.

**basilica** an oblong building typically with a broad nave flanked by colonnaded aisles or porticoes and ending in a semicircular apse. It was used in ancient Rome especially for a court of justice and place for public assembly, later as a church building of similar construction (I, chap. 16, 150). It has come to mean a place of worship of unusual importance.
*Greek:* "royal."

**basilosaur** "A basilosaur swimming up from the open sea would not have astounded me more" (IV, chap. 32, 261).

*History:* a slender-bodied Eocene whale of the Gulf of Mexico area. (The most abundant remains have been found in Alabama and Florida.)

**batardeau** a large knife whose hilt is of the same piece of steel as the blade (V, chap. 41, 291). From the late 16th century.

**Bear Tower** an outer tower of the Citadel, located on the western side, near the Matachin Tower. Between the Bear Tower and its neighbor the Red Tower is a gap in the curtain wall. The Bear Tower, originally a zoetic transport ship in the Age of the Monarch, houses the beast handlers during the Age of the Autarch. It is likely that they supply animals to such gaming establishments as the nearby lion pit, located on the other side of the Gyoll (I, chap. 10, 99). The beast handlers have their own guild, and in the elevation of their masters, the candidate stands under a metal grate trod by a bleeding bull. Each brother eventually takes a lioness or bear sow in marriage, after which he shuns human women (I, chap. 4, 41).
*History:* the detail about the grate and the bull is similar to the initiation rites for the Persian god Mithra, whose mystery religion was brought to Europe by the soldiers of Alexander the Great. Mithraism was later taken up by the Romans, especially the soldiers, who spread it throughout Europe and into Britain.

**Becan** a pioneer peasant, husband of Casdoe, father of Severa and LITTLE SEVERIAN (III, chap. 14, 113). He went out hunting the alzabo that had eaten Severa and was himself eaten.
*Onomastics:* "small" (Celtic).

*History:* there are two Saints Becan, both 6th century: one, a relative of Saint Columba, founded a monastery at Kill-Beggan, but perhaps the more pertinent one was an Irish hermit near Cork.

**Becca** narrator's grandchild in "The Old Woman Whose Rolling Pin Is the Sun" (IA, 42).
*Onomastics:* short form of "Rebecca," possibly "a snare" (Hebrew) or perhaps derived from an Aramaic name.

**Bega** Hallvard's grandmother (IV, chap. 7, 55).
*History:* Saint Bega (died 698?) lived in Northumbria and founded a convent in Cumberland. She is said to have been a daughter of an Irish king, who fled from marriage to a Norwegian prince and then received the veil from Saint Aidan.

**Bell Keep** a tower in the Citadel, on the western side near the Matachin Tower (I, chap. 2, 22). It houses the great cistern in which the apprentice torturers clandestinely swim.

**belt of weightlessness** a "thick affair of linked metal prisms" that enables the giant Baldanders to float in the air (III, chap. 37, 288).

**belvedere** "the view through the dusty windows of the belvedere" (II, chap. 11, 99). A building overlooking a fine view.

**berdiche** a staff-mounted axe used by foot-soldiers in Russia and the Baltic during the 16th and 17th centuries (II, chap. 11, 92).

It has a long, narrow curved head twenty-four to thirty-two inches long. It was also used by the Turks and in the Near East.

**beryl** the elfstone (I, chap. 18, 168), a transparent precious stone of a pale-green color, distinguished only by color from the more precious emerald.

**Bethor** the name the Hierodules use for the planet Jupiter (IV, chap. 31, 247). See SOLAR SYSTEM TABLE.
*Myth:* in alchemical lore, one of the seven angels (or Olympian Spirits) who rule over the 196 provinces of heaven, Bethor is lord of the planet Jupiter and commands 29,000 legions of spirits. He rules forty-two provinces and commands kings, princes, and dukes.

**Beuzec** small trader traveling with Hethor (II, chap. 13, 112). He saw Severian perform twice (113) meaning he saw the execution of Agilus in Nessus and the group at Saltus, so he might be the small ALGOPHILIST who gave Severian an asimi. Beuzec has escaped the antechamber and is hiding in the loft of a closet when Severian next sees him (II, chap. 19, 174), but from there he escapes into the walls and is not seen again.
*Onomastics:* a fanciful derivation of the name is "saved from the waters."
*History:* Saint Budoc (6th century), said by unreliable sources to be the son of King Goello (Brittany) and Azenor (daughter of King of Brest), raised in a monastery near Waterford, Ireland. Name sometimes spelled Beuzec or Budeaux.

**Big Blossom** not mentioned in the Urth Cycle directly, but the likely term for what we call "the Big Bang." Severian comes close in describing how the universe "blooms" (IV, chap. 34, 241). From the story "Procreation": "stop thinking about the Big Bang. Think about the Big Blossom instead. Think of that primeval fireball unfolding and scattering out stuff that slowly picks up speed" (ES, 347). See GRAND GNAB.

**bijoux** plural of *bijou,* a jewel, a trinket; a "gem" among works of art (II, chap. 14, 120).

**Bird of the Wood** a princess on Urth, she is loved by Spring Wind and gives birth to Frog and Fish in "Tale of the Boy Called Frog" (III, chap. 19, 148).
*Myth:* (Roman) Rhea (a type of bird) Silvanus ("of the wood") is the mother of Romulus and Remus.

**Black Killer** a friend of Frog's in "Tale of the Boy Called Frog," he seems to be a panther. He ransoms Frog with gold (III, chap. 19, 156).
*Myth:* the panther is associated with Dionysus and Jesus Christ. The panther also has an ancient connection with honey, which is golden in color and highly valued.
*Literature:* Bagheera the panther is Mowgli's friend throughout Kipling's Jungle Books.
*History:* Bagheera and Black Killer may both be symbols for slavery, especially that practiced in the United States.

**Black Sun** another name for the Conciliator (III, chap. 8, 66).

**Blaithmaic** author of *Lives of the Seventeen Megatherians*, a folio in green cloth (I, chap. 6, 64).
*Onomastics:* related to blythe, "the very happy [joyful] one" (Old English).
*History:* Saint Blaithmaic (died 823) was an Irish abbot slain by invading Danes.

**Blue Flower Island** name of an isle in the Xanthic Lands (V, chap. 46, 327). Eata seems to have escaped his carrack indenture by jumping ship here. He lived in the area for two years.

**boatman** a passing boatman along the Gyoll when Severian nearly drowned, who asks if he saw a woman underwater (I, chap. 2, 26); the boatman on the Lake of Birds who tells of looking for his wife, "Cas" (I, chap. 22). They are surely the same man, DORCAS'S HUSBAND.

**Bolcan** given as a very common name in the Commonwealth, along with Alto (II, chap. 15, 130).
*History:* Saint Bolcan (died 480) sent to Gaul for study by Saint Patrick, he returned to become bishop of Derkan (northern Ireland) and to develop a brilliant school in his own see.

**Bona Dea** a goddess-like being who is somehow a personification of nature, akin to Mother Nature, in "The Old Woman Whose Rolling Pin Is the Sun" (IA, 45).
*Onomastics:* "the Good Goddess" (Latin).
*Myth:* an ancient Roman goddess, she presided over both virginity and fertility in women, and at her festivals in Rome no man was

allowed to be present. Consecrated serpents were kept in her temple at Rome, indicating her phallic nature. See FAUNA, GEA.

**Book of Exulted Families** a tome that lists all of the exultant family names (I, chap. 7, 74). It is 746 pages long, with an average of two names per page, so there are around 1,492 exultant families.

**Book of Gold** the volume that leads a young reader to join the curator's guild (I, chap. 6, 62).

**Book of Mirrors** a man-sized tome in the Second House (II, chap. 21, 186). The pages are mirrors leading to somewhere else, perhaps YESOD, the higher universe. This seems to offer a shortcut which Severian declines to take, even as autarch, when he chooses to travel by ship instead. A wise choice on his part, since it seems more likely that all magic mirrors lead to the same place: that ghost-region at the end of the universe.
*History: Mar'ot ha-Zove'ot* ("Book of Mirrors") was a 14th-century kabbalistic book.

**Book of the New Sun** (1) A single volume of stories told by the Conciliator to his followers in the time of Typhon, written down by a student named Canog (V, chap. 37, 266). Although thought to be long lost by the time of Appian's reign, Dr. Talos claims to have read it, and based his play *Eschatology and Genesis* upon it; in addition there is a copy at the Library of Nessus (see FOURTH BOOK); and finally it seems likely that Casdoe had a copy from which she read to LITTLE SEVERIAN. (2) An autobiographical work

**Book of the Wonders of Urth and Sky**

composed by Severian the Great in the tenth year of his reign, translated into four volumes by Gene Wolfe.

**Book of the Wonders of Urth and Sky** see BROWN BOOK.

**bordereau** [birduh-ROW] one of the "common words" that Master Gurloes mispronounces (I, chap. 7, 78); see also SALPINX and URTICATE.
*French:* a memorandum, detailed statement, or schedule (in this case, a list of documents).
*History:* the word was once heavy with associations of corruption and betrayal. Linked to the infamous Dreyfus treason case that convulsed France for a decade (1894–1904), "bordereau" was internationally understood as meaning one thing only: the key document of the case, the secret plans that were allegedly drawn up by Dreyfus.

**Borges, Jorge Luis** this South American author inspires mirrors, books, Kabbalah, paradoxes, and mystery within the Urth Cycle. Gene Wolfe wrote a poem about Borges, "Last Night in the Garden of Forking Tongues" (*Plan[e]t Engineering,* 138), but the following points are more specific:

- The Borges collection *The Book of Imaginary Beings* has a lot of relevant material (see its entries on Alzabo, Baldanders, and Fish).
- The Borges story "Circular Ruins" ties into "The Tale of the Student and His Son."
- The title character of "Funes the Memorius" has photographic memory, like Severian (Clute, *Strokes,* 152).

❧ "The Library of Babel" ties into the Library of Nessus (Wolfe, *Plan[e]t Engineering*, 4; Clute, *Strokes*, 156).

❧ The story "Tlon, Uqbar, Orbis Tertius" offers a kind of blueprint for *The Book of the New Sun* in its opening paragraph, and it is a model for Wolfe's non-Urth story "Useful Phrases" (collected in *Strange Travelers*).

**bosquets** pleasant thickets (I, chap. 35, 296).

**Botanic Gardens** (of Nessus) located on an island near the west bank in the living section of the city, a large, multifaceted glass dome that houses a number of gardens, among them the gardens of Sleep, Pantomime, Antiquities, Sand, Delectation, Jungle, and Endless Sleep (I, chap. 19, 174). Each garden seems to exist in a different time and place: the Garden of Endless Sleep is rumored to be spatially located on the other side of the world, while the Garden of Antiquities boasts many hundreds of extinct plants, some not seen for tens of millions of years. In the Garden of Endless Sleep there is the Lake of Birds, and near the lake is the Cave of the Cumaean. See CUMAEAN.

**bothy** a small hut for farm hands, or in this case, a shepherd (III, chap. 27, 218).

**Boy Who Hooked the Sun, The** a tale from the BROWN BOOK that is ostensibly set on the emerald-studded east coast of Atlantis, where a boy (whose father trades with the barbarians of Hellas) hooks the sun while fishing. Several people try to talk him into letting it go (the richest man, the strongest man, the cleverest man, the magic woman, the most foolish man) before he finally

does so at the urging of his mother, but even then, he reasons "the time must come when I live and she does not; and when that time comes, surely I will bait my hook again." The boy resembles Severian dragging the New Sun across space; the others are perhaps Vodalus, Baldanders, Typhon, the Cumaean, (no guess for 'most foolish'), Earth as the mother, and Urth as the dead mother. The structure is seven-part, suggesting the seven planetary bodies of the week, but otherwise the history and mythology seem right up front in the form of "Atlantis" and "Hellas."
*Commentary:* emeralds harken back to the Green Empire, which also seems to be the eastern of the two nations in EFF. This story appeared as a Cheap Street chapbook (1985), then in *Weird Tales* #290, Spring 1988, and was later collected in SS.

**brachet** a kind of hound that hunts by scent; always feminine and extended to any kind of hound; a bitch hound (II, chap. 4, 31).

**Branwallader** archivist whom Rudesind served as an apprentice (I, chap. 5, 52).
*History:* Saint Branwallader (6th century?) is said to have been a bishop on the Isle of Jersey.

**braquemar** a sword with a simple guard and a wide, short, double-edged blade (I, chap. 28, 245). Used in the 16th century.

**breeches and hose** (I, chap. 25, 221) Severian's lower body clothing.

**Bregwyn** the Typhon-era hetman of Vici, father of Herena (v, chap. 28, 199; v, chap. 29, 203).
*Onomastics:* site of Arthur's eleventh battle.
*History:* Saint Bregwin (died 764), also known as Breguivine, was the twelfth archbishop of Canterbury, England.

**Briah** Odilo writes, "As every thinking man acknowledges, mighty powers move through this dark universe of Briah, though for the most part hidden from us by its infinite night" (ES, 221). The universe that Urth inhabits, first named by Severian only after he has left it (v, chap. 14, 104).
*Myth:* from the Jewish Kabbalah, Briah is the second of the four created worlds: Atziluth, world of Supernals (containing the sefiroth Kether, Binah, and Chokmah); Briah, world of Creation (containing Chesed, Geburah, and Tiphereth); Yetzirah, world of Foundation (containing Hod, Netzach, and YESOD); and Assiah, world of Action (containing Malkuth). See SEFIROTH.

**Brook Madregot** a "stream" that flows from Yesod to Briah, as water flows down a hill, and as energy seeks a lower state (v, chap. 40, 285).
*Myth:* in kabbalistic writings, reference is made to the Four Rivers, each running from the godhead of Ein Soph to one of the Four Created Worlds. These rivers are not considered among the paths that crisscross the Tree of Life, connecting the sefiroth to each other; rather, the rivers are like direct lines to God, or expressways. Two of them are associated with rivers in the physical world.

| Name | River | Element | World |
|---|---|---|---|
| Pison | none | Fire | Atziluth |
| Hiddikel | Tigris | Air | Briah |
| Gihon | none | Water | Yetzirah |
| Phrah | Euphrates | Earth | Assiah |

If the Brook Madregot were one of these, it would most likely be "Hiddikel," which links Briah to the godhead.
*Occult:* "Madregot" is a kabbalistic term for "levels of mystic ascent," according to Epstein (*Kabbalah,* Shambhala, 1988, glossary).

**brown book** *The Book of the Wonders of Urth and Sky, Being a Collection from Printed Sources of Universal Secrets of Such Age That Their Meaning Has Become Obscured of Time* (I, chap. 6, 63). A standard work of short stories published three or four centuries prior to the reign of Severian. The Urth Cycle contains many of the complete stories (see separate entry for each). Other stories are summarized and there are about a dozen lesser fragments.

COMPLETE STORIES

- The Boy Who Hooked the Sun (alluded to: V, chap. 33, 232).
- Empires of Foliage and Flower (alluded to: II, chap. 31, 265).
- The God and His Man.
- The Old Woman Whose Rolling Pin Is the Sun.
- Tale of the Boy Called Frog (III, chap. 19).
- Tale of the Student and his Son (II, chap. 17).
- Tale of the Town That Forgot Fauna (V, chap. 33, 232).
- To which Severian adds "The Two Sealers" (IV, chap. 7), "The Cock, the Angel, and the Eagle" (IV, chap. 9), "The Just

Man" (IV, chap. 11), and "The Armiger's Daughter" (IV, chap. 13).

STORY SUMMARIES

- Tale of an angel killed by a child's arrow, "Had I known we might perish, I would not at all times have been so bold" (I, chap. 18, 162).
- Tale of a great sanctuary veiled by a diamond-sprinkled curtain lest man see the face of the Increate and die (V, chap. 47, 331), which sounds similar to Flaubert's *Salambo.*
- Tale of a man who drank the waters of another world and never returned (V, chap. 17, 119).
- A section listing the keys of the universe, one of which is "everything has three meanings" (I, chap. 32, 271).

FRAGMENTS

- Afterlife: the notion that a region of mist separates the living from the dead (V, chap. 27, 195).
- Ancient times: "These times are the ancient times, when the world is ancient" (II, chap. 28, 266).
- Angels: an argument about amschaspands (III, chap. 27, 220).
- City: "There is nothing stranger than to explore a city wholly different from all those one knows, since to do so is to explore a second and unsuspected self" (III, chap. 2, 16).
- Culture: a passage to the effect that culture is an outgrowth of the Increate's vision (I, chap. 30, 261).
- Democracy: "It was thought of Thalelaeus the Great that the democracy desired to be ruled by some power superior to itself, and of Yrierix the Sage that the commonality would never permit one differing from themselves to hold high

office. Notwithstanding this, each is called the Perfect Master" (I, chap. 10, 97).

- Hell: "Hell has no limits, nor is circumscribed; for where we are is Hell, and where Hell is, there we must be" (II, chap. 28, 266). This is line 553 of Christopher Marlowe's *Faustus.*
- History: the Legend of the Historians, "which tells of a time in which every legend could be traced to a half forgotten fact" (I, chap. 6, 64).
- Wisdom: a passage about man and wisdom (III, chap. 33, 265).
- A tale with the quote, "Behold, I have dreamed a dream more; the sun and the moon and eleven stars made obeisance to me" (V, chap. 38, 267), which is directly from the Bible at the beginning of Joseph's adventures (Genesis 37 to 50). Briefly, Joseph was wrongfully sold into slavery by his brothers who were jealous of his dreams; in Egypt he gained a position of authority in his master's household, but was then imprisoned in the Round Tower on the false accusations of his master's wife; Joseph was released after interpreting Pharaoh's dream of the lean and fat kine, and he became governor of Egypt; the famine years came, and Joseph gave grain to his brothers, forgiving their abuse of him.
- "Again she leaped, and twisting round the columns of the carapace . . . " (III, chap. 29, 226).
- "soulless warrior!" (II, chap. 28, 266).
- "lucid yellow" (II, chap. 28, 266).
- "by noyade" (II, chap. 28, 266).
- A possible quote, "Men to whom wine had brought death long before lay by springs of wine and drank still, too stupefied to know their lives were past" (V, chap. 46, 326).

OTHER DETAILS

- A description of the nature of a hologram (I, chap. 6, 65).
- Pictures of sikinnis and sylphs (III, chap. 6, 50).
- Pictures of centaurs (IV, chap. 22, 180).
- Several stories that seem to imply colonies of cacogens on Urth (III, chap. 14, 107).

*Commentary:* "And because of this constant searching upon one matter, I had come but a while back, upon a little book of metal, very strange and ancient, that had lain forgot in a hid place in the Great Library through ten hundred thousand years, maybe, or less or more, for all that I had knowing.

"And much that was writ in the book was common knowledge, and set mostly to the count of fairy-tales and such like, even as we of this age take not over-surely any belief in Myths of olden times" (Hodgson, *The Night Land).*

**Bull** a constellation of Urth's ZODIAC (IV, chap. 23, 190). See GREAT BULL.

**burgess** "some . . . veneal burgess had been delivered to the mercy of the guild" (I, chap. 2, 24).
History: the representative of a borough in a legislative body.

**burginot** a type of open helmet having a rounded, longitudinal crest (I, chap. 35, 291).

**Burgundofara** a young woman from Liti who signed aboard the ship of Tzadkiel, only to be sent back to Urth by Gunnie after one trip to Yesod (V, chap. 26, 183). Burgundofara is the Conciliator's companion, but she gravitates towards Captain Hadelin, betrays the Conciliator to the soldiers of the monarch, and later begs forgiveness. She plans to settle down in Liti with Hadelin and have children, but the Conciliator sees her future: restlessness will come again. She is "as lovely as a red roe" (v, chap. 37, 263). See GUNNIE.

*History:* Saint Burgundofara (died 657) was blessed by Saint Columbanus in her infancy and early developed a religious vocation in spite of her noble Frankish father, who in the end founded for her the nunnery of Brige (Brie).

**Butcher** a character in "The Tale of the Boy Called Frog" who causes trouble for the infant hero (III, chap. 19, 151). He is a smilodon (or sabertooth cat) in whole, in part, or perhaps only figuratively.

# C

**cabochon emeralds** "Thecla was . . . stroking a bracelet formed like a kraken, a kraken whose tentacles wrapped the white flesh of her arm; its eyes were cabochon emeralds" (1, chap. 8, 81).
*History:* emeralds polished without cutting, as was the way of all gems in the ancient world.

**cacogen** literally, "those filthy born" (1, chap. 2, 23). More broadly, degenerate. An ethnic slur aimed against those born off-world. *Extrasolarian* is the neutral term.
*History:* an antisocial person.

**Cadroe of the Seventeen Stones** a monomachist at the Sanguinary Field (1, chap. 27, 235). Note that seventeen has a sinister charge in the Urth Cycle: the seventeen megatherians written about by Blaithmaic were "great beasts"; and Ascia is ruled by the Group of Seventeen. (For other monomachists, see LAURENTIA OF THE HOUSE OF THE HARP and SABAS OF THE PARTED MEADOW.)
*History:* Saint Cadroe (died 976) was a Scots prince who became a Benedictine monk.

**Caesalipinia sappan** a botanical sign in the Jungle Garden (1, chap. 19, 178).
*History:* a tropical tree from which the heavy wood brazilwood is obtained. Brazilwood is used as red and purple dyewoods and in cabinetwork.

**Caesidius** a military leader who married Autarchia Valeria during her regency in Severian's fifty-year absence (v, chap. 46, 328). He died the year before Severian returned from Yesod. ("Dux" is his title, meaning "battle leader" and related to "Duke.")
*Onomastics:* "of the steel-gray eyed" (Latin).
*History:* Saint Caesidius was martyred on the shores of Lake Fucino in the 3rd century.

**caique** a light boat or skiff propelled by one or more rowers, much used on the Bosphorus (I, chap. 13, 127). Those used on Acis River have eight oars.

**Caitanya** [chai-TUN-yuh] "Possibly we all come to such a time, and it is the will of the Caitanya that each damn herself for what she has done" (IV, chap. 2, 21). Under the usual questioning, Wolfe answers that he means a goddess of consciousness and intelligence (akin to Athena and Minerva), who is called Wisdom in Bible translations.
*Onomastics:* "spirit, consciousness, especially higher consciousness," "Supreme Being" (Sanskrit).
*History:* an Indian mystic (A.D. 1485–1533) of this name led a Hindu sect focused in part on the love of Krishna and his consort Radha as the archetype of mystical union. He is regarded by his followers as an incarnation of both Krishna and Radha in a single form.
*Commentary:* this name is spoken by Thecla, on the one hand showing her esoteric and/or syncrestic knowledge, and on the other hand showing her unguessed powers of prophesy: Severian and Thecla themselves are later united in one body. Other

prophesies-come-true include her sitting on the throne and her desire to create a new religion.

**caldarium** a (Roman) hot bath or bath-room (III, chap. 7, 59).

**Calendar** the Commonwealth calendar of thirteen months (twenty-eight days each) is based on the lunar year and as there are no non-calendar days it is not reconciled with the solar year. According to Wolfe, months can be designated by expected, historic, or natural events; for example, we might refer to our own 20th century American November as "Thanksgiving," "Blackout," or "Sleet," depending on what we were talking about. Wolfe goes on to write that people in the Commonwealth simply aren't as time conscious as we are; there is too much history for anyone to learn (or care about) any but recent history, and it's generally assumed that next year will be very much like this one. The only month named in the Urth Cycle is that of the Spading Moon (ES, 211), which seems to derive from the agricultural activities of fall.

It is difficult to map the calendar under these circumstances. Most holidays are assumed to be both seasonal and "floating," so that, for example, the Feast of Holy Katharine will fall sometime after the middle of winter but not in spring. In addition, it is not known if the seasons are all of equal length (around 91.25 days), since the dying sun might cause the winter cooling to be greater and summer heating to be less, perhaps causing years with long winters and short summers. But without any clues from the text, the following calendars assume that each season is equal, having about three months and one week: the year is exactly fifty-two weeks long and begins (at least one time) in the middle of summer.

## Calendar

At the Matachin Tower they use numbered days to track the progress of the month (a detail revealed when Roche says it is the eighteenth, not even three weeks since his elevation [1, chap. 8, 82]) but while out in the field Severian periodically notices the moon phase of Lune. This helps track things in some cases, but causes vexing problems in others (for example, to the untrained observer the Moon can appear "full" for three nights before Full Moon). The following table illustrates the assumptions made in using moon phase data to patch gaps in the calendars.

| Symbol | Phase | Days | Moonrise/Moonset Times |
|---|---|---|---|
| ● | New | 1 to 7 | New Moon in sky during day (rises when sun rises, sets when sun sets). |
| ◖ | 1st Q. | 8 to 14 | Waxing Moon rises about mid-day, sets around midnight. |
| ○ | Full | 15 to 21 | Full Moon rises when sun sets. |
| ◗ | 3rd Q. | 22 to 28 | Waning Moon rises around midnight. |
| [ ] | | | Implied phase. |

*Notes*

Symbol Column: the symbols for First Quarter (Waxing) and Third Quarter (Waning) are reversed from their usual Northern Hemisphere positions to better approximate the Southern Hemisphere orientation of the Commonwealth.

Days Column: at times it seems as though the Commonwealth month is so linked to the phases of Lune that one can assign days of the month in this manner. Because New Year's Day seems to come on a New Moon, it seems to follow that the Commonwealth month begins at the New Moon.

## Four Fragmentary Calendars of Events in *The Book of the New Sun*

### **First Calendar:** from near-drowning to Echopraxia (2 P.S.)

| Week | Events |
|---|---|
| 1 | New Year's Day at middle of summer. |
| 8 | Fall starts. |
| 14 | Middle of fall, the fall when Severian saves Vodalus. |
| 21 | Winter starts. |
| 27 | Middle of winter. Severian meets Triskele, later Valeria. |
| 30 | 1st: Feast Day (elevation of Drotte & Roche). * |
| 31 | 13th: Thecla arrives (1, chap. 7, 71). |
| | 14th: Journeymen sent to House Absolute. |
| 32 | 15th: Severian visits Library. |
| | 17th: Severian called to Gurloes. |
| | 18th: Severian's first visit to Echopraxia, snow. |
| 34 | Spring starts. |
| 47 | Summer starts. |

### **Second Calendar:** from tower to gate ("the last year" or 1 P.S.)

| Week | Events |
|---|---|
| 21 | Winter starts. |
| 28 | Waitress (future Jolenta) begins her job at the cafe. |
| 30 | 1st: Feast Day (elevation of Severian). † |
| | 2nd: Prisoner Marcellina arrives. |
| | 3rd: Thecla tortured, Severian betrays guild, confesses. |
| | 5th: Trial. |
| 31 | 14th: Exiled to Thrax, night with Baldanders. |
| 32 | 15th: Meet Agia, Dorcas. Fight in duel. |
| | 16th: Awaken in lazaret. |
| | 17th: Execution of Agilus, the flying cathedral, the play. |
| | 18th: Meet Hethor, Jonas. |

## Calendar

**Third Calendar:** from Saltus to the stone town (spring of 1 P.S.)

| Moon | Events |
|---|---|
| | Day 1: Jonas and Severian arrive in Saltus. Water into wine. |
| | Day 2: Saltus Fair. Help Green Man, execute Morwenna. ‡ |
| [◑] | Day 3: Severian and Jonas taken to Vodalus, feast of Thecla. |
| | Day 4: Given horses in morning. |
| | Day 7: Fourth morning of travel, arrive at House Absolute. |
| | Day 8: Escape antechamber. |
| | Day 9: The play partially performed. Moon near full. § |
| ○ | Day 10: Rejoin troupe, night of undine on Cephissus. ** |
| | Day 11: Walking through cane. |
| | Day 12: Walking on the pampa, sleep at herdman's hut. |
| | Day 13: The stone town. Moon past full (II, chap. 31, 278). |

* The feast day falls in "fading of winter" (I, chap. 11, 104), which is here interpreted as meaning sometime after the middle of winter (week 27) but before the beginning of spring (week 34).

† Here the assumption is that the feast day is always on the first of that month, as seems the case in the previous year.

‡ Severian tells the Green Man that he left Nessus a few days earlier (II, chap. 3, 26), so the "Day 1" might be the 20th of the month.

§ "Quarter moon hangs low in the eastern sky [after sunset]" (II, chap. 23, 209), taken here to mean that the First Quarter (Waxing) Moon week is nearly over.

** Sunrise comes at about the same time as moonset (II, chap. 27, 258; chap. 28, 264).

## **Fourth Calendar:** from Thrax to throne (I P.S. to S.R. I)

| Week | Moon | Events |
|---|---|---|
| 40?–45 | | In the latter part of spring, Severian and Dorcas travel from stone town to Thrax (III, chap. 1, 14), riding with a caravan (IV, chap. 36, 294). |
| 46 | ☽ | First week in Thrax. * |
| 47 | ● | Court in session (New Moon). Cyriaca sees Severian at court. Summer begins. |
| 48 | ☾ | Third week in Thrax.<br>27th: Two fire murders in Thrax.<br>28th: Last day of court in session. Full Moon that night (III, chap. 1, 14). Three fire murders in Thrax (III, chap. 4, 38) |
| 49 | ○ | 1st: Dorcas tours prison. Alzabo eats Severa. (See note on anomaly, next page.)<br>2nd: Dorcas at Duck's Nest. Archon's party. †<br>3rd: Into the mountains.<br>4th: The widow's house. (Alzabo eats Becan.)<br>5th: Severian adopts little Severian.<br>6th: Circle of the Sorcerers.<br>7th: Sleep. |
| 50 | [?] | 8th: Skirts of the mountain.<br>9th: Climbing.<br>10th: Cursed town.<br>11th: Typhon killed.<br>12th: On high paths.<br>13th: Shepherd's bothy (evening).<br>14th: Lake Diuturna (evening). |

* Here the assumption is that the minimum time was spent in Thrax, but they could have arrived in earlier weeks.

† "Under the waning moon [the water of the vincula] seemed almost a lake" (III, chap. 12, 95). Technically the Moon is "waning" the second after it becomes Full Moon, so this does not require the Moon to be Third Quarter (Waning).

## Fourth Calendar (continued)

| Week | Moon | Events |
|---|---|---|
| 51 | ○ | 15th: The hetman's boat. |
| | | 16th: Gathering islands and assault on castle. (Moon waning *). |
| | D | 17th: The search for the Claw begins. |
| | | 18th: The Claw found (no food). |
| | | 19th: Deep into the hills. |
| | | 20th: Dead soldier. |
| | | 21st: Walking to lazaret/fever night. |
| 52 | D | 22nd: Meet Foila, etc. |
| | | 23rd: Introduce Miles to Foila, etc. Hallvard's story. |
| | | 24th: Melito's story. |
| | ☽ | 25th: Loyal's story. |
| | | 26th: Foila's story. Mannea by moonlight (IV, chap. 14, 113). |
| | | 27th: On the way to Last House. † |
| | | 28th: Last House. |
| 01 | ● | 1st: Mid-summer, New Year's Day, S.R. 1. |
| | | 2nd: Find survivors of lazaret. |
| | | 3rd: Wandering. |
| | | 4th: Wandering. |
| | | 5th: Find rusty falchion, join military group. |
| 02 | ☾ | ? : Patrol, followed by other patrols and days of idleness. |
| | | 13th: Day before battle, moon waxed nearly to the full. |
| | | 14th: Third Battle of Orithyia. |

* Waning moon slightly more than half full (III, chap. 36, 287).

† "The old moon had died while I lay in the lazaret and the new would not be born for several days" (IV, chap. 15, 118).

(The fourth calendar anomaly at weeks 49 to 52 might be solved if week 49 was changed to a New Moon, making week 50 a 1st Quarter Waxing, week 51 a Full Moon, and week 52 a 3rd Quarter Waning.)

## Fourth Calendar (conclusion)

| Week | Moon | Events |
|---|---|---|
| 03 | ○ | 15th: Down in flier, caught by Ascians, rescued by Agia, hit by Agia.<br>16th: First visit by old leech.<br>17th: Strong enough to rise.<br>18th: Second visit by leech, visit by Agia.<br>20th: Strong enough to look out window in day, bat bite at night.<br>21st: Taken before Vodalus. |
| 04 | [D] | March through jungle for seven days. |
| 05 | [●] | 1st: Meet Ascian horde.<br>2nd: Catch up with rearguard. Midnight interview.<br>3rd: Severian becomes autarch, escapes, walks on beach, gets passage on Samru (20 days). |
| 06 | [◖] | Passage on Samru. |
| 07 | [○] | Passage on Samru. (Summer ends by count of weeks.)<br>21st: See Dorcas in mourning. |
| 08 | [D] | 22nd: Arrive at Citadel.<br>23rd: Bad Gold and Burning. The Trason incident.<br>24th: Across the River Again. |

**caliver** a non-lethal rifle-weapon used on the ship of Tzadkiel, the caliver fires a binding cord (v, chap. 2, 13). As the stricken creature struggles, the cords tighten. It is used to capture escaped animals.
*History:* a type of long gun without a rest, used principally for military purposes in the late 16th and early 17th centuries. The barrel length is 39 inches. The overall length is 4.5 feet. The bore is 17.

**calotte** a skullcap (IV, chap. 28, 193), or a caplike architectural construction, especially the interior of a small cupola or a cup-shaped vault (II, chap. 17, 148).

**caloyer** "A caloyer in red stood beside the scaffold clutching his little formulary; he was an old man, as most of them are" (II, chap. 4, 33).
*History:* a Greek monk, especially of the order of Saint Basil.

**camarilla** ("little room") a cabal, or kitchen cabinet, i.e., a group of secret schemers or unknown advisors (I, chap. 25, 223).

**camisias** the shirt worn by Arabs and other Mohammedans (I, chap. 20, 181).

**Camoena** a peer of Ossipago, Barbatus, and Famulimus, so either a Hierodule or a godling (III, chap. 33, 265).
*Myth:* (Roman) a minor goddess of prophecy, either one of the Camenae (ancient Italian nymphs of springs and fountains, sometimes identified with the Greek muses) or the mother of the Camenae.

**cangues** yoke for oxen, porter's yoke, or wooden collars having holes for the neck and hands, used to restrict a person's movement (I, chap. 30, 258).

**Canog** a student imprisoned in the prison-hulk cell next to the Conciliator in the reign of Typhon (V, chap. 37, 264). He had killed a shopkeeper while trying to burglarize the shop at night.

After overhearing the Conciliator speaking to his followers, he writes (Canog's) *The Book of the New Sun* (266).
*History:* Saint Canog (Cynog), eldest son of King Brychan of Brecknock, died in 492 at Merthyr-Cynog.

**cantle** the protuberant part at the back of a saddle; the hindbow (I, chap. 25, 297).

**capote** a long shaggy cloak or overcoat with a hood, worn by soldiers, sailors, travelers, et cetera (I, chap. 16, 153). Or a long mantle reaching to the feet, worn by women.

**captain of the Alycone** see HADELIN.

**captain of the jibers** there is brief mention of a mutiny leader when Purn says, "If there's a captain of the jibers, we've never heard of him till now" (V, chap. 11, 81). The other sailors are silent, which might mean that they dare not admit knowing more.

The best candidate for such a leader is the giant winged creature that kills Severian in the spiracle (V, chap. 9, 65). This monster seems too big and powerful to be one of the zoo creatures in the ship's hold, but it might be one that escaped confinement during the power outage. Furthermore, the hierogrammates themselves can be giant and have wings, suggesting that the monster is a type of fallen angel. So it is possible that the monster is Tzadkiel, which makes more sense if it is related to little Tzadkiel, the one who was subsequently exiled to Brook Madregot.

**captain of the Samru** a sly-faced man with a craquemarte (IV, chap. 32, 255), a sword that he lends to Severian (258) for his brief trip into the ruins of Oldgate, to the south of living Nessus.

**captain of the tender** a human male commanding the spaceship taking Severian and Burgundofara from starship to Urth (V, chap. 27, 191).

**Capulus** the wall that closes off the Acis valley and forms the southern boundary of Thrax (III, chap. 2, 18).
*Latin:* "the sword haft."

**capybara** the largest extant rodent quadruped, closely related to the guinea pig; it lives around the rivers of tropical South America and has habits much like those of the muskrat (I, chap. 11, 105).

**caracara** a South American bird similar to the vulture (I, chap. 2, 21).

**caravel** "the carrion-eating teratornises . . . each borne on wings as wide as the main yard of a caravel" (III, chap. 17, 137).
*History:* a small, light sailing ship of the kind used by the Spanish and Portuguese in the 15th and 16th centuries.

**carcanet** Severian writes of the carved mountains of Urth, each a monument to an autarch, and how he imagined them with "crystal streams like carcanets" (III, chap. 2, 20).
*History:* an ornamental collar or necklace.

**carillon** a set of bells so hung and arranged as to be capable of being played upon either by manual action or by machinery (II, chap. I, 8).

**Carina** the personal name of the contessa, a character in Dr. Talos's play *Eschatology and Genesis* (II, chap. 24, 224). Her maids are Kyneburga, Lybe, and Solange.
*Onomastics:* "beloved," "a keel" (Latin).
*History:* Saint Carina (died 360) was wife of Saint Melasippus, mother of Antoninus, all three martyred by Julian the Apostate.
*Commentary:* for names which also detail parts of ships, see PEGA.

**cariole** a light four-wheel open or covered one-horse carriage; or a light covered cart (II, chap. I, 7).

**carnelian** "A snake with carnelian eyes came gliding onto the path, lifted a venomous head to look at us, then slipped away" (I, chap. 20, 180).
*History:* reddish semiprecious stone.

**carnifex** "Lesser places have no more than a carnifex, who takes life and performs such excruciations as the judicators there decree" (I, chap. 13, 123).
*History:* an executioner. Note that carnificate means "to hang."

**carnificial sword** the executioner's sword (I, chap. 4, 39).
*History:* the blade is square-tipped and double-edged. Often it is engraved with illustrations depicting Justice, scenes from the Bible, or methods of execution.

**carrack** a big square-rigged merchant ship, used in the 14th, 15th, and 16th centuries; a galleon (I, chap. 15, 141).

**carronade** Severian sees one among the cargo in Tzadkiel's ship (V, chap. 3, 17).
*History:* a short piece of ordnance, usually of large caliber, having a chamber for the powder like a mortar. It is mainly used on ships. (From Carron, near Falkirk in Scotland, where originally cast.)

**carthartidae** zoological family of vultures (II, chap. 29, 271).

**caryatid** a draped female sculpture serving as a pillar (I, chap. 9, 87).

**Cas** the name DORCAS'S HUSBAND uses for his long-dead wife.

**Casdoe** wife of Becan, mother of little Severian and Severa (III, chap. 15, 114). Her mother is Herais of Thrax. After Becan is eaten by an alzabo, she tries to hold the family together, but she is killed by zoanthropes.
*History:* Saint Casdoe (of the group Dadas, Casdoe, and Gabdelas) was wife of Dadas (a noble Persian). All three were martyred under Shapur II.

**Casdoe's father** the old man at the widow's house (III, chap. 15, 114). At about the same age as Palaemon, he was a boyhood friend of Fechin and seems to have known the artist before Rudesind met him. Severian assumes he is Casdoe's father (III, chap. 15, 115; III, chap. 17, 137), but there is no explanation given as to why

Casdoe's mother Herais is still in Thrax if her husband is with Casdoe. That is, the old man may more logically be Becan's father and Casdoe's father-in-law.

**casern** one of a series of small (temporary) buildings between the ramparts and houses of a fortified town for the accommodation of troops; barracks (I, chap. 16, 151).

**castellan** the commander of the Citadel at Nessus (I, chap. 12, 115), an old soldier, silver-haired and lame (IV, chap. 33, 265). Aquastor Malrubius says to Severian the new autarch, "You are not ready. . . . You were nurtured in the Citadel of Nessus — what are the words for its castellan?" (IV, chap. 31, 245). *History:* the governor or warden of a castle or fortress; one who administers the affairs of a stronghold but is not the owner.

**Cat, The** a short story of Urth, first published in the *1983 World Fantasy Convention Program Book,* later collected in ES. Written by Odilo (II), it tells the strange history of Sancha.

**catachtonian** a misspelling of catachthonian, subterranean (III, chap. 6, 54).

**catafalque** a coffin support used in elaborate funerals (V, chap. 9, 64).

**catamite** a boy used in homosexual (pederastic) relations (III, chap. 35, 279).

**cataphract** a soldier in full armor, typically chainmail (I, chap. 12, III).

**Catherine** a monial who left her order, she became pregnant by Ouen (IV, chap. 37, 305–306). While imprisoned in the Matachin Tower for reasons unknown, she gave birth to Severian the Great. She is said to be dark complexioned. Severian has a memory of her nursing him in a grey cell (II, chap. 27, 257). She is probably the MAID WHO PLAYS THE ROLE OF KATHARINE on the feast days of the torturers. See KATHARINE, HOLY.
*Commentary:* she probably was a Pelerine (hence Severian's bastard exultant lineage) and her reason for leaving the order (of "professional virgins," as Agia called it) may well have been her carnal knowledge of Ouen and resulting pregnancy. The reason for her arrest, aside from the cryptic protection of the unborn Severian, may relate to preserving exultant bloodlines.

If she had been a Pelerine, she must be an exultant, an armigette, or a rare optimate. If she is an exultant, this would explain Severian's semi-exultant height, as well as her own exultant stature.

The connection between Dorcas's family and the Pelerines is through the enameled crucifixes manufactured by Dorcas's father and brother, sold by Dorcas and her husband, and presumably bought by the Pelerines whenever they were in the area. This is precisely the scenario described by Ava as the way in which the rare optimate enters the Pelerines: an optimate family having a long relationship with the monials. Yet there is no indication that the Pelerines would take an infant as a postulant, if, for instance, Dorcas had died giving birth to a daughter.

Catherine may be a khaibit, yet a virginal khaibit seems possible only if, hypothetically, her "original" died at an early age and the khaibit was released from service to the throne into service with the Pelerines. This could give the government reason to pursue a woman who had left an order of monials: to control exultant bloodlines and punish breach of contract.

Then again, the old autarch was unmanned in Yesod and did not begin prostituting his khaibit harem until "about the year you [Severian] were born" (IV, chap. 24, 194), which allows for a lot of virginal khaibits.

Perhaps Catherine was not really a monial at all, but only a khaibit who escaped the Well of Orchids (or the opening night of the House Azure) while in costume, in the same way that Cyriaca escaped Thrax. An escaped khaibit, impregnated by a commoner, might be enough of a crisis to warrant her stay in the tower.

**Catodon** another mysterious godling mentioned in passing in *Urth* (V, chap. 43, 306).
*Onomastics:* "down-tooth" (Greek).
*History:* a genus of cetaceans, including the sperm whale, so called from the fact of its having teeth in the lower jaw only.
*Myth:* another name for Leviathan, as in Job 41:1. Rhetorically, the speaker in *Urth* is asking whether the human race has god-like power; whether it can catch Leviathan with a hook and tame him with a bit.

**catoptric armor** ("mirror" armor) reflective to the point of chameleon-like invisibility, this full-body armor is used only by the Praetorian guards at the House Absolute (II, chap. 14, 118).

Probably of stellar technology, its name is given much later (v, chap. 38, 271).

**cavalry** the mounted forces of the Commonwealth travel an average of fifteen leagues a day through friendly areas (i, chap. 28, 243) and are organized into iles, baceles, and xenagies. The armor worn by destrier and rider is usually of a composite material similar to Kevlar. The pyrotechnic weapons fire jets of a substance which is like napalm but burns at a higher temperature, at ranges of twenty-five to fifty yards. For more detail see the article "Cavalry in the Age of the Autarch" in CD. For Ascian cavalry, see TALLMAN RIDERS.

**cavy** any of various short-tailed or apparently tailless South American rodents of the family *Caviidae,* which includes the guinea pig and the CAPYBARA (iii, chap. 27, 222).

**Ceallach** one of the best wood-carvers in the village Gurgustii of Typhon's era (v, chap. 33, 236). He and Anian make the staff for Severian the Conciliator (v, chap. 30, 209).
*Onomastics:* "bright headed" (Irish/Gaelic; the Anglicized form is "Kelly"); "warrior" (Gaelic); "strife" (Irish).
*History:* there are several saints Ceallach. One, a disciple of Saint Kieran of Clonmacnoise in the 6th century, served as bishop of Killala and then retired as a hermit.

**celeriac** a turnip-rooted variety of garden celery (v, chap. 5, 31).

**celestine** a delicate blue, the color of heaven (i, chap. 31, 268).

**celure** "This affair will wear out the night, and at dawn, if the archon is still enjoying himself, they'll . . . perhaps even raise the celure over the garden" (III, chap. 5, 46).
*Latin:* ceiling, canopy.

**cenobite** a member of a religious order living in a community, as opposed to an anchorite, who lives in solitude (II, chap. 4, 36).

**cenotaph** an empty tomb; a sepulchral monument erected in honor of a deceased person whose body is elsewhere (II, chap. 14, 122).

**Cephissus** a tributary of Gyoll (II, chap. 28, 262). It lies north of the HOUSE ABSOLUTE and probably forms its boundary. Severian later recalls "the glossy leaved hardwoods of the tropical forest we had left behind on the south bank of the Cephissus" (III, chap. 13, 91), suggesting that the House Absolute is covered by a tropical garden.
*Geography:* a river in Greece, near Athens.
*Myth:* (Greek, "the river of gardens") a river god who was the father of Narcissus, also attributed to a river surrounding the Garden of Eden. Furthermore, in the myth of Deucalion's Flood, after the ark lands on a mountain top, the last humans (Deucalion and Pyrrha) pray at the shrine of Themis, beside the river Cephissus. At Themis's instruction, they throw stones over their shoulders, and these become the men and women of the new human race.

**cerbotana** a blowgun of South America (II, chap. 1, 11). From the Italian and Spanish name for the blowgun.

**cerise** a shade of dark red, the color of ripe cherries (I, chap. 27, 235). "A reminder of the dying of the old sun" (CD, 246).

**Ceryx** [KAY-rooks] the mountebank mage of Os, the necromancer who re-animates Zama (V, chap. 30, 210).
*Onomastics:* "a herald" (Greek).
*Myth:* (Greek) Ceryx was a son of Hermes and either Pandrosus or her sister Herse. A messenger of the gods like his father, he was the ancestor of the Kerukes, a family of priests in Athens.
*Commentary:* Ceryx's power would appear to be telekinetic in nature. See MAGIC IN THE URTH CYCLE.

**Chad** son of Morwenna and Stachys, killed by Morwenna (II, chap. 1, 7).
*Onomastics:* "warlike," "warrior" (Old English).
*History:* Saint Chad (died 672) was the first bishop of Mercia and Lindsey at Lichfield.

**chain** see MEASUREMENT TABLES.

**chalcedony** a precious (or semiprecious) stone that in its various tints is largely used in lapidary work, having the luster nearly of wax and being either transparent or translucent (I, chap. 1, 16).

**champian** [SHAM-peean] "the tent-cathedral had been pitched on a champian surrounded by semi-fortified houses" (I, chap. 19, 170).
*History:* an expanse; flat or open country.

**chandler** one who sells marine supplies, a ship-chandler (I, chap. 35, 293). The word was originally used for one who makes and sells candles.

**chapel** a ruinous building in the Grand Court of the Citadel complex where the torturers celebrate their feast days. With broken pews and lacking a roof altogether, the chapel is perhaps a chiliad old, and Severian's curious vision of its earlier state, with roof and ruby lamps (I, chap. 11, 110) is one of his first visits to the corridors of Time.

**Chara** name of the female dog in the constellation the Hounds (IA, 44).
*Astronomy:* the southern dog of Canes Venatici, her name means "dear to the heart" of her master. This part of the constellation contains the two brightest stars.

**chatelaine** [SHAT-lane] polite form of address for a female exultant.
*History:* (English from French) the lady of a chateau (a French castle or large country house).

**chatoyant** "at first it was the colorless light of the creature, then a rapid alternation of chatoyant pastels — peacock blue, lilac, and rose" (III, chap. 9, 74).
*History:* play of colors in a mineral.

**chechia** [SHASH-ya] "It was Dr. Talos. He appeared to be in funds, and he had dressed himself for the occasion in a capot of red velvet and a chechia of the same material" (IV, chap. 36, 291).

*History:* a cylindrical brimless cap of Arab origin often having a tassel on the crown. From Shash, a town in Persia where it was manufactured in medieval times.

**cherkaji** "lightly armed cherkajis whose formations were seas of plumes and flags" (IV, chap. 22, 172).
*History:* light cavalry of Persia.

**chiliad** [KILL-ee-ad] one thousand years. See MEASUREMENT TABLES.

**chiliarch** [KILL-ee-ark] commander of 1,000 men; roughly, a colonel (the officer in charge of a column) (I, chap. 28, 243). See MILITARY ORGANIZATION.

**chiliarch of the Xenagie of the Blue Dimarchi** "The chiliarch had tried to hand me my fee instead of casting it on the ground at my feet (as is customary), and I had to dissuade him for the sake of his reputation" (I, chap. 31, 266). The authority who sentences Agilus to death. The blue-armored horsemen who respond to the disturbance at the Piteous Gate (II, chap. 1, 8) are almost certainly his men.

**Chimera** [kih-MERE-uh] the figures painted on the breastplates of the Septentrions (I, chap. 17, 156) apparently consist of winged women with the paws and hindquarters of lions, and while Severian calls this design a Chimera, such a design might also be termed a variety of sphinx.

*Myth:* a fire-breathing monster of Greek mythology, usually described as either constantly shifting in form, or as being part lion, part goat, and part dragon.

**choralcelo** a keyboard instrument like the piano but with electromagnets vibrating the strings and producing an organlike effect with string quality (ES, 216).

**chrism** oil mingled with balm, consecrated for use as an unguent in the administration of certain sacraments in the Eastern and Western churches (I, chap. 10, 102). The chrism of the torturers is blood.

**chrisos** the gold coin of the Commonwealth, stamped with the profile of an autarch (I, chap. 3, 31). A chrisos will purchase a good mount. See MEASUREMENT TABLES.

**chronon** "as if some unimaginable power had acted in the interval between one chronon and the next (III, chap. 8, 67). A moment.
History: the hypothetical smallest unit of time, according to a theory that time is not continuous but rather made up of tiny particles jammed together like beads on a string. The chronon is calculated to be $10^{-24}$ seconds (one million, million, millionth of a second).

**Chuniald** a male servant of Thea who serves her in the woods (II, chap. 10, 86).
*History:* Saint Chuniald (7th century) was an Irish or Scottish missionary who evangelized southern Germany and Austria.

**Cilinia** (entry from EATA'S MAUSOLEUM) a character from Wolfe's *Book of the Long Sun* and *Book of the Short Sun,* and as such, beyond the scope of this work. However, it turns out her coffin lies in the Citadel's necropolis.

**Cinnia** wife of Bregwyn, mother of Herena, living in Typhon's era (v, chap. 29, 203).
*Onomastics:* "beauty" (Irish).
*History:* Saint Cinnia (5th century), a princess of Ulster, Ireland. She was converted to Christianity by Saint Patrick, who also gave her the veil when she entered a convent.

**Citadel of the Autarch** an ancient fortress located near the center of Nessus, on top of Citadel Hill, on the northern edge of the Algedonic Quarter, east of the Gyoll. Near the heart of the citadel is the Atrium of Time. Within the citadel are the Great Keep, the Broken Court, the Blue Hall, the Flag Tower, the Tower of Healing, the Drum Tower, the Chapel, the Library, and the Grand Court. In back (to the west) of the citadel proper stand two towers on the Old Yard: the Witches' Keep and the Matachin Tower. Further west is the curtain wall, in which there is an ancient breach between the Red Tower and the Bear Tower. Beyond the wall of unsmeltable metal lies the necropolis, which slopes down to meet the river Gyoll, just beyond the Potter's Gate.
*Commentary:* the citadel complex was probably a starport during the First Empire period of the Age of the Monarch. During the reign of Typhon, when all the functional spaceships fled the planet, the remaining hulks were used as buildings, marking the transition from port to citadel. Jonas suggests in his interrupted

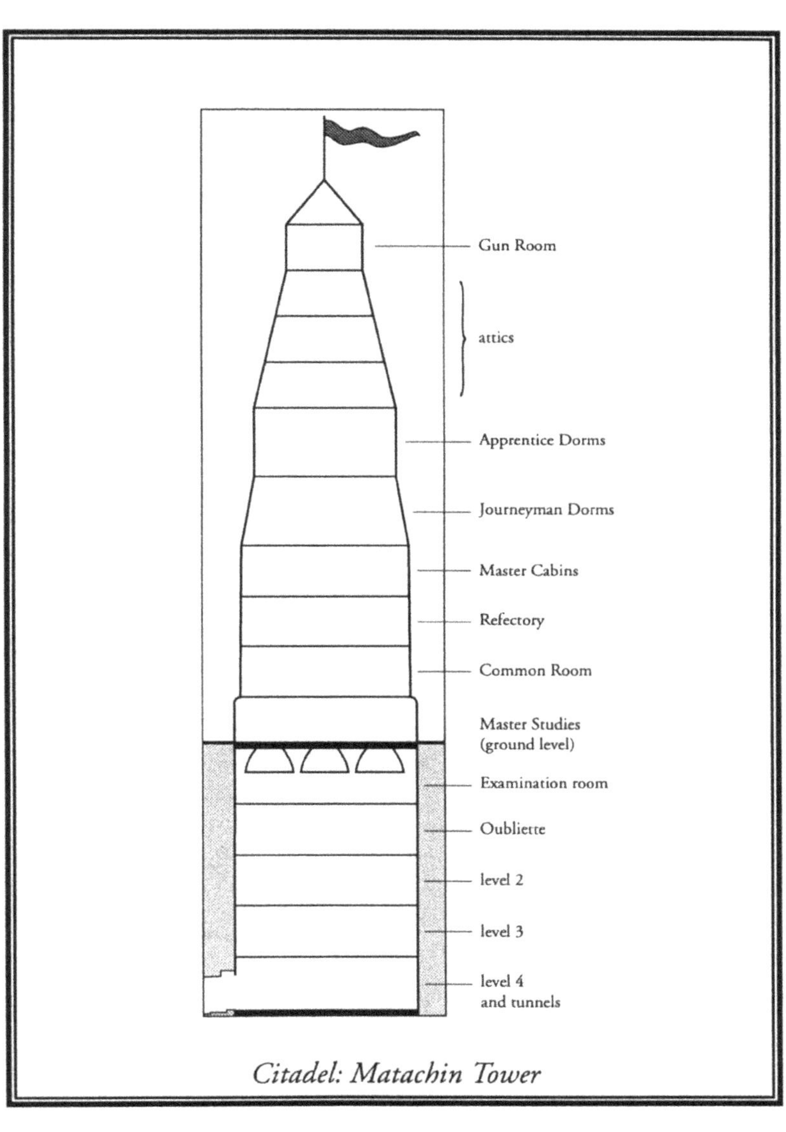


*Citadel: Matachin Tower*

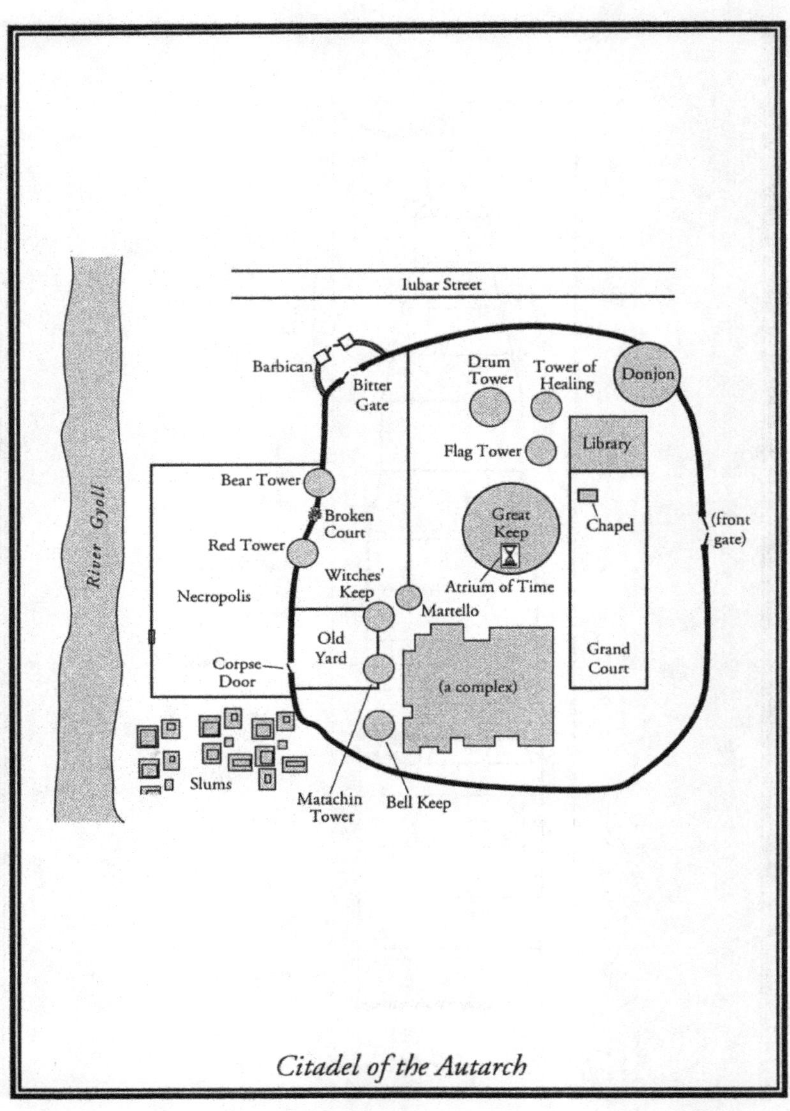
Iubar Street
River Gyoll
Barbican
Bitter
Gate
Drum
Tower
Tower of
Healing
Donjon
Flag Tower
Library
Bear Tower
Broken
Court
Great
Keep
Chapel
(front
gate)
Red Tower
Witches'
Keep
Atrium of Time
Necropolis
Martello
Old
Yard
Grand
Court
Corpse
Door
(a complex)
Slums
Matachin
Tower
Bell Keep

*Citadel of the Autarch*

tale (I, chap. 35, 273) that the Citadel and Wall of Nessus were constructed (in the Age of Myth or the Age of the Monarch) to protect the despotic leader from his own subjects.

**cithara** an ancient musical instrument of triangular shape with seven to eleven strings, not unlike the lyre or phorminx (V, chap. 24, 173).

**citrine** a pale-yellow variety of quartz, resembling topaz, or the greenish-yellow color of a lemon (I, chap. 3, 31).

**citron** fruit trees related to orange and lemon trees, and their fruit (I, chap. 16, 151). The trees in the text were grown in pots and taken inside during the winter.

**clava** (Latin) a staff or cudgel (IV, chap. 37, 297).

**clave** a key the size of a small crowbar, used by the clavigers (III, chap. 2, 39). Because of its size, it serves as a club as well as an emblem.
*Latin:* from clavis, key.

**claviger** literally "one with keys," a guard of the Vincula (II, chap. 29, 275). Clavigers also act as detective police. See also SERGEANT OF THE VINCULA.
*History:* applied to the key-bearers of Janus, Roman god of portals.

**Claw of the Conciliator** a relic given by the Conciliator to a group of soldiers in the era of Typhon, it became at some point

the duty of the Pelerines to care for it. Nearly everyone thinks that the Claw itself is a kind of gem, mistaking the beautiful monstrance for the relic itself.
*Commentary:* regarding the sack that Severian carries the Claw in, the text gives it as being made of doeskin at one point (III, chap. 1, 13) and human skin at another point (III, chap. 21, 173). This curious detail is seen by Malcolm Edwards and Robert P. Holdstock in *Realms of Fantasy* (1983) as a concrete example of how Wolfe uses careful signals to cast doubt upon Severian's memory.

**clerestory** the upper part of a cathedral containing a series of windows admitting light to the central part of the building (II, chap. 23, 208).

**cloisonné** the boatman says he and his wife Cas had a cloisonné shop (I, chap. 22, 199). See ROOD.
*History:* decorative enamelwork in which metal filaments are fused to the surface of an object (jewelry, vases, and other decorative accessories) to outline a design that is filled in with enamel paste. The word comes from Old French *cloison* (meaning "divided into compartments"), from Latin *clausion-* (meaning "closed, locked").

**coati** an American carnivorous mammal somewhat resembling the civet and the raccoon, with a remarkably elongated and flexible snout (IV, chap. 4, 33). Two species exist: the Brazilian (original) and the Mexican or brown coati.

**Cobblers Common** "That purple creeper you're so proud of—I met it growing wild on a hillside in Cobblers Common" (I, chap. 19, 176). An area of Nessus that Agia is familiar with, thus within the living city.

**Cock, the Angel, and the Eagle, The** story told by Melito (IV, chap. 9). It is a barnyard animal fable about a wounded rooster who won't give up the fight, even against an angel. Hallvard sees that the rooster is a symbol for the badly wounded Melito (IV, chap. 9, 72).

**coffle** a train of men or beasts fastened together, specifically a gang of slaves chained and driven along together (I, chap. 3, 35).

**cohort** one of the ten divisions of a Roman legion, consisting of 300 to 600 men (V, chap. 44, 314). See MILITARY ORGANIZATION.

**columbine** a saucy, fantastically dressed young lady (I, chap. 20, 182).

**comfits** hard, candied fruits (I, chap. 18, 165).

**Commonwealth** the Urth nation in which most of Severian's narrative takes place. Located in the southern hemisphere, its largest city is Nessus, its northern boundary is Lake Diuturna, and its southernmost territories are the Southern Isles. The autarch rules from the House Absoute.

The economy is based on agriculture, on small farms (like Melito's) and ranches (like Foila's). The Commonwealth is a poor country getting poorer, because every year the pampas claims more farmland. In such a society, poor and relatively stable over centuries, power becomes concentrated in particular families.

**Conciliator** in the Commonwealth, a historical messianic figure who lived in the age of Typhon, a chiliad before the time of Severian the Great (I, chap. 19, 171). A precursor or herald of the New Sun, the Conciliator first appeared in a small village called Vici, where he healed a girl deformed from birth. At Gurgustii he healed a man on his deathbed, and at the town of Os he fought a duel with a necromancer and won. At Saltus he was betrayed by a woman, captured by soldiers, and imprisoned at Nessus. He was taken before Typhon and disappeared shortly thereafter.
*History:* one who brings together or unites otherwise opposing elements; a peacemaker.

**Conciliator's followers** (in order of appearance):
- Burgundofara.
- Herena.
- Declan.
- cook of the *Alcyone.*
- mate of the *Alcyone.*
- sailor, brawny man of the *Alcyone.*
- Gaudentius's chiliarch of the Praetorians.

**condottiere** a professional military leader or captain who raises a troop and sells his services to states or princes at war; the leader of a troop of mercenaries (IV, chap. 19, 150).
*History:* the name arose in Italy, but the system prevailed broadly over Europe from the 14th to the 16th centuries.

**Conexa** a Pelerine rank, for example "Conexa Epicharis" (IV, chap. 10, 78).
*Latin:* "conexus," a connection, union.

**Constellations of Urth's Southern Hemisphere** Cross, the Crotali, the Eight (three stars), Great Bull, the Hounds, the Hunter, Hydra, Ihuaivulu, Little Wolf, Septentrion ("great bear"), Swan, Unicorn, and Wolf. Severian also names a few of his own: Amphisbaena and Peryton.

**contarii** a unit of contus-bearing soldiers (IV, chap. 19, 150).

**Contessa** a role in the play *Eschatology and Genesis* (II, chap. 24, 211). Outside of the play, Severian glimpses a woman who seems to be playing the role in real life at the deluge of House Absolute (V, chap. 41, 293). She has black hair and an oval face with olive complexion.
*History:* the Italian form of "countess." Her male counterpart is *conte.*

**contus** one of the many pyrotechnic (i.e., Urth technology level) "pole arms," this energy weapon is probably the simplest of them all (IV, chap. 20, 156). It has a range of twenty-five to fifty yards, and can be fired at least sixty times before needing a recharge.
*History:* Roman term for a long pole with a metal tip used for taking soundings, pushing a boat, and performing other maritime operations. Synonymous with words meaning "javelin" and "spear," the contus was used by the Roman cavalry under Vespasian (A.D. 9–79), and the mounted soldiers thus armed

(contarii) formed the wings of battle formations. Its features and functions were close to those of the later boarding pike and boat hook.

**conventicle** a secret or unauthorized meeting or assembly house (I, chap. 16, 150).

**Cook, Brother** cook for the torturers (I, chap. 3, 33). Perhaps the same person as Aybert. He is a guild member who does not actually do any torturing (see also AYBERT, BROTHER; CORBINIAN, BROTHER; and PORTER, BROTHER).

**cook of the Alcyone** a greasy, close-faced woman, she is in the group that visits Severian in the hulk (V, chap. 34, 245). "Please" is the only word he ever hears from her (V, chap. 37, 265).

**cook of the Inn of Lost Loves** said to be male by Abban ("I'll have the cook begin his preparations now" [I, chap. 25, 220]) and to be female by the pot boy ("Trudo's gone, Cook says. She was out fetchin' water . . . and seen him runnin' off" [I, chap. 26, 233]). Presumably Abban is lying in order to make his establishment sound more upscale than it is.

**Corbinian, Brother** an apothecary of the torturers (II, chap. 7, 58). He is a guild member who does not actually do any torturing (see also AYBERT, BROTHER; COOK, BROTHER; and PORTER, BROTHER).
*Onomastics:* "crow," "raven" (Latin, from "corvus").
*History:* Saint Corbinian (A.D. 670–725), born in Chartres, France, sent by Pope Gregory II to evangelize Germany.

**cordwain** a soft, fine-grained leather made of horsehide (I, chap. 6, 64). Originally applied to goatskin from Cordoba, according to John Brunner.

**cornet** a military ranking among the UHLAN of the Commonwealth.
*History:* the fifth grade of commanding officer in a British Cavalry troop who carried the standard, or the lowest commissioned rank in the U.S. Cavalry.

**coronas lucis** "They lit candelabra with crystal lenses and coronas lucis suspended from the upper limbs of the trees" (III, chap. 5, 41).
*History:* "crown of lights," a kind of firework.

**Correct Thought** the adult Ascian practice of speaking only by quoting from APPROVED TEXTS.

**corridors of Time** there are several episodes in *The Book of the New Sun* featuring the mysterious corridors of Time. The first is when Severian is drowning, during which he sees Malrubius and Juturna, and he hears a woman (presumably Catherine) crying (I, chap. 2, 16). In tracing out the intricate pattern in the tunnels below the oubliette, he enters the Atrium of Time (I, chap. 4, 33 and IV, chap. 38, 271). Severian enters the corridors briefly after the feast of his elevation and smells the perfume of Thecla's khaibit, then sees the CHAPEL restored and Malrubius again (I, chap. 11, 93). After the performance of the play at Ctesiphon's Cross he is visited by Malrubius and Triskele (I, chap. 33, 256), who have come from the corridors. While alone in the mountains, Severian senses Hethor looking at him (III, chap. 13, 256), probably by way of the corridors. Ossipago, Barbatus, and Famulimus travel in their saucer-like ship from Baldanders's tower into the corridors (III, chap. 35, 255). Through a fever in the lazaret at Media Pars, Severian enters the corridors and sees Roche, Malrubius, the Cumaean, Merryn, Hethor, Hunna, Juturna's hand, and Triskele (IV, chap. 4, 23). Of this group, all but Roche, Hethor, and Hunna are known time travelers. Hethor spies on Severian in the mountains, so he may have some limited power, but Roche and Hunna are apparently drawn in by the power of Severian's mind. The way to the Last House involves the same sort of time-maze that leads to the Atrium of Time (IV, chap. 15, all), and the second floor of the Last House looks out on a landscape many thousands of years in the future. Between fainting and waking, Severian has a vision of the Old Autarch as a minotaur (IV, chap. 24, 161), which must be his corridor analog. The Green Man, Malrubius, Triskele, and a flier appear from the corridors to take Severian from behind Ascian lines (IV, chap. 30).

**corselet** a breastplate (III, chap. 4, 40).

**coruscant** glittering, sparkling, gleaming (IV, chap. 25, 201).

**coruscate** to sparkle; glitter (I, chap. 4, 37).

**coryphaeus** the leader of a chorus (IV, chap. 22, 173).

**coryphee** the chief dancer in a ballet (I, chap. 20, 182).

**coryphodon** [ko-RIFF-o-don] a large hippopotamus-like creature, about seven and a half feet from nose to base of tail, possessing tusk-like eyeteeth (III, chap. 19, 151). Lived in and around rivers of North America and Europe during the Late Paleocene.

**cothurni** plural of cothurnus, a thick-soled boot reaching to the middle of the leg, worn by tragic actors in the ancient Athenian drama; a buskin (IV, chap. 33, 266).

**coutel** a short knife or dagger in use during the Middle Ages (IV, chap. 1, 14). Carried by irregular troops in the 13th and 14th centuries.

**coypu** a South American aquatic rodent nearly equal in size to the beaver (V, chap. 49, 347).

**craquemarte** (French) a large cutlass (IV, chap. 32, 255). Used in the 17th century.

**crenelations** details of castle architecture: embrasures, loopholes; battlements (I, chap. 28, 242).

**Cross** a constellation of Urth, visible in spring and summer, mentioned along with the Unicorn (III, chap. 18, 131; V, chap. 49, 350).
*Astronomy:* our Crux, or Southern Cross. Because it is a Polar Star of the Southern Hemisphere it is visible all year round.

**crotal** a kind of rattle (III, chap. 27, 221).

**Crotali** (the rattles) a constellation seen in the winter skies of the Commonwealth, but seen in the springtime in the era of Apu-Punchau (V, chap. 49, 346).

**Ctesiphon's Cross** an area in Nessus, in the undeveloped land between the Sanguinary Field and the highway to Piteous Gate (I, chap. 16, 149). Dr. Talos's players give a performance here.
*Geography:* Ctesiphon is the name of the Parthian capital (near Baghdad) captured by Trajan in his war against the Parthians (A.D. 113–17).
*History:* according to a tradition, the Apostles had seven disciples, among them Ctesiphon, who were sent to evangelize Spain. Ctesiphon worked at Verga (possibly Vierzo). Most of them suffered martyrdom.

**cubicula** "cubicula of moiraic women long dead" (III, chap. 6, 54).
*Latin:* cubiculum, a small sleeping chamber.

**cubit** see MEASUREMENT TABLES.

**cucurbit** "The cucurbit in which it floated was about seven spans in height and half as wide; the homuncule itself no more than two spans tall" (IV, chap. 35, 282).
*Latin:* cucurbita, a gourd, a cupping glass.

**cuir boli** (from French *cuir-bouilli)* leather boiled or soaked in hot wax and, when soft, molded or pressed into any required form; on becoming dry and hard it retains the form given to it,

and offers considerable resistance to cuts, blows, et cetera (IV, chap. 22, 177).
*History:* this may be a misspelling, but the OED lists so many versions (quir-, quyr-boilly, -boyly, -boile, boy[l]e, quere-boly, qwyrbolle, coerbuille, -boyle) that I cannot be certain. John Brunner suspects it to be Provencal.

**cuirass** armor made originally of leather and covering the body from neck to girdle; especially one consisting of a coupled breast-plate and backpiece (I, chap. 3, 33).

**culina magna** (Latin) main kitchen (ES, 210).

**cultellarii** cutthroats in 12th century France (II, chap. 2, 18).

**culverin** a type of artillery used by the Autarch's armies (IV, chap. 15, 118).
*History:* a large cannon, very long in proportion to its bore: length 10 to 13 feet; diameter 5 to 5.5 inches; and weight of shot 17 to 20 pounds.

**Cumaean** [cue-ME-un] an extrasolarian residing on Urth, a hundred-eyed reptile disguised as an old woman. She is counted among the witches as one of their own, but she seems quite independent. Hildegrin says she stays at times in a cave overlooking the Lake of Birds in the Garden of Endless Sleep.
*Myth:* the Cumaean Sibyl, earliest of the sibyls in classical mythology, was said to have come from the East and resided at Cumae (a Greek colony in Italy, northwest of Naples). She

escorted Aeneas to the underworld by way of the nearby Avernus cave. She sold the Sibylline books to Tarquin in this manner: she offered him nine books of prophesies regarding the future destiny of Rome; he refused, saying the price was too high; she burned three of them and offered the rest for the original price; he refused again; she burned three more; finally, Tarquin bought the remaining three books for the price of all nine. The books were kept at Rome in the Capitol, which was destroyed by fire in 83 B.C.
*Commentary:* the Cumaean leading Severian to meet Apu Punchau is similar to the scene in *The Aenead* where the sibyl leads Aeneas to meet the dead. The detail about the many eyes recalls Argus, the hundred-eyed giant of Greek myth. Argus was sent by Hera to guard Io, but at Zeus's command Hermes slew him. Hera then took his eyes and placed them into the tail of the peacock.

**curators** the curators' guild includes the Library's Ultan and Cyby; the picture-cleaner Rudesind; and the gardeners of the Botanic Garden, including the old man in the chair in the corner (I, chap. 19, 176).

**curtelaxe** a short axe (IV, chap. 28, 229).

**cuvee** a bulk wine, especially wine in casks or vats so blended by the vintner as to ensure uniformity and marketability: usually used of French wine (Burgundy, for example); or a blend of still wines prepared for use in secondary fermentation in the production of champagne (III, chap. 6, 50).

**Cyby** Ultan's apprentice curator (I, chap. 6, 56). He is stocky, forty years old, and has a flat, pale face. His forehead is high and square with receding gray hair (58).
*History:* Saint Cybi, aka Cuby and Kabius, was a 6th century Welsh abbot.

**Cygnet, the** an inn near River Gyoll in the living city of Nessus, north of the Citadel (ES, 32). A cygnet is a young swan, so the inn must have one on its sign. Simulatio stays here before and after his treasure hunt.

**cymar** a robe or loose light garment for women; especially an undergarment, a chemise (I, chap. 16, 153). See also SIMAR.

**cynaeous** "the magenta-breasted, cynaeous-backed parrot that flapped from tree to tree" (I, chap. 20, 179), probably a typo of "cyaneous," sky-blue.

**cynocephalus** one of a fabled race of men with dog's heads, or a kind of ape having a head like that of a dog: the Dog-faced Baboon (I, chap. 28, 242).

**Cyriaca** [kir-ee-UCK-uh] the wife of an armiger whose villa is near Thrax (III, chap. 5, 41). Her adulterous behavior is so embarrassing that the archon Abdiesus orders her execution. Her husband is away in Nessus when Severian meets her, but he had been in Thrax a week earlier, the occasion when Cyriaca saw Severian in court (45). She had been a postulant of the Pelerines but left before taking vows. She must be around thirty-five years old, and as she is not of exultant stature, to qualify for the

Pelerines she must have been an armigette by birth. Severian allows her to escape and then flees the city himself.
*Onomastics:* "dedicated to the Lord"?
*History:* two Saints Cyriaca: one (died 249) was a wealthy Roman widow who sheltered the persecuted Christians (scourged to death for her charity), and the other (died 307) was one of six Christian maidens who perished at the stake in Nicomedia.
*Commentary:* Cyriaca's connection to the Pelerines and her flight to Nessus while wearing a Pelerine's costume make a strong link to Catherine. But when she says that she might almost be Severian's mother if she had conceived within a year or two of when her menses began (III, chap. 12, 92), there is a suggestion that Cyriaca's situation could be a more direct re-enactment of what happened to Catherine.

# D

**damassin** in the autarchial quarters of the Citadel, Severian finds "a voluminous damassin cape embroidered with rotting pearls" (IV, chap. 33, 266).
*History:* a type of woven damask with gold and silver flowers.

**Danaides** "For the love of Danaides, be quiet" (V, chap. 2, 13).
*Myth:* the fifty daughters of Danaus, son of Belus and brother of Aegyptus, from whom he fled to Argos. By extension, of or belonging to the Greeks (before Troy).

**Daria** the fox-haired trollop, a mercenary in Guasacht's unit (IV, chap. 19, 151).
*Onomastics:* "rich" (Greek/Latin, feminine form of "Darius," a Persian royal name).
*History:* Saint Daria (3rd century) was originally a priestess of Minerva, until she married Saint Chrysanthus and converted to Christianity. Both were successful at converting others, so they were tortured and demeaned by order of the tribune Claudius.

**Daughters of War** a voluptuous group of warrior women from somewhere in the Commonwealth, who ride atop baluchithers and lead their foot-soldiers in battle, much like modern tanks each leading a group of infantry (IV, chap. 22, 176).
*Myth:* the legendary Amazons, who aided Priam in the Trojan War, counted Ares (god of war) and Artemis (goddess of the

Moon) as their chief deities and were led by their queen Penthesilea, daughter of Ares.

**dead assassin in the Second House** a corpse found by Severian, dead for a year at least (v, chap. 41, 291). After being resurrected he kills Valeria, wounding Severian in the process.

**dead soldier** a cadaver Severian finds (iv, chap. 1, 14). The soldier had been dead for a short time, presumably of disease. At time of death he was armed with a falchion and was wearing a simple barbute. With his blond hair, blue eyes, and pale complexion, he is probably from the south, perhaps from the Southern Isles (if so we would expect him to have a Scandinavian name). He might be from the same group of blond soldiers Severian saw at Saltus (ii, chap. 1, 11–12). His unfinished letter says he is a hundred leagues north of where he last wrote, mentions that his friend Makar fell ill, and reports that his group was harassed by Vodalarii for three nights (iv, chap. 1, 15). When resurrected, he becomes Miles.

**dead woman in the necropolis** a recently buried female body, presumably a Vodalarius, that is stolen by Vodalus, Hildegrin, and Thea (i, chap. 1, 14). She may be the mother of the nameless volunteer who said, "I'm going to watch over my mother. We've wasted too much time already. They could have her a league off by now" (i, chap. 1, 12). She may be related to the volunteer with the axe, the man killed by Severian. She may have been a tribade (see comment by WALDGRAVE). Severian is reminded of this woman when he first meets Master Ultan, who seems like a ghost in the underworld (i, chap. 6, 55–56).

*Commentary:* compare with the dead woman at the beginning of *Nightside the Long Sun*, who may be Hyacinth's mother.

**Declan** an old man of Gurgustii with a lethal tumor, he is healed by the Conciliator and becomes a follower (v, chap. 29, 207).
*Onomastics:* (DECK-lan) "goodness" (Irish).
*History:* Saint Declan (5th century) bishop in the district of Ardmore.

**Declan's relative** a big man with a loud voice, he demands an answer from Severian and is beaten by the crowd (v, chap. 29, 205).

**decollation** beheading, from "decollate," to behead (III, chap. 4, 35).

**decolletage** a low neckline on a garment (II, chap. 25, 237).

**Decuman** the sorcerer who enters a duel of magic with Severian and is killed by Hethor's slug (III, chap. 21, 170). His staff is hollow, and with the head removed it forms a blowgun for shooting poisoned darts. See MAGIC IN URTH.
*History:* Welsh saint who lived as a recluse until he was martyred in 716. Decuman is also an adjective that means "every tenth," thought of as the largest in a series; huge, enormous, especially waves.

**Deeses** icons representing the Heavenly Court (I, chap. 35, 297).

**defenestration** the act of throwing something out of a window, usually a person who is being executed (I, chap. 30, 258). Defenestration has not been performed by a member of the torturers' guild in living memory (III, chap. 4, 35).

**delator** "You mean the delator who was brought in with you?" (IV, chap. 26, 215)
*History:* an informer or accuser.

**delta** an island formed by silt deposited at the mouth of a river (I, chap. 13, 127). "It is usually triangular, like the Greek letter of its name" (CD).

**deluge** complementing the echoes of Eden scattered throughout *The Book of the New Sun* are intimations of civilization-destroying floods in the past (the XANTHIC LANDS as a remnant of a drowned continent) and in the future (the renewed world of Ushas).

- The underwater palace of the undines (I, chap. 15, 140–41).
- "I dozed, and dreamed that the world had been turned upside down. Gyoll was overhead now, decanting all its flood of fish and filth and flowers over us. I saw the great face I had seen under the water when I had nearly drowned" (I, chap. 30, 260).
- "I feel now that I'm traveling through the Citadel in a flood, solemnly rowed" (II, chap. 9, 76).
- Jonas says, "Kim Lee Soong would have been a very common kind of name when I was [ . . . ] a boy. A common name in places now sunk beneath the sea" (II, chap. 15, 130).
- The undine says, "My sisters and I will show you the forgotten cities built of old, where a hundred trapped generations of

your kin bred and died when they had been forgotten by you above" (II, chap. 28, 262).

- The chapter titled "Following the Flood," wherein the Claw lights up like a lamp after the water pours through the Vincula (III, chap. 12).
- "The remaining [floating] islands were separated now, and though the boats moved among them and sails were bent to every limb, I could not but feel that we were stationary under the streaming clouds, our motion only the last delusion of a drowning land" (III, chap. 32, 253).

**demagogue** popular leader or leader of the mob (I, chap. 31, 264).

**demilancer** "Not a cataphract, or they wouldn't have got you so easily. The demilancers?" (IV, chap. 33, 266). A type of military unit in the Commonwealth.
*History:* the light cavalry of the late 15th and early 16th centuries.

**demilune** a weapon, probably pyrotechnic, used on Urth by Ascian infantry (IV, chap. 28, 230).
*History:* a pole arm with a crescent-shaped blade at right angles to the shaft.

**Demiurge** "We who are worn [like a cloak by a god] are seldom aware that, seeming ourselves to ourselves, we are yet Demiurge, Paraclete, or Fiend to another" (II, chap. 24, 217).
*Myth:* a name for the maker or creator of the world, in the Platonic philosophy; in certain later systems, such as the Gnostic, the Demiurge is considered a being subordinate to the supreme being, and sometimes as the author of evil.

**deodand** on Urth, a deodand seems to be a person exiled to the wilderness for his crimes, "the deodands mourning their unspeakable abominations in the wilderness" (III, chap. 5, 42).
*History:* a thing forfeited or to be given to God; specifically in English law, a personal chattel which, having been the immediate occasion of the death of a human being, was given to God as an expiatory offering; i.e., forfeited to the Crown to be applied to pious uses, such as being distributed in alms.
*Commentary:* this word and the context in which it appears (a masque) strongly echo a scene in "Turjan of Miir" from Jack Vance's *The Dying Earth:* "In the shadow of a balcony a girl barbarian of East Almery embraced a man blackened and in leather harness as a Deodand of the forest" (Lancer Books edition, 12). The Vancean Deodands appear in subsequent stories as loathsome monsters, hungry for human flesh.

**Destiny** "Destiny crowned in chains" (IV, chap. 25, 204). A figure of allegory rather than mythology.

**destrier** these mounts are highly modified horses, possessing clawed feet (for better traction) and large canine teeth, sometimes referred to as "tushes," or tusks (I, chap. 28, 242). They are capable of running at 100 miles per hour, and are at least partly herbivorous.
*History:* a warhorse, a charger.

**dhole** the wild "red dog" of the Deccan in India *(Cuon alpinus dukhunensis)* (I, chap. 1, 13). They are famous for group attacks.
*Onomastics:* probably from the Kannada word meaning "wolf."

*Literature:* dholes appeared in Kipling's "Red Dog" (*The Second Jungle Book)* as a threat to Mowgli's wolf pack.

**dhow** a native vessel used on the Arabian Sea, generally with a single mast, and of 150 to 200 tons burden; a kind of lateen-rigged trading boat (I, chap. 12, 114).

**diakka** ghosts who trouble the souls of the blessed (likely from Sanskrit) (ES, 216).

**diatryma** [DIE-ah-TRY-mah] a dangerous flightless bird bred in the Bear Tower of the Citadel for bloodsports, where its beak is sheathed in steel (I, chap. 3, 33). The plural is diatrymae [DIE-ah-TRY-me].
*History:* rapacious ground birds of the Paleocene, they stood seven to eight feet tall, had strong four-toed feet, and deep, powerful beaks. They roamed throughout Europe and North America.

**Didugua** "the ford of Didugua," a geographical location between the Green and Yellow Empires in EFF (SS, 247).
*Latin:* from *diduco* "to cause to come apart, divide, split, separate" or *diduco causam* "to decide."

**dimarchi** in the Commonwealth, dimarchi serve as an archon's uniformed police as well as his troops, and are often given such duties as escorting prisoner trains to the Matachin Tower (I, chap. 3, 35). Severian sees the dimarchi at the fortress near the Sanguinary Field and at the Piteous Gate adorned in blue (the Blue Dimarchi), whereas the dimarchi of Thrax wear scarlet capes (III, chap. 13, 98). They are "organized along infantry lines and

commanded by a chiliarch" (CD, 246), so their XENAGIE has a nominal strength of 1,000 (double the usual 500).
*History:* literally, "those who fight in two ways." A species of dragoons formed by Alexander the Great, soldiers trained to act as infantry or cavalry. Usually this meant riding to the front lines and dismounting to fight on foot. In contemporary (post-WWII) terms, mechanized infantry.

**Dis** the Urth name for the outermost planet of the solar system, presumably our (former) planet Pluto (III, chap. 25, 200). See SOLAR SYSTEM TABLE.
*Myth:* from the Latin name meaning "riches," a translation of Pluto, the Greek word for riches and an alias for Hades.

**Discontent** "Discontent with her staff and glass" (IV, chap. 25, 204). An allegorical figure rather than a goddess.

**Diuturna, Lake** the northernmost part of the Commonwealth, forty leagues (as the bird flies) from Thrax. The Shore folk live in a village called Murene. The Lake folk live on floating islands. On the north shore stands the PELE TOWER of Baldanders. According to the map in *Plan[e]t Engineering,* the lake is drained by the river Fons. The lake has fish but also a species of fresh-water seals hunted by the Lake folk: their pelts provide cloaks (III, chap. 31, 247) and their shoulder bones are fashioned into spearheads (250). (Fresh-water seals are found in Lake Baikal in Russia and Lake Iliamna in Alaska.)
*Latin:* lasting a long time; of long duration.

**dolman** a long robe open in front, with narrow sleeves, worn by the Turks, or the uniform jacket of a hussar, worn like a cape with the sleeves hanging loose, or a kind of mantle with cape-like appendages instead of sleeves, worn by women (I, chap. 16, 151).

**Domnicellae** the highest rank of Pelerine, the "chief priestess" (III, chap. 5, 43). Severian and Agia meet the Domnicellae after the destruction of the altar in the Cathedral of the Claw (I, chap. 18, 167). At the costume party in Thrax, Severian mistakes Cyriaca for a Domnicellae (III, chap. 5, 43). At the lazaret in Orithyia, the Domnicellae is away, leaving Mannea in charge (IV, chap. 14, 114).

The Domnicellae they meet can tell that Severian is being truthful and Agia is lying. She says, "The Claw has not vanished in living memory, but it does so at will and it would be neither possible nor permissible for us to stop it." As a result of this loss during her stewardship, she has the cathedral burned (IV, chap. 10, 83), an action first floated by the TEA SELLER at Saltus. *Commentary:* this seems to be a word of Wolfe's invention. The word *domnicella* (Late Latin young noblewoman, a diminutive of Latin *domina*, noblewoman) is an appropriate term for the supreme Pelerine, since they are nearly all aristocrats (exultants and armigettes), and while not all of them are young, they are all virgins. But for this word, *domnicellae* would be the plural form ("young noblewomen"), which seems an odd term to apply to a single person (unless it is used in imitation of the terms of plurality applied to the autarch). Looking at the Latin roots, *domni* (ruler) added to *cellae* (inner temples) might make "Priestess of the Sanctuaries," creating a near pun that conflates a high priestess with a group of damsels.

**Domnina** a friend of young Thecla (1, chap. 20, 181). When Thecla was thirteen years old, Father Inire found Domnina admiring herself in a mirror, so he showed her something frightening about the magic mirrors in the Presence Chamber. *History:* Saint Domnina (died 460) was a consecrated virgin who lived in a shed, leaving only to attend Mass. Known for keeping her face covered at all times and refusing to look at the faces of others.

**Dorcas** a teenager who lived in the Oldgate quarter of Nessus, forty years before Severian met her. After nearly four years of marriage (according to Dorcas's husband), she died in childbirth (according to Ouen) at the age of sixteen or seventeen (Agia's guess of her age), implying that she married at age thirteen. Her only known surviving child is Ouen. Her body was interred in the Lake of Birds in the Botanical Garden of Endless Sleep, but she is resurrected roughly forty years later when Severian falls into the lake (1, chap. 23, 204). Dorcas and Severian are traveling companions and lovers for most of Severian's travel from Nessus to Thrax, but in Thrax they part company. She is haunted by a chair she sees in Thrax, a piece of furniture looted from her home in Oldgate, now within the deserted section of Nessus.

> "a few families, or perhaps a few people living alone, remained behind when the quarter died. They were too old to move, or too stubborn. I've thought about it, and I'm sure some of them must have had something there they could not bear to leave. A grave, perhaps" (1, chap. 11, 82).

Dorcas's husband finally left the house they had lived in, and so her observation is an intimation of his life without her: that he held on as long as he could, even after the quarter had died, such that only recently the chair was looted.

Dorcas is blonde and often has flowers in her hair: first a water hyacinth (I, chap. 24, 210), then a daisy followed by a moonflower (I, chap. 30, 258), later white tree blossoms (II, chap. 22, 196), a white peony (III, chap. 2, 16), a scarlet poppy (IV, chap. 32, 258), and finally an arum (IV, chap. 32, 260).

*Onomastics:* "gazelle" (Greek).

*Literature:* in the Bible, Dorcas (or Tabitha) was a widow and a disciple at Joppa in the 1st century. She died of illness but was resurrected by Saint Peter.

*Commentary:* in the final analysis, Dorcas is Severian's paternal grandmother. During Severian's vigil with the dead soldier he recalls Dorcas saying, "Sitting in a window . . . trays and a rood. What will you do, summon up some Erinys to destroy me?" (IV, chap. 2, 19). The first sentence is her answer to the question of what she remembers from her life before, and describes the cloisonné shop (see ROOD); the second is a line from the play *Eschatology and Genesis* (II, chap. 24, 218). Because the Erinys were traditionally summoned to torment persons who committed serious crimes such as murder, perjury, and violations of filial piety, it seems that Severian might have intimations that he has committed incest with Dorcas.

**Dorcas's father** made cloisonné with his son; Dorcas and her husband sold these goods at their shop (I, chap. 22, 196). He was an optimate.

**Dorcas's husband** searches for "Cas" in the Lake of Birds, forty years after her death (I, chap. 22), and is probably the BOATMAN who passes by when Severian recovers from almost drowning in Nessus. He sleeps in a loft belonging to a man he met years after Dorcas died. The little shop he ran was on Signal Street. They ran it "four years, less a month and a week" before Dorcas died (I, chap. 22, 199). He tried to keep a locket and Cas's combs, but everything is gone. Dorcas finds his corpse and funeral bier in their old house, implying that he died there on his own or was brought there as a final favor from the man who owns the loft.

**Dorcas's son** see OUEN.

**drachm** a unit of measurement equal to sixty minims or one dram, also known as a *drachma* (I, chap. 6, 66). See MEASUREMENT TABLES.
*History:* from the weight of an ancient Greek coin called "drachma."

**dray** a low cart used for heavy loads (I, chap. 18, 161).

**dream** "It moved like tyrian smoke, but very much faster, and in an instant had enveloped the giant . . . the visions . . . are said to leave soldiers dazed and helpless, a burden to their cause" (II, chap. 25, 239). Called the rarest weapon, it is stellar in origin, and produces a cloud of smoke that envelops its target and assails it with debilitating visions.

**Drotte** a captain of the apprentice torturers when Severian was a boy (I, chap. 1, 9). He is raised to journeyman a year before Severian, suggesting that he is one year older.
*History:* Saint Drotte (Droctoveus) (died c. 580) was abbot of Saint-Germain-des-Pres.

**Drum Tower** a tower of the citadel that rumbles at the solstice (IV, chap. 23, 189).

**dryad** an oak-nymph (II, chap. 10, 88). Ash-nymphs, by the way, are called *meliae.*

**dulcimer** a stringed musical instrument of trapezoidal shape encompassing two or three octaves and played with light hammers held in the hands (I, chap. 19, 171).

**dulcinea** a mistress, sweetheart, lady of one's devotion (originally from *Don Quixote*) (I, chap. 20, 182).

**dux** probably a high-level military title, but could be a rank of exultant (V, chap. 46, 328).
*Latin:* a leader, ruler, commander; this word gave rise to the title *duke.*
*History:* Tiberius (A.D. 578–82) divided the Byzantine army into three forces to correspond to the country's three main geographical regions, basing one in the East, one in Illyria, and one in Thrace. Each army was commanded by a dux and was made up of from six to eight regiments each numbering three to four thousand men. In contrast to the civilian governor of a district, a dux was given control over an area often consisting of several

provinces or districts, and while he was responsible for the overall military organization, it was the *strategus* (regimental commander) who was entrusted with the actual conduct of military operations.

**Early Summer** queen on a mountaintop beyond Urth, but probably still within the solar system (III, chap. 19, 147). She was made pregnant by a rose and gave birth to Spring Wind in "The Tale of the Boy Called Frog."
*Myth:* Juno (who gave her name to the month of June, which is "early summer") is the Roman Queen of the Sky, made pregnant with Mars by a flower.
*Astronomy:* Juno (1804) was the third asteroid to be discovered. (This meets the criteria of being a "mountaintop" beyond Urth, yet still within the solar system.)

**Eata** a boyhood friend of Severian and fellow apprentice (I, chap. 1, 9), Eata drew the arms of a great northern exultant clan above his cot in the belief he was descended from that family (I, chap. 2, 21). (This links him to Thecla, if only by association, since her family is a member of such a clan.) He is tow-headed (I, chap. 1, 11), with freckles on his arms (9). He became a sailor before the guild was reformed. Eata is the hero of "The Map," wherein he says he feels he wasted too much of his life, and Maxellindis's, in searching for buried treasure on a map he had found (ES, 34). He was convicted of smuggling (circa S.R. 7) and sentenced to serve on a carrack. He jumped ship and lived on or near Blue Flower Island for two years until a food riot killed his girlfriend, then he got a ride back to Nessus. He survives the deluge caused by the arrival of the White Fountain (IV, chap. 46, 324). It seems likely that he died at sea, around the time that

Severian left him and his ship; in any event, he is not one of the gods of Ushas. Or perhaps the Sleeper is a blend of Eata and Severian. See also LAETUS, MAXELLINDIS, and SYNTYCHE.
*History:* Saint Eata (died 686) was an English bishop.

**Eata's mausoleum** apprentice Severian knows that just as he has his secret mausoleum, so do his friends have private hiding places in the necropolis. Since Eata drew the exultant arms above his cot, we can infer that he found them at his own mausoleum. This place, in turn, becomes the most likely candidate for being the mausoleum housing Cilinia's coffin, but of course there are also all the mausoleums that they share in common during their play. See MAUSOLEUM.

**echidne** "We have books here bound in the hides of echidnes, krakens, and beasts so long extinct . . . that no trace of them survives unfossilized" (I, chap. 6, 60). A typo for *echidna,* the spiny anteater (CD, 237).

**Echopraxia** the name of a specific brothel in the Algedonic Quarter of Nessus, or more likely, a category of brothel where the theme is mimicry (I, chap. 8, 83). At the one in question, the House Absolute is mimicked as the House Azure.
*History:* habit of repeating the actions of others as if echoing them; mimicry, imitation.

**eclectic** in the Commonwealth, the mixed-race descendants of settlers from the south and autochthons (III, chap. 2, 18). Analogous to the mestizos of Latin America.
*History:* borrowing or borrowed from diverse sources.

**Eden** just as there are references to the deluge scattered throughout *The Book of the New Sun*, there are also some definite allusions to the Garden of Eden across Severian's narrative:

- The House Azure has a door showing the Temptation (I, chap. 9, 88).
- The Lake of Birds scene with Severian, Agia, and Dorcas has echoes of Adam, Lilith, and Eve (I, chap. 23).
- Breakfast at Ctesiphon's Cross has Severian offering Dorcas an apple, which prompts her to say "Red as the apples of . . . " but she cannot remember the name Eden (I, chap. 34, 288). The fact that Severian has eaten a pomegranate points to the notion that since apples are not native to the Middle East, the fruit must have been a pomegranate.
- The first act of the play *Eschatology and Genesis* (II, chap. 24, 211–18) has characters analogous to Adam, Eve, and Lilith.
- At the deluge, a soldier reports to Autarchia Valeria that "certain cacogens have landed a man and a woman from one of their ships" (V, chap. 42, 301).

**Egino** an exultant bearing the title "Starost" whom Thecla thinks may be present at her upcoming punishment (I, chap. 7, 71). He is not.
*History:* Egino (12th century) Bishop of Chur, Switzerland, sided with Pope Alexander III during the quarrel with Frederick Barbarossa and was, in 1170, awarded the title of prince of the empire (a detail which seems to fit with the title STAROST).

**eidolon** an unsubstantial image, specter, phantom (I, chap. 3, 36). See AQUASTOR.

**Eight, the** a constellation of three stars which "hang forever over the southern ice" (IV, chap. 25, 209).
*Astronomy:* our Octans, or Octant, the pole-stars of the Southern hemisphere.

**Eigil** a journeyman torturer (I, chap. 3, 30).
*Onomastics:* "inspires fright" (Norse).
*History:* Saint Eigil (died 822) was abbot of a monastery in Fulda, Germany.

**Einhildis** a Pelerine friend of Cyriaca who wrote her the letter saying that the Pelerines were in Orithyia (III, chap. 12, 90). She might well be the unnamed NURSE.
*History:* Blessed Einhildis (8th century) served as Benedictine abbess of Niedermunster, Germany.

**eisegesis** the interpretation of a text (for example, the Bible) by reading into it one's own ideas (III, chap. 6, 54).

**ell** a unit of measurement, roughly forty-five inches (I, chap. 14, 129). See MEASUREMENT TABLES.

**embrasure** a slanting or beveling in the sides of an opening to a wall or window, so that the inside profile of the window is larger than that of the outside (II, chap. 17, 153).

**emerald bench** an artifact located in the most ancient part of the Citadel (IV, chap. 35, 282).
*History:* alchemical writings of the medieval period are full of references and allusions to the Emerald Table of Hermes. According to the legends, the original emerald slab carved with the Thirteen Precepts of Hermes was discovered in the tomb of Hermes by Alexander the Great. The Precepts are as follows.

1. Speak not fictitious things, but that which is certain and true.
2. What is below is like that which is above, and what is above is like that which is below, to accomplish the miracles of one thing.
3. And as all things were produced by the one word of one Being, so all things were produced from this one thing by adaptation.
4. Its father is the sun, its mother the moon; the wind carries it in its belly, its nurse is the earth.
5. It is the father of perfection throughout the world.
6. The power is vigorous if it be changed into earth.
7. Separate the earth from the fire, the subtle from the gross, acting prudently and with judgment.
8. Ascend with the greatest sagacity from the earth to heaven, and then again descend to the earth, and unite together the powers of things superior and things inferior. Thus you will obtain the glory of the whole world, and obscurity will fly far away from you.
9. This has more fortitude than fortitude itself; because it conquers every subtle thing and can penetrate every solid.
10. Thus was the world formed.

11. Hence proceed wonders, which are here established.
12. Therefore I am called Hermes Trimegistos, having three parts of the philosophy of the whole world.
13. That which I had to say concerning the operation of the sun is completed.

John Reed, *Prelude to Chemistry,* 54.

**Emilian** a gallant of the Autarch's court, known by Thecla, healed by the Claw in the lazaret at Orithyia (IV, chap. 8, 65).
*Onomastics:* "eager" (Latin).
*History:* there are eight saints of this name.

**Empires of Foliage and Flower** a long story from the brown book, collected in SS. The Cumaean alludes to it, saying, "In ancient days, in a land far off, there stood two empires, divided by mountains. One dressed its soldiers in yellow, the other in green. For a hundred generations they struggled —" and Severian finishes the summary, "an eremite came among them and counseled the emperor of the yellow army to dress his men in green, and the master of the green army that he should clothe it in yellow. But the battle continued as before" (II, chap. 31, 289).

The main character of EFF is an eremite named Father Thyme who ages as he walks west and grows young as he walks east. He finds a young child playing at war and peace and takes her on a quest to end the conflict between the two empires. The child ages as she travels with Thyme, such that she is seduced as a young woman by the green Prince Patizithes; gives birth to a son in the mountains the next day; and enters the yellow capital as an old woman with a teenage son. Barrus, the son, is taken hostage by the Yellow Emperor, and Thyme takes the child back east, leaving her at the yard where he had found her, an infant again.

**enchor** seems to be synonymous with AUTOCHTHON, "even as tribes of enchors" (III, chap. 16, 126).
*History:* from "enchorial" meaning "native, endemic": thus native things, native people, or perhaps even "common" people.

**energy mace** a stellar-level melee weapon used by Baldanders (III, chap. 37, 288). It makes a high-pitched whine when in operation. This sound may create the aura of fear that surrounds the wielder.

**entheal** "I put away the gem at last, a little ashamed at having toyed with so entheal a thing as if it were a bauble" (III, chap. 28, 226).
*History:* inspired by an indwelling god.

**ephemerid** a mayfly (ES, 27).

**ephor** a judge (or perhaps more properly, "referee") at the Sanguinary Field (I, chap. 25, 220).
*History:* (Greek) a judge.

**Epicharis** a Pelerine with the rank or title of Conexa (IV, chap. 10, 78).
*History:* Saint Epicharis (died 300), said to have been the wife of a Roman senator, was put to death at Byzantium during the Diocletian persecution.

**epitagm** "By then I had remembered that I held honorary commissions in half a dozen legions and epitagms, all of which I could employ as incognitos without a lie" (V, chap. 44, 312).
*Greek:* a reserve force or subsidiary force; literally "command," the command of some officer, not forming a regular unit.
*Commentary:* in response to pestering, Wolfe writes, "Let's make one up: three companies of heavy infantry, with twenty crossbowmen, fifty slingers from the Balearic Isles, and about a hundred barbarian cavalry. That's an epitagm. Or the militia of the towns and village of the Halys valley, from the springs to the sea."

**eponym** one who has given his or her name to a group or place, such as a tribe or town (I, chap. 19, 171).

**epopt** a "beholder"; a person fully initiated into the ancient Greek Eleusinian mysteries; an initiate (I, chap. 10, 102).

**equerries** the stables belonging to a royal or princely household; the body of officers in charge of the stables (V, chap. 25, 178).

**Erblon** Guasacht's second in command (IV, chap. 19, 150), he is tall and thus of exultant blood. He dies at the Third Battle of Orithyia (IV, chap. 22, 182).
*History:* Saint Erblon (died 720?) was born in Noyon, France.

**Erebus** one of the Great Lords opposed to the New Sun (I, chap. 1, 15). He is an ice demon and Mount Erebus in Antarctica is the seat of his power. Ships of Erebus raid the Southern Isles, coming behind a mist. See OTHER PEOPLE.

*Myth:* the proper name of "a place of darkness, between Earth and Hades." Also an ancient Greek god, son of Chaos (god of darkness) and Nox (goddess of night).

**eremite** literally, "desert dweller," one who has retired into solitude for religious motives; a recluse, a hermit (II, chap. 14, 121). Or a quasi-religious mendicant, a vagabond.

**erentarii** light infantry (II, chap. 1, 11).

**Erinys** the Furies of Roman mythology (II, chap. 24, 218; IV, chap. 2, 19).

**eschatology** the department of theological science concerned with the four last things: death, judgment, heaven, and hell (II, chap. 24, 211).

**Eschatology and Genesis** Dr. Talos's play, based upon his reading of (Canog's) *Book of the New Sun,* performed once at Ctesiphon's Cross in Nessus (I, chap. 32) and once at the House Absolute (II, chap. 24). Wolfe gives a list of players and most of their roles in his article "Onomastics" (CD, 255).

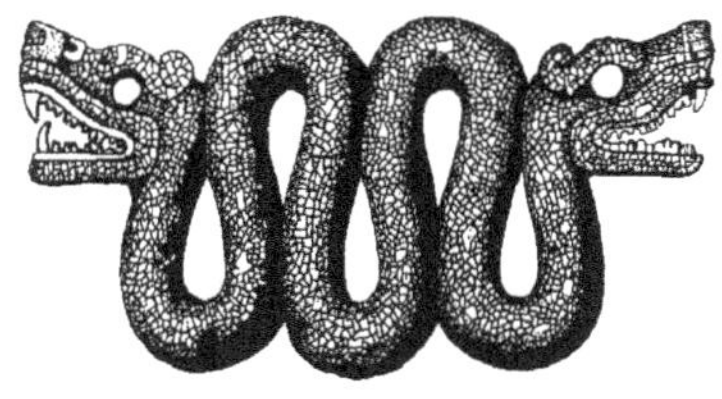

| The Players | Their Roles |
|---|---|
| Dr. Talos | Gabriel, Autarch, Ivo (First Soldier), Inquisitor, Old Sun |
| Baldanders | Nod, Statue |
| Severian | Meschia, Second Soldier, Prophet, Generalissimo, Familiar, New Sun |
| Dorcas | Meschiane, Lybe (Maid), Second Demon, an Angelic Being (?), Moon (?) |
| Jolenta | Jahi, Carina (the Contessa), First Demon, an Angelic Being (?) |

The play seems to be made up of seven segments.

*Scene I* (the garden above the House Absolute)

The scene begins with Gabriel announcing the last night of the old sun. Nod enters, looking for Meschia's son to marry Nod's daughter. Meschia, Meschiane, and Jahi enter. They are fully grown but have no memory. Gabriel leaves. The Autarch enters. Meschia mistakes the Autarch for God. The Autarch tries to seduce Meschiane, then Jahi. The women argue and run offstage, fighting. The Autarch realizes that Meschia mistakes him for God. The Contessa and her Maid arrive. Meschia strikes her for interrupting his conversation with "God" and the Autarch escapes. The Contessa tries to seduce Meschia but fails.

*Commentary:* a lot of Scene I is pre-figured by events in the Botanical Gardens of Nessus (I, chap. 23) involving Severian (as Meschia), Dorcas (as Meschiane), Agia (as Jahi), and Hildegrin (as Autarch); with cameo by the nameless boatman (as Gabriel).

*Scene II* (under a rowan tree, by a door in a hill)

The scene opens with Meschiane and Jahi lying under a rowan tree. In their fight, Meschiane was victorious. Two soldiers find them, and Meschiane escapes with one man in pursuit. Jahi tries to seduce the remain soldier. When that fails, she makes it snow. She seduces a passing statue into being her champion, but the soldier flees underground with Jahi over his shoulder. The statue, weeping, begins to dig with his hands.

*Commentary:* the comedic surprise here is that "nice girl" Meschiane won in the fistfight with "tough girl" Jahi. (Note that rowan is identified as quickbeam, aka "tree of life," in Graves's *The White Goddess.*)

*Scene III* (throne room of the House Absolute)

Scene begins with the Autarch on his throne, surrounded by his court. The Prophet enters and they discuss strange events of recent days. Nod enters to explain the situation as he knows it. The Generalissimo enters, gives his report, and then chases after an escaping Nod. Nod returns with a laser burn across one cheek and fights with the Autarch. Two Demons disguised as merchants arrive to save the Autarch at the last second. They counsel him to kill Meschia and Meschiane so he can rule Ushas himself. He calls down ships to raze the garden above.
*Commentary:* this scene is echoed at the end of Typhon's reign, with Typhon as "Autarch" to Conciliator as "Prophet" (v, chap. 39); and even more clearly at the Deluge, with Valeria as "Autarch" to Jader's sister as "Prophet," with Baldanders reprising

his role as "Nod" (v, chap. 42). The fight between Nod and Autarch, wherein "the Autarch strikes him with his scepter; each blow produces an explosion and a burst of sparks" (II, chap. 24, 225), has clear and obvious connections to the fight between Baldanders and Severian (III, chap. 37) as well as the puppet theater dream which foretold it (I, chap. 15, 141–42).

*Scene IV* (torture chamber of the House Absolute)

Scene opens with the Inquisitor and his Familiar in the torture chamber. The Contessa is brought in. She describes the strange man she saw on the Road of Air. Then Meschiane is brought in and prepared for torture. The Contessa admits she hopes Meschia will take her as a replacement for Meschiane, then leaves. Jahi is brought in, then Nod is brought in. Jahi escapes while Meschiane is being tortured. The Familiar releases Nod to hunt her down and return.

*Commentary:* when "Contessa" in the play speaks of being with guards and seeing a strange man from the Road of Air, she mirrors the moment when Severian, on the Path of Air, sees a hauntingly familiar woman surrounded by Praetorian Guards (v, chap. 41, 293).

*Scene V* (corridors of the House Absolute)

Scene opens with Nod running through the corridors, chasing Jahi. He runs offstage and she enters from the other side, with Second Demon at her side. They argue. Nod returns.

Unsuspecting, he sits on the trunk she is hiding in. It begins to splinter.

*Scene VI* (torture chamber)

Scene opens with the Familiar torturing Meschiane on the rack. The Autarch enters, his robes torn and bloodstained. He is saddened to discover that the Familiar does not recognize him. Nod enters with Jahi, but madness is upon him. The Familiar chains him but he starts crushing Jahi, so the Familiar beats him until he releases her. The Familiar presses the Autarch into holding Jahi, then returns to torturing Meschiane. Nod breaks his chains, fights with the Familiar. The scene ends with Nod breaking the Familiar's back.

*Scene VII* (presumably the arrival of the new sun)

This scene is never performed. The characters include Angelic Beings, the New Sun, the Old Sun, and the Moon.

*Commentary:* because this section of the play is never revealed, we are left with only echoes from the text (primarily *The Urth of the New Sun)* to work with. "Angelic Beings" would easily describe Tzadkiel, Apheta, and Venant. It is interesting that on Ushas, Severian "dreams" that Valeria is weeping over him, and wakes to rain from a cloud covering Lune; the linkage of Valeria to Moon might also be a part of the scene where Valeria is assassinated and pinned to Severian: she is Moon to Severian's New Sun, and their pinning is like a solar eclipse.

| Scene | Day/Celestial Body |
|---|---|
| I | Monday/Moon: Meschiane as Moon? |
| II | Tuesday/Mars: appearance of soldiers. |
| III | Wednesday/Mercury: underworld and prophets. |
| IV | Thursday/Jupiter: Jove sentences vanquished titan (Sisyphus, Ixion, Prometheus) to torture. |
| V | Friday/Venus: Jahi in the Descent of Venus. |
| VI | Saturday/Saturn: autarch usurped (as Saturn was by Jupiter), unrecognized in his own palace. |
| VII | Sunday/Sun: arrival of New Sun. |

**escritoire** a writing-desk constructed to contain stationery and documents (v, chap. 6, 41).

**Eskil** a Typhon-era soldier (v, chap. 35, 249–51). The Conciliator breaks his neck, then heals him.
*Onomastics:* "vessel of the gods" (Norse).
*History:* Saint Eskil (died 1080) was a fellow missionary of Saint Sigfrid in Sweden (both were English) and was stoned to death for protesting against a heathen festival at Strengnass. He reclaimed for the faith many who had lapsed since the time of Saint ANSKAR.

**espalier** a kind of latticework or framework of stakes upon which fruit trees or ornamental shrubs are trained (II, chap. 21, 192).

**estafette** a courier on horseback (III, chap. 29, 235).

**esthete** variant of *aesthete;* one who professes a special appreciation of what is beautiful, and endeavors to carry his ideas of beauty into practical manifestation (II, chap. 21, 190).

**estoc** a small stabbing sword (III, chap. 35, 281). Having a long, narrow, quadrangular blade, it was used from the 13th to the 17th century.

**estrapade** a torture consisting of attaching a person's hands and feet to a rope, drawing him up by them to a great height, and then letting him fall suddenly (I, chap. 30, 258).

**ethnarch** Severian, after being imprisoned by the villagers of Murene, expects that they will "deliver me to some petty ethnarch" (III, chap. 29, 235). It is an exultant title (III, chap. 2, 19).
*History:* a governor of a nation or people; a ruler over a province.
*Commentary:* "Ethnarch was a title of little honour; the commoner who presided over Jewish affairs in Alexandria was also called the Ethnarch" (Graves, *King Jesus,* 160).

**Eusebia** a woman of Saltus (II, chap. 1, 7). Jealous that the younger woman Morwenna has taken Stachys away from her, she accuses Morwenna of murdering Stachys and Chad. Morwenna plants poison in Eusebia's bouquet.
*Onomastics:* "Godliness" (Greek).
*History:* there are three Saints Eusebia. One (late 3rd century) was a maiden of Bergamo, in Lombardy, niece of Saint Domnio, martyred under Maximian Herculius; another (died 680) became abbess at Hamage (Hamay) at the age of twelve; the third (died 731), an abbess of a nunnery at Marseiles, was put to death by Saracens at Saint-Cyrj.

**Eusignius** a young torturer's apprentice (I, chap. 3, 31).

*History:* Saint Eusignius (died 362) was an old soldier in the army of Constantius Clorus. At the age of 110, he refused to sacrifice to idols at the bidding of Julian the Apostate and was scourged and beheaded at Antioch in Syria.

**evzone** "It seemed a long time before the Ascian evzones saw them" (IV, chap. 25, 208).
*History:* a member of a select infantry corps in the Greek army.

**exarch** an ecclesiastic ranking between patriarch and metropolitan (I, chap. 7, 71). An exultant title (III, chap. 2, 19).

**externs** foreigners; those born on Urth outside of the Commonwealth (I, chap. 14, 132).

**exultant** the class of high-born people (I, chap. 1, 17). Exultants are ironically taller than the common folk in the Urth Cycle, and although they are renowned for their ancient lineage, Jonas suggests that they are the most recent to arrive on Urth (II, chap. 10, 78). So they would appear to be descendants of invaders from space.

Exultants in the text include Abdiesus, Barbea, Catherine (possibly), Domnina, Egino, Gracia, Guibert, Lelia, Leocadia, Lollian, Nympha, Talarican, Thea, Thecla, Ultan, and Vodalus.

There are approximately 1,492 names listed in *The Book of Exulted Families*, and they seem to be grouped into clans, for example the "exultant Northern clans" (I, chap. 2, 21).

Chatelaine, contessa, ethnarch, exarch, and starost are exultant titles ("Vodalus, in whose veins flowed the undefiled blood of a thousand exultants — exarchs, ethnarchs, and starosts" [III, chap. 2, 19]); dux and tetrarch might be as well.

Yet the distinction must be made between exultant status and exultant blood: all exultants have exultant blood, but not all those people with exultant blood have exultant status. When Severian uses the term "true exultant," he signals that the character in question is a member of the exultant class; whereas when he uses a simple "exultant" or "tall" he is commenting on exultant blood rather than class. This is important in that there seem to be plenty of impoverished families of exultant blood, allowing Severian to reasonably suppose that the tall prostitutes of the House Azure are local girls, along with the MAID WHO PLAYS THE ROLE OF KATHARINE.

Because of the importance height plays in identifying an exultant, here are some details on exultant height:

- Severian's height is 6'1" (according to Wolfe in *Thrust no. 19*, winter/spring 1983, 8), and this puts him within the height range of an exultant bastard.
- Thecla at age thirteen or fourteen was as tall as Severian, i.e., 6'1" (IV, chap. 4, 34).
- If adult Thecla is 6'11" tall (which seems the least she could be), then Severian comes up to her chin. This fits with Severian's recollection "how Thecla had bent over me when we embraced, and how I had kissed her breasts [while standing upright]" (IV, chap. 14, 114).
- Thecla's khaibit is "somewhat shorter" than Thecla (I, chap. 9, 90).
- The maid who plays Katharine is "tall" but not as tall as Thecla (I, chap. 11, 106), suggesting that if she is an exultant,

she must be younger than Thecla and/or a khaibit. Or she could be an exultant bastard.

- Barbatus and Famulimus are both "a good head taller than [Severian], as tall as exultants" (III, chap. 33, 262). Assuming that they are nine inches taller, this would make them 6'10" tall.
- Master Ultan is a head and a half taller than Severian (i.e., 7'3"), a true exultant (I, chap. 6, 55).
- Mannea is "a good two heads taller [than postulant Ava] — a true exultant, as tall has Thecla had been" (IV, chap. 14, 114). If Mannea is 6'11" tall, then subtracting eighteen inches would make the optimate's daughter Ava 5'5" tall.

Based on these figures, true exultant height seems to be around 7' tall, with women averaging 6'11" and men averaging 7'3".

**exultant bastard** "There's an exultant's bastard in that family a generation or so back" says Master Gurloes to a young Severian about Ia, the tall armigette (II, chap. 7, 57). The tall fat algophilist at Agilus's execution is introduced as being "taller than I, surely the illegitimate son of some exultant" (I, chap. 30, 256). This, together with the notes on exultant heights, implies that exultant bastards are taller than non-exultants yet not so tall as true exultants. Severian's height is in the range for exultant bastards, perhaps running from 6' to 6'10". Characters who are "tall" are possible candidates. Another character who might be an exultant bastard is Erblon.

**faille** a light kind of ribbed silk fabric (II, chap. 17, 144).

**falchion** a type of sword that first appears with the DEAD SOLDIER (IV, chap. 1, 14). Severian later finds one on the ground, dropped "in some campaign of the year before" (IV, chap. 19, 146), and this one becomes his sword during his brief soldiering career. Since the military kits have a certain ethnicity about them, it seems likely that the dead soldier was a new replacement for the same group that had suffered losses there the year before. *History:* a European sword with a broad, curved, single-edged blade that is wide near the point, with the back joining the edge in a concave curve. Stone calls it a "sword of the middle ages."

**family trees** a collection of genealogical charts sifted from the text:

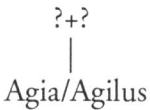

There are few details about the family of twins Agia and Agilus other than the fact that they inherited their rag shop.

**family trees**

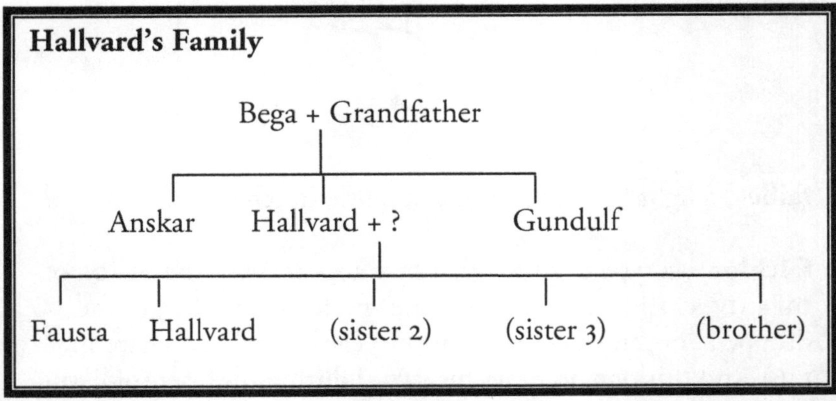


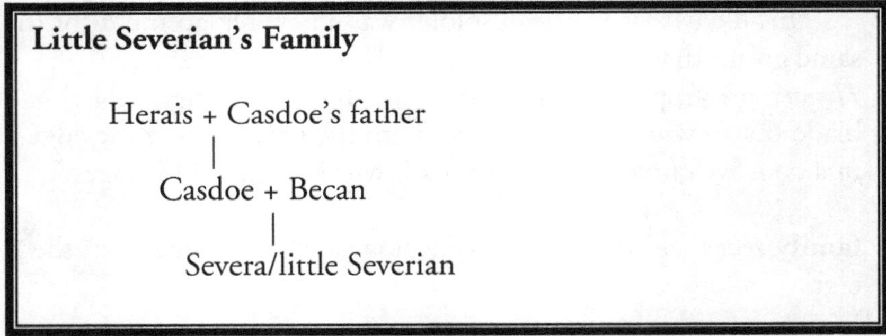

Little Severian's Family
Herais + Casdoe's father
Casdoe + Becan
Severa/little Severian


Herais may be the nameless innkeeper of the Duck's Nest Inn. Then again, while Casdoe talks of her mother in Thrax, we aren't entirely sure that the old man Severian identifies as her father is really her father or instead perhaps her father-in-law.

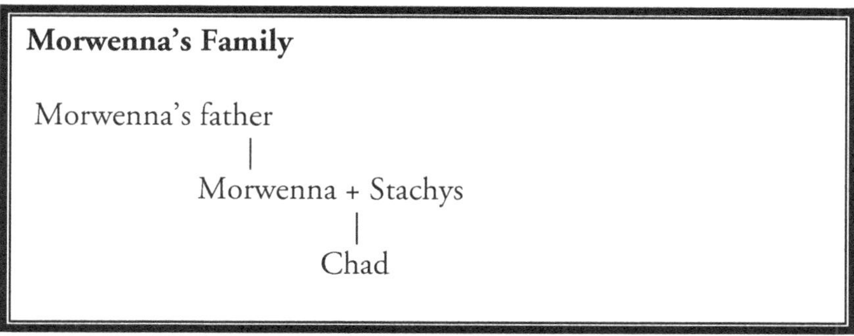


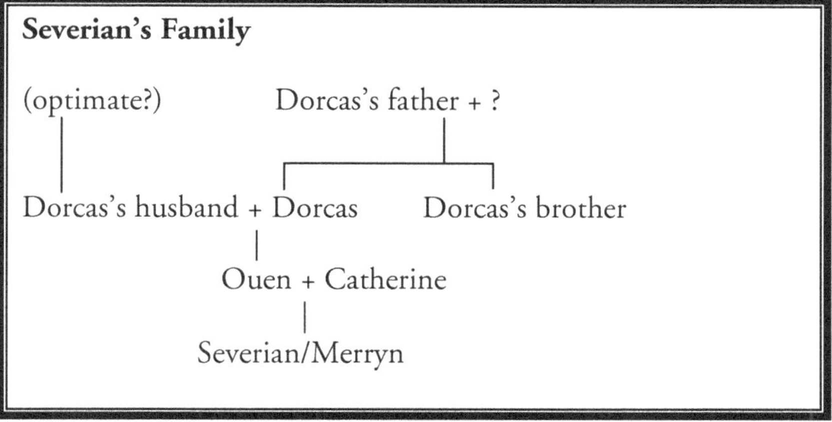


Hildegrin says Dorcas looks "noble"; the appendix says there are hints she was an optimate in her previous life. The fallen pelerine Catherine may or may not be a khaibit, but this is the best position as the source for the "exultant blood" that Severian seems to have.

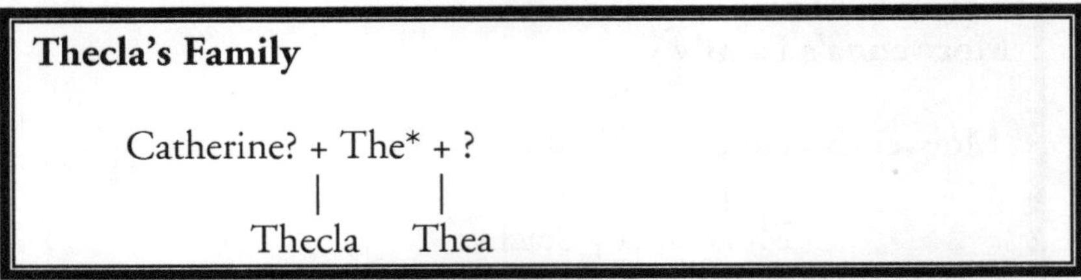


Thea and Thecla are half sisters. The recurrence of "T-H-E" in their names might suggest that their common parent is named "The*" (i.e., Theo, or a similar name). Thecla's father died before she was taken to the Matachin tower.

The controversial placement of Catherine within the Thecla tree is an experiment that answers the following needs: first, the linkage of bloodlines between Severian and Thecla, so that the book of her family history, which Severian brings to her in her cell, is also in some literal way his own family history (that is to say, beyond the fact that he will later absorb her memories); second, if Severian's biological mother Catherine is, in fact, a khaibit, this helps to show how exultant bastard lines can branch out on the female side as well as on the male side. But then again, the common parent of Thea and Thecla could well be their mother. The "burning rose" perfume used by both Thecla and her khaibit forms a link to Catherine in the fiery "Catherine Wheel" combined with the eruption of roses from the wheel during the play on the feast day.

**famula** the female servant of a medieval scholar or magician (III, chap. 7, 59).

**Famulimus** of the group Ossipago, Barbatus, and Famulimus, travelling back in time with their flying saucer. Famulimus is the

female hierodule. Severian thinks her voice is like that of a bird at first; later he specifies a lark (v, chap. 5, 32). Beneath her hideous masks, her face has the sort of calm beauty that inspired the faces of the House Absolute's walking statues (II, chap. 24, 273).
*Myth:* (Roman) a minor god who looked after a boy's reputation.

**Famulorum** a village near the House Absolute (v, chap. 40, 284). One of Severian's childhoods (presumably that of the old autarch) was spent here. Its name suggests that this village has a tradition of supplying the House Absolute with stewards and servants.
*Latin:* "famulor" to be a servant, to minister (to), serve or be subject (to), be at the orders (of).

**fantassin** "You have fantassins aboard your ship, surely. Once line the walls with horrors, and we will be safe for a century" (III, chap. 33, 264).
*History:* a foot-soldier.

**Fauna** "It was Fauna, the Bona Dea, some say, who sent the she-wolf that . . . Well, never mind. Nature, we call her now" (IA, 45). A powerful figure in the stories "The Town that Forgot Fauna" (v, chap. 33, 232) and "The Old Woman Whose Rolling Pin Is the Sun," especially in the latter, where she is shown to be bent and stern, yet taller than the trees, and to have lions at her command. Her husband, a shadowy, frightening figure unnamed in "The Old Woman Whose Rolling Pin Is the Sun," is probably Thyme (also known as Father Time) of EFF.
*Myth:* ancient Roman earth-mother and fertility goddess usually termed the Bona Dea (the Good Goddess), and considered the

wife, sister, and/or daughter of Faunus. She was identified with Terra, Tellus ("earth"), or Ops ("plenty").
*Commentary:* she also forms a link between the Urth Cycle and Wolfe's *Soldier* series, which addresses the earth-mother goddess at length. A goddess "who sent the she-wolf" hints at the Romulus and Remus legend (see TALE OF THE BOY CALLED FROG) and the ancient Roman goddesses Acca Larentia (see LAURENTIA OF THE HOUSE OF THE HARP) and Rhea Silva (see BIRD OF THE WOOD).

**Fausta** one of Hallvard's sisters (IV, chap. 7, 55).
*Onomastics:* "fortunate" (Latin).
*History:* Saint Fausta (died 303) was a thirteen-year-old girl martyred during the Diocletian persecution.

**fearnought** a thick, heavy overcoating made of wool (often mixed with shoddy) that has a rough, shaggy surface; and a garment made of this material, called also "dreadnought" (I, chap. 23, 208).

**feast days** the torturers have three types of feast days, "lofty" (when a journeyman is elevated to mastership), "lesser" (at least one apprentice is elevated to journeyman), and "least" (no elevation takes place) (I, chap. 11, 104). It is likely that all guilds follow the same pattern.

**Feast of Saint Catherine, The** originally Gene Wolfe planned to write a forty-thousand-word novella with this title, in the hope of placing it in Damon Knight's *Orbit* anthology series. But it grew into a novel, and then a trilogy, before finally becoming *The Book of the New Sun.* (See article in CD for more detail.)

**Fechin** an artist of the period two generations prior to Severian, at least two of his paintings hang at the Citadel or in the House Absolute (I, chap. 5, 52).

Casdoe's father was a friend of Fechin in his youth (III, chap. 15, 115), and he tells Severian several details. Fechin had red hair on his hands and on his arms "like a monkey's arms" (115), yet "he was handsome and could get food or money from a woman" (116). As a boy he saw Fechin steal his mother's copper-bottomed pan (115). Later he gave Fechin half of his rare piece of paper (116).

Fechin painted a portrait of Rudesind when the latter was a boy, and this painting hangs in the Citadel or in the House Absolute (II, chap. 20, 179).

A second painting by Fechin shows three girls dressing a fourth girl with flowers (I, chap. 5, 51). See also QUARTILLOSA.
*Onomastics:* "young raven" (Irish).
*History:* Saint Fechin (died 665) was born in Connaught, Ireland.

**Felicibus brevis, miseris hora longa** a phrase from the Atrium of Time, which Valeria translates as "Men wait long for happiness" (I, chap. 4, 44).
*Latin:* "Happiness is brief, misery's hours long."

**felucca** a small vessel propelled by oars or lateen sails, or both, used mainly in the Mediterranean for coasting voyages (III, chap. 2, 23).

**fen** "a dark lake in an infinite fen" (I, chap. 22, 195). Marsh or bog. The peat bogs of northern Europe have amazing preservative powers, as shown by the ancient corpses discovered therein.

**fennec** an animal *(Canis zerda)* found in Africa, resembling a small fox, but having very long ears (IV, chap. 19, 147).

**fiacre** a small four-wheeled carriage for hire; a hackney-coach; a French cab, usually drawn by two animals (I, chap. 8, 84).
*Commentary:* the patron saint of cabdrivers is Saint Fiacre (died 670). His legend made him a misogynist in life and after death, a possible link to his patronage of those who suffer venereal disease. The cabs got their name because they plied their trade from the hotel Saint-Fiacre in Paris.

**fibula** an ornamental safety pin; a brooch (I, chap. 19, 171).

**Fiend** arch-enemy of mankind; the devil (II, chap. 24, 217).
*Literature:* "The Gates . . . belching outrageous flame . . . since the Fiend pass'd through" (Milton, *Paradise Lost*).

**figurantes** female extras in a theatrical production; also, female spear carriers (I, chap. 20, 182).

**Fish** twin brother to Frog in "The Tale of the Boy Called Frog" (III, chap. 19, 149).
*Myth:* Fish plays a role similar to that of (Roman) Remus, but also has elements of (Sumerian) Gilgamesh (as the city-dwelling brother).

*History:* American Indians taught the Pilgrims to plow the fish into the fields to ensure a good crop.

**Fish's Mouth** the Cumaean says that there is an ancient and acute mind on the one surviving world of this star (II, chap. 31, 280). Presumably this entity remembers Apu Punchau.
*History:* Fomalhaut (meaning "Fish's Mouth" in Arabic) is the brightest star in the Piscis Austrinus constellation. Although classified as an A3-type white star, it has a reddish color just as Severian reports. It is one of the four ancient Royal Stars (Aldebaran, Regulus, Antares, and Fomalhaut). See VENANT.

**flagae** ethereal light creatures seen in mirrors of the Hall of Meaning (I, chap. 20, 184). They have some link to the lower universe, and are perhaps the lowest life form there. See ABADDON, YESOD: THE MECHANICS OF HYPERSPACE.
*History:* spirits visible only in mirrors (the reverse of the vampire legend), they are usually summoned to reveal the future.

**flageolet** musical instrument played by beggars on the bridge connecting the Algedonic Quarter with the living city of Nessus (I, chap. 14, 132).
*History:* a small wind instrument with a mouthpiece at one end, six principal holes, and sometimes keys. Similar to a recorder.

**flambeau** a torch, especially one made of several thick wicks dipped in wax; a lighted torch (I, chap. 2, 22).

**flier** dart-like aircraft of Urth that are relics of a forgotten level of technology (IV, chap. 24, 198). They can fly 10,000 leagues in a day, and each one has a mind in the form of a thinking machine. Their lift is supplied by the antimatter equivalent of iron held in a magnetic cage, and since the anti-iron has a reversed magnetic structure, it is repelled by promagnetism. Most have the shape of a cherry leaf, but in the period of Typhon, some are locust shaped.

**Fluminis** the stream leading from Vici through Gurgustii to Os, where it empties into Gyoll (v, chap. 30, 211).
*Latin:* a river or stream.

**Foila** female soldier in the lazaret who had been in the light cavalry of the Blue Huzzars (IV, chap. 5, 40). She is courted by Hallvard, Melito, and Loyal to the Group of Seventeen. All are killed in the attack on the lazaret, but which suitor would she have chosen? Her story suggests she would pick the third suitor.
*History:* Saint Foila (6th century) was sister of Saint Colgan and her shrine is at Galway, Ireland.

**Folia** a typo for Foila, used in the magazine version of her contest story ("Folia's Story: the Armiger's Daughter," *Amazing Stories,* November 1982).

**folio** a very large book, in the range of 12 x 15 inches to 15 x 24 inches (I, chap. 7, 71).

**Fons** a river depicted on the map entitled "Northwest Area of the Commonwealth" in *Plan[e]t Engineering.* It is not mentioned anywhere in the Urth Cycle. (On the map it links Lake Diuturna with the River Gyoll about five leagues east of Saltus.)

*Latin:* a spring, fountain; fresh or spring water. It also came to mean "origin," "source," like the English "fount."
*Myth:* Roman goddess of fountains.

**Fors** a rural area of the Commonwealth, to the south of the House Absolute. The chatelaine Sancha weds the heir of Fors in around 62 P.S. (ES, 215).
*Latin:* luck, chance.

**Fortunate Cloud** the ship that Jonas served on (II, chap. 15, 130). Severian initially supposes it to have been a gambling ship. He later wonders if Jonas and Hethor knew each other: "Perhaps they were from the same ship. Or perhaps it was only that each would have known the other by some sign, or that Hethor at least feared they would" (III, chap. 15, 119). Hethor served on the *Quasar.*
*Commentary:* "Fortunate Cloud" sounds like a Chinese name on its own, but in James Clavell's multi-novel Asia Epic, the Struan family of Far East traders has a tradition of surnaming all their ships "Cloud," for example *China Cloud, Resting Cloud,* and *Lasting Cloud,* to honor the founder's mother, a McCloud. This bit of trivia seems hauntingly appropriate: the Strauns represent Westerners living and working in the Asian sphere for generations, while the First Empire of the galaxy has an Asian feel to it and Hethor himself seems to be a Caucasian whose mother tongue is Asian.

**fourragere** a shoulder ornament or award, usually made of cord (III, chap. 18, 144).

**fourth book** the prisoner Thecla requests four books: the brown book, the saffian book, the green book, and the obscure "fourth book" (I, chap. 6, 67). It is green but not as small as the green book (I, chap. 7, 71). In his essay "Books in *The Book of the New Sun*" (PE; also in Wright's *Shadows of the New Sun)*, Gene Wolfe writes, "The fourth book, as the astute reader will have guessed long ago, is *The Book of the New Sun* itself" (PE, 15). See CANOG.

**fricatrice** "One can imagine an ideal servant who serves out of love for his master, just as one can an ideal rustic who remains a ditcher from a love of nature, or an ideal fricatrice who spreads her legs a dozen times a night from a love of copulation. But one never encounters these fabulous creatures in reality" (I, chap. 35, 294).
*History:* a lewd woman.

**Frog** the hero of "The Tale of the Boy Called Frog" (III, chap. 19, 149), who is raised by wolves and builds an empire, probably the First Empire.
*Myth:* Frog is a combination of (Roman) Romulus and (Sumerian) Enkidu.
*Literature:* Kipling's Mowgli (whose name means "frog") is another model for Frog.

**fulgurator** "Master Gurloes would appear trailing three or four journeymen and perhaps an examiner and a fulgurator" (I, chap. 7, 74). At the Citadel, a priest (or technician?) commonly employed by the torturers whenever the electrical devices are to be used.

*History:* a priest who interprets lightning. See LIGHTNING.

**fuligin** a sooty color, powdered black (I, chap. 4, 39).
*Commentary:* the descriptions of this color as being "blacker than black" (aside from the powerful sin aspect) indicate to Michael Swanwick that it is actually "selective black," a black that absorbs light beyond the visible spectrum and into the ultraviolet. Selective coatings are used on solar collectors to maximize absorption of radiation. It is a notion that engineer Wolfe would definitely be familiar with, and the seeming paradox having a practical explanation would fit his sense of humor. Presumably a fuligin cloak would be unusually warm.

**Fulstrum** a reference point of some kind on the Lake of Endless Sleep in the Botanical Gardens of Nessus (I, chap. 22, 197).
*Latin:* a marker, most likely a buoy, in a lake or along a beach (Late Latin).

**fuscina** "In translating these [terms for weapons], I have endeavored to bear in mind the radical meaning of the words employed as well as what I take to be the appearance and function of the weapons themselves. Thus *falchion, fuscina,* and many others" (IV, appendix, 314). It seems to appear only in the appendix.
*Latin:* a trident.

**fusil** a type of energy rifle used by the Autarch's MAN-BEASTS, it is capable of slaughtering half a dozen men with a blast (IV, chap.

20, 162). Undoubtedly of stellar-level technology, it has a range of 500 yards.
*History:* a 17th-century flintlock, whose name means "fusing, melting." More advanced than the arquebus and the caliver, it fired a .65 caliber ball and weighed around nine pounds.

**galleass** a heavy, low-built vessel, larger than a galley, using both sails and oars, chiefly employed in war (IV, chap. 37, 301).

**gallipot** an old slang word for those assistants or apprentices who pounded drugs, rolled pills, collected herbs, et cetera, for an apothecary (I, chap. 1, 11). From the term for a small earthen glazed pot used by apothecaries for ointments and medicines.

**gamboge** a strong and brilliant yellow, originally from a gum-resin based pigment of the same name (I, chap. 27, 235). "No doubt supplied here by the remaining three quarters of the sun breaking through the clouds" (CD, 246). Here is a case where sunlight on Urth is definitely yellow in color.
*History:* John Brunner reports that the word comes from the name Cambodia, origin of the resin.

**Gandharvas** "For an instant it seemed to me that I heard the voices of the Gandharvas, the singers before the throne of the Pancreator" (V, chap. 15, 108).
*Myth:* in the Hindu Veda, a deity who knows and reveals the secrets of heaven and divine truths in general, thought by some to be a personification of the fire of the sun. The Gandharvas generally have their dwellings in the sky or atmosphere, and one of their offices is to prepare the heavenly soma juice for the gods.

**Garden Landing** a location in Nessus, on the River Gyoll near the Botanic Gardens (I, chap. 18, 164).

**Garden of Everlasting Sleep** one of the Botanical Gardens of Nessus, designed to look like the mouth of a dead volcano (I, chap. 23, 208). The Lake of Birds is at the center, surrounded by fens, and there are trees up to the rim. The Cave of the Cumaean is located here, so this garden's time/space coordinates would appear to be on the Italian peninsula, several centuries B.C.

**gateaux secs** the cookies or biscuits served at the Inn of Lost Loves (I, chap. 25, 222). "Gateau secs" (French term meaning "dry cakes") are simple cookies.

**Gaudentius** the Praetorian vingtner (V, chap. 39, 279) who repeatedly strikes the Conciliator at the order of his chiliarch.
*Onomastics:* "the blissful one" (Latin).
*History:* there are six Saints Gaudentius; the earliest was martyred by the Arians in 360.

**Gaudentius's chiliarch** the Praetorian orders Gaudentius to hit the Conciliator several times (V, chap. 38, 271–72). He is later tormented by Typhon for allowing the Conciliator to have the dirk; he is freed by the Conciliator and given the Claw; he and his men vow to join the rebels against Typhon (V, chap. 39, 279). This group of the chiliarch and his men thus becomes the precursor to the Pelerines in bearing the Claw.

**Gea** the mother of Nod, in Dr. Talos's play *Eschatology and Genesis.* This draws a parallel between Baldanders, who plays that part in the play, and the offspring of Gea. See BONA DEA; FAUNA.
*Myth:* (Greek) goddess personifying the Earth, she sprang from primeval Chaos, and in turn bore Ouranos ("sky"). Mating with Ouranos, she bore the Titans, the Cyclopes, and the HECATONCHIRES. In resentment against Ouranos, she set her sons, the Titans, to revolt against him. Chronos, the youngest, led the revolt and castrated his father. Her name is sometimes spelled Gaiea.
*Commentary:* the Urth Cycle is a complicated skein marking the transformation of our mother Earth (Gea) first into Urth (Norn of the past, a withered crone) and then into Ushas (a sexy goddess of the dawn).

**gegenschein** a faint elliptical nebulous light in the sky best seen during September and October when in the constellations Aquarius and Pisces (III, chap. 17, 136).

**genicon** an imagined sexual partner (I, chap. 30, 257).

**Gentle Right** in a contest between two gentlemen, the right of a man knocked down to rise and rearm before being attacked again (I, chap. 27, 239).

**Gerbold** Ultan's master at the Library of Nessus (I, chap. 6, 59).
*History:* Saint Gerbold (died 690) was a Benedictine bishop who founded the abbey of Livray, and then was made bishop of Bayeux, France.

**giddypate** "and Aude was but a giddypate, who knew the chatelaine only when she was old" (ES, 214). "Giddy" is frivolous and light hearted, flighty; "pate" is head.

**Gildas** a former captain of apprentices, he was long since a journeyman torturer at the time of Severian's elevation (I, chap. II, 106).
*Onomastics:* "serves God" (Celtic); "gilded" (English); a name from Arthurian legend.
*History:* born in Scotland, Saint Gildas (A.D. 500?–570?) was an ascetic in Wales who wrote on the moral degradation that he felt had despoiled Britain.

**Glacies** easternmost of the Southern Isles of the Commonwealth; home to Hallvard (IV, chap. 7, 54).
*Latin:* ice.

**glaive** a kind of halberd; a pole arm with a head like the blade of a sword (I, chap. 4, 43). Used in the 12th and 13th centuries.

**glamour** a spell affecting outward appearances but not reality (I, chap. 16, 149).

**gligua** a term used in Chile for a worker of black magic (ES, 216).

**glyptodon** [GLIP-tow-don] the Atrium of Time has statues of glyptodons (I, chap. 4, 43).
*History:* a South American prehistoric quadruped similar to a cat-headed armadillo the size and shape of a Volkswagen Beetle.

Covered with a solid carapace, this odd creature also had fluted teeth and a clublike tail.

**gnomon** a pillar, rod, or other object that serves to indicate the time of day by casting its shadow upon a marked surface (I, chap. 4, 43).

**Gnosticism** Gnosticism seems to have a place on Urth. The witches openly dabble with it; Severian, visiting their tower, sees that "Gnostic designs in white, green, and purple had been chalked on the walls" (II, chap. 30, 257). Even sixteen year old Dorcas talks along Gnostic lines: "The world is filled half with evil and half with good. We can tilt it forward so that more good runs into our minds, or back, so that more runs into this [lake of death]" (I, chap. 24, 188). While actively recruiting Severian to his cause, Vodalus also alludes to certain ideas of later Gnosticism: "I want you to conceive now of two autarchs — two great powers striving for mastery. The white seeks to maintain things as they are, the black to set Man's foot on the road to domination again" (II, chap. 10, 75). But it is Famulimus who first openly questions this worldview, when she asks Severian, "Is all the world a war of good and bad? Have you not thought it might be something more?" (III, chap. 34, 251).
*History:* a religious philosophical dualism that professed salvation through secret knowledge, or "gnosis." The movement reached a high point of development during the 2nd century A.D. in Rome and Alexandria. The origins of gnosticism have been attributed to a number of sources: the Greek mystery cults; Zoroastrianism; the Kabbalah of Judaism; and Egyptian religion.

The gnostic sects presented their teachings in complex systems of thought. Characteristic of their position was the doctrine that all material reality is evil, and one of their central convictions was that salvation is achieved by freeing the spirit from its imprisonment in matter. Elaborate explanations were given on how this imprisonment came to be, as well as how the deliverance of the soul could be accomplished.

Gnosticism was denounced by the Christian theologians Irenaeus, Hippolytus, and Tertullian, and from the 3rd century, it gradually merged with Manichaeism (which focused on the undetermined battle between Light and Darkness).

**Gobar** the seamstress of Vert who makes a gown for the child in EFF (SS, 252).

**God and His Man, The** a short story, probably contained within the brown book. Collected in ES, it was originally published in *Isaac Asimov's SF Magazine* (Feb. 1980), thus the first Wolfe story to mention Urth. It may be a kind of overture to Severian's Narrative, but in some ways it seems to be the antithesis. It tells of a god named ISID 1000 100E who takes a man of Urth to the planet ZED and tries to tell him what to do. See also MASER and TARNUNG.

**gonfalon** a banner or ensign, frequently composed of or ending in several tails or streamers, suspended from a cross-bar instead of being directly fastened to the pole (I, chap. 24, 217).

**Goslin** the Pelerine slave who recruited Winnoc thirty years before Severian met him (IV, chap. 12, 97).

*History:* Saint Gozzelinus or Goslin (died 1153) was the second abbot of a Benedictine monastery near Milan, Italy.

**gosport** communication tube on a ship, leading below decks to the engine room (II, chap. 17, 154).

**government** Master Malrubius teaches that there are seven principles of government, from lowest to highest (I, chap. 33, 283).

| Focus | Example |
|---|---|
| abstraction (highest) | ideal government |
| greater/lesser board of electors | representative government |
| law only | government by law |
| code legitimizing state | constitutional government |
| royal state | absolute monarchy |
| bloodline/rules of succession | hereditary monarchy |
| monarch (lowest) | charismatic monarchy |

**gowdalie** "And so he took up his gowdalie and went to a certain pool" (I, chap. 21, 189).
*History:* a three-pointed fish spear.

**Gracia** a prostitute at House Azure, the khaibit of an inner-circle exultant at the House Absolute (I, chap. 9, 89). Her hair is white; her complexion is dark. Roche chooses her (90). See also BARBEA, THEA'S KHAIBIT, and THECLA'S KHAIBIT.
*Onomastics:* "favor," "blessing" (Latin).
*History:* Saint Gracia (died 1180?), daughter of the Moslim caliph of Lerida, Spain, was converted by her brother, changing her name from Zaida to Gracia.

**graisle** "Like most cavalry helmets it left the ears bare to better hear the graisle" (I, chap. 27, 237).
*History:* a trumpet used in signaling.

**Grand Court** a part of the Citadel of the Autarch that contains the Chapel and probably the Pinakotheken and Library as well.

**Grand Gnab** "Then would you see the Grand Gnab, when the universe shall fall into itself?" (CD, 278). From *gnab(b)le,* a variant of *knabble,* meaning to nibble. (It is also "bang" spelled backwards.) The counterpart to the Big Bang, coming at the end of the universal day. See BIG BLOSSOM and MANVANTARA.

**gravid** "You are gravid with the knowledge" (V, chap. 23, 165).
*History:* pregnant.

**Great Bull** a constellation of Urth's zodiac (III, chap. 18, 146), visible from the Commonwealth in spring and summer (IV, chap. 23, 161).
*Astronomy:* our constellation Taurus, a spring sign in the northern hemisphere and a fall sign in the southern hemisphere.

**green book** "A green book hardly larger than my hand . . . appeared to be a collection of devotions, full of enameled pictures of ascetic pantocrators and hypostases with black haloes and gemlike robes" (I, chap. 6, 67). This book, one of the four that Thecla is allowed to read while in the Matachin Tower, is a euchologion or formulary of prayers (PE, 12). Gene Wolfe mentions that the enamel of the pictures forms a link to Dorcas's family (PE, 9).

**Green Man** time traveler from the Age of Ushas or beyond. His green pigmentation comes from a form of symbiotic algae (pond scum) that provides nourishment. Severian first meets him at the Saltus fair, where he is a prisoner and sideshow attraction (II, chap. 3, 25). Severian gives him half of a whetstone, the means to escape, and later the Green Man returns the favor: first aiding Agia in rescuing Severian from the Ascians (IV, chap. 30, 241) and later opening the tomb of Apu Punchau in the Age of Myth to let Severian out (V, chap. 51, 365). The Green Man represents the triumph of the New Sun, in contrast to Master Ash.
*Myth:* fairies often have such green skin and a magical connection to nature.
*Commentary:* the Green Man represents the next evolutionary stage of man toward the Hiero, guided by the hammer and tongs of the HIEROGRAMMATES. The Green Man says, "In us, the tiny plants live and die, and our bodies feed from them and their dead and require no other nourishment. All the famines, and all the labor of growing food, are ended" (II, chap. 3, 20), attesting to his peace with Fauna, and his ability to walk the corridors of Time at will proves his atonement with Thyme.

**Green Room** Severian is told that Dr. Talos and his company are in the Green Room at the House Absolute (II, chap. 20, 179), and he is surprised when he finds that while it is green, it is not actually a room.
*History:* in theater parlance, the Green Room is the room (regardless of color) in which the actors wait before going on stage. In *Return of the Straight Dope,* Cecil Adams writes, "Legend has it that the green room, also styled greenroom or green-room, goes

back to the Elizabethan era, when the actors lolled away the time between entrances on the lawn behind the theater, or 'on the green.'" Adams then debunks this legend by showing that the earliest use of the term comes from 1701, yet we shake our heads in wonder at the fact that the autarch's green room is like the legendary one.

**Grimkeld** the sailor on Tzadkiel's ship who shoots the life-line to Severian and Gunnie (v, chap. 23, 168). He takes them to the captain's quarters (v, chap. 24, 172).
*Onomastics:* Grimkel (lacking final "d") is a saga name for a son of Ulf (Norse).
*History:* in a group (Theodore and Companions) martyred by invading Danes, Grimkeld (died 870) was a 100-year-old Benedictine.

**Group of Seventeen** the rulers and cultural focus of Ascia (IV, chap. 5, 38).
*History:* the Ascian obsession with authorized texts and Correct Thought points toward a totalitarian system along the lines of Marxist-Leninist Communism, the result being the utter suppression of the individual in favor of the group/government. The number seventeen alludes to the Soviet politburo, which typically had seventeen members (eleven to twelve full members and six to nine alternate members).

**Guasacht** condottiere of the Eighteenth Bacele of the Irregular Contarii (IV, chap. 19, 150). See also DARIA, ERBLON, LACTAN, MESROP, and URSINE MAN.
*Onomastics:* "peril" (Gaelic).

*History:* Saint Guasacht (4th century), a son of the man under whom Saint Patrick was a slave in Ireland. He was converted and served as a missionary bishop of Granard, Ireland.

**Guibert** the friend of Thecla who handed her the scourge and lash prior to their cruel game against the prisoners in the antechamber (II, chap. 16, 135).
*History:* Saint Guibert (died 962), a Lotharingian noble and military hero who became a hermit, then established a monastery on his estate.

**guilds** there are countless guilds in Nessus, each one having a different Patron Saint. A handful of them (curators [I, chap. 6, 57] and others [I, chap. 11, 104]) are as follows:

| Guild | Patron | Tinct |
|---|---|---|
| Curators' | Jerome* | gray |
| Matrosses' | Barbara | — |
| Seekers' | Katharine | fuligin |
| Soldiers' | Hadrian | — |
| Witches' | Mag | — |

*Jerome is not named, but would fit the pattern.

Among the torturers it seems that apprentices become journeymen at around the age of twenty-one. While one would expect a journeyman to be elevated to master in his thirties or forties, masters may be limited in ratio to the number of journeymen, just as grand masters may be limited in ratio to the number of masters. The guild of torturers has two masters, twenty journeymen, and many apprentices. This is a ratio between journeymen and masters of 10:1.

**Gundulf** Hallvard's uncle, who murdered his brother Anskar (IV, chap. 7, 54). He had loved Nennoc and intended to marry her, for which Anskar called him "oath-breaker" since he had told their dying father he would not marry.
*History:* Saint Gundulf (6th century) was a Gallic bishop.

**Gunnie** a middle-aged woman who is a sailor on Tzadkiel's starship (V, chap. 2, 13). "Gunnie" is her ship-board sailor name, a shortened form of Burgundofara. She is described as cow-eyed (V, chap. 3, 18) and also as a blue bird (V, chap. 3, 20). When she was a girl newly signed on the Ship she had a lover named Severian (V, chap. 26, 185). She meets Severian the Great on Tzadkiel's ship and takes him under her wing. (She also nearly kills him while helping Idas.) When the ship returns to Urth, Gunnie sends Burgundofara (a new shipmate, her earlier self) with the rejuvenated Severian. Gunnie searches for the illusion that love is more than it is. Like MASTER ASH, who is undone when he steps outside of the Last House, so might Gunnie dissolve after her younger self Burgundofara leaves the ship . . . or if Burgundofara leaves Urth again to sail on the Ship, then the circle will be closed.
*Commentary:* once we know Burgundofara's story as the betrayer of the Conciliator, we can see how Gunnie tries to aid Severian on the ship, yet accidentally betrays him by helping Idas. Even though she tries to redress her previous mistake, still she seems cursed to betray him again. Her character combines elements of Judas (the betrayer) and Magdalen (the enigmatic female disciple).

**Gurgustii** the name of a village located on Fluminis between Vici and Os (v, chap. 29, 204).
*Latin:* plural of *gurgustium*, hut, hovel.

**Gurloes** a master torturer (I, chap. 1, 9). He is roughly forty years older than Severian (I, chap. 7, 62), and thus around sixty. When he tells a younger Severian he has been master for twenty years (II, chap. 7, 57), it seems he was elevated at around the age of thirty-five. In the triumvirate of the torturers he is the "son," aged Master Palaemon is the "father," and dead Master Malrubius is the "ghost." He has a remarkably small head for so large a man (II, chap. 7, 58), with square yellow teeth like those of a dead nag (I, chap. 10, 103), and eyes brighter than any woman's (I, chap. 7, 78).

Master Palaemon says that torture "Must be done by good men . . . what is intolerable is that it should be done by bad men" (IV, chap. 33, 268). Gurloes seems to illustrate this paradox through the various details we know about him.

Gurloes is a complex man trying to be simple: he eats too much and too seldom; he reads when he thinks no one knows of it; and he visits prisoners, including an insane one on the third level, to talk of things none of his eavesdroppers could understand. He suffers nightmares when he drinks heavily; he is the only one in the guild who is not afraid of the voices at the top of the tower (I, chap. 7, 78). He was a coward for fearing he could not carry out the sentence of sexually abusing Ia (II, chap. 7, 58), yet on another occasion he proved spontaneously capable on short notice (59). The fact that he mispronounces the "common" words BORDEREAUX, SALPINX, and URTICATE might indicate that

these three terms are secret keys to his character. He is still alive in the tenth year of Severian's reign, but he looks unwell to Severian (I, chap. 7, 78).
*History:* Saint Gurloes (died 1057) was a Benedictine monk, prior of Redon Abbey, who in 1029 became abbot of Sainte-Croix of Quimperlé in Brittany.

**Gwinoc** illustrator of the brown book (I, chap. 6, 64).
*History:* Saint Gwinoc (6th century) and his father Saint GILDAS were Welsh monks; the son wrote a number of Celtic poems.

**gymnosophist** one of a sect of ancient Hindu philosophers of ascetic habits who wore little or no clothing, denied themselves flesh meat, and gave themselves up to mystical contemplation (III, chap. 5, 42). Known to the Greeks through the reports of the companions of Alexander.

**Gyoll** a major river of the Commonwealth (I, chap. 1, 10). The name comes, perhaps, from "gyo," meaning "gully" or "creek." The Gyoll has several tributaries, among them the CEPHISSUS and the FLUMINIS, and runs roughly from north to south, where it meets the ocean. "Gyoll, below Thrax but above Nessus, flows too swiftly to foul its channel . . . hemmed by rocky hills on either side, it runs straight as a spar for a hundred leagues" (V, chap. 33, 235), and at the center of the flood along this length, a ship can float downstream at three leagues per watch (around seven miles per hour).
*Myth:* "Gjoll," meaning "icy" or "freezing," is the river of death in Norse mythology, one of the eleven rivers flowing from the primal spring Hvergelmir. The others are Svol (cool), Gunnthra

(defiant), Fjorm, Fimbulthul (bubbling), Slid (fearsome), Hrid (storming), Sylgar, Ylg, Vid (broad), and Leiptr (lightning flash). (In this regard, see PHLEGETHON.) But there are two other Gjolls in Norse mythology: the horn worn by Heimdall (analogous to Gabriel's trumpet) and the boulder to which Fenrir the wolf is chained.

**gyves** (jives) shackles (III, chap. 28, 228).

*Huanaco*

**Hadelin** a middle-aged man, captain of the *Alcyone* in Typhon's era (v, chap. 30, 213). When the reanimated Zama attacks Severian in his room, Hadelin is among those who respond (217). When Severian resurrects Zama, Hadelin is the last man to flee (219), and Burgundofara leaves soon thereafter. Hadelin and Burgundofara spend the night together. Hadelin later visits Severian in his cell at the old hulk (v, chap. 37, 261).
*Onomastics:* possibly the diminutive of a Germanic word for combat.
*History:* Saint Hadelin (died c. 690) of Gascony was one of the scholarly, mostly Irish monks who preached Christianity and started conversion work in what is now Belgium under the pagan invaders. He founded the monastery of Celles.

**Hadid** an android sailor on the ship of Tzadkiel.
*Onomastics:* not a name, it is the word "iron" (Arabic).

**Hadrian** patron saint of the Autarch's soldiers (I, chap. 11, 104).
*Onomastics:* variant of Adrian "from Adria" (Latin).
*History:* there are several Saints Adrian (or Hadrian), the most pertinent being a pagan officer of the imperial court at Nicomedia who befriended the Christian prisoners and was himself thrown into prison, where he died in 304. Patron saint of soldiers and butchers.

**Hagith** (entry from SOLAR SYSTEM TABLE) ruler of the planet Venus and one of the Seven Olympian Spirits, Hagith rules twenty-one or thirty-five of the 196 Olympian Provinces. He commands 4,000 legions of spirits and has the power of transmuting metals.

**Hall of Justice** part of the fortress complex near the Sanguinary Field of Nessus (I, chap. 28, 242). Executions and excoriations take place in front of it. It seems to be occupied by the same Blue Dimarchi who later appear at the disturbance at the Piteous Gate.

**Hallowmass Eve** Halloween, the evening preceding All Saints' Day. In the Lunar calendar of the Commonwealth, this date falls in "the full of the Spading Moon" (ES, 21).

**Hallvard (the elder)** Hallvard's father (IV, chap. 7, 54).

**Hallvard** one of Foila's suitors, along with Melito and Loyal to the Group of Seventeen (IV, chap. 5, 40). He is from Glacies, one of the Southern Isles. His father is Hallvard, and Fausta is his sister. His uncles are Anskar and Gundulf. (See FAMILY TREES.) He tells the story of "The Two Sealers" (IV, chap. 7).
*Onomastics:* "fought in the Battle of Hafursfjord" (Norse).
*History:* Saint Hallvard (died 1043) was a Norwegian trader in the Baltic, who was asked to give refuge on his ship to a woman pursued by three men who said she was a thief. Although he offered to make up any loss they may have suffered, they shot her and Hallvard. He is the patron of Oslo.

**hanger** a loop or strap on a sword belt from which the sword is hung; also (as is this case) the generic term for the sword so worn (II, chap. 7, 60).

**harena** (Latin) arena, named after the sand that covers the floor (III, chap. 1, 9).

**hastarii** spearmen, a unit of hastarus-equipped men (II, chap. 14, 122).
*History:* Roman legionaries or spearmen.

**hastarus** a pyrotechnic weapon of Urth level technology, held like a thrusting spear (IV, chap. 33, 266).
*History:* the Greek spear.

**hatif** "He told me a shaft had been driven into a hillside [near Saltus] about a year ago upon the advice of a hatif that had whispered in the ears of several of the principal citizens of the village" (V, chap. 34, 245).
*Myth:* (Arabic) a familiar spirit, like Socrates's daemon.

**haubergeon** a sleeveless coat or jacket of mail or scale armor, originally smaller and lighter than a hauberk, but sometimes applied to the same (IV, chap. 19, 148).

**hecatonchires** "as though hecatonchires roved the gloomy corridors and deserted rooms, their thousand fingers smeared with noctilucence to light their way" (ES, 26).
*Myth:* (Greek) three giants (Briareus, Cottus, and Gyges), each having 100 arms.

**heliotrope** moderate, light, or brilliant violet to moderate or deep reddish purple (II, chap. 22, 194).

**hellebore** a name given by the ancients to certain plants having poisonous and medicinal properties, and especially reputed as cures for mental disease (III, chap. 33, 260). This group includes the Christmas Rose.

**heptarch** "Such rituals are divided into seven orders according to their importance, or as the heptarchs say, their 'transcendence'" (IV, chap. 28, 225).
*History:* a ruler of one of seven divisions of a country; one of the rulers of the Heptarchy. Since the heptarchs mentioned in the text are authorities on transcendence, they are probably the seven Olympic Spirits (Kabbalah), whose names are used by the Hierodules on the SOLAR SYSTEM table.

**Herais** Casdoe's mother, a woman of Thrax (III, chap. 14, 113). Perhaps she is the innkeeper of the Duck's Nest Inn. (See INNKEEPERS.)
*History:* Saint Herais (died 202) was a young girl burned to death in Alexandria around the time Saint Plutarch was killed, during the persecution of Septimus Severus.

**Herena** a girl of Vici whose withered arm is healed by the Conciliator (V, chap. 28, 199). She becomes a follower.
*History:* Saint Herena (3rd century) was martyred in Africa in the persecutions of Decius.

**Hermas** a great historian of earlier times, remembered by Master Ultan (I, chap. 6, 65).
*Onomastics:* "mercury," "gain," "refuge" (Hebrew).
*History:* there are a few Saints Hermas, but a 2nd century Christian writer who was not a saint seems most appropriate. Hermas's book *The Shepherd* was held in highest regard by the early Church Fathers, some of whom considered it scripture, though most of them rightly held it to be worthy of respect but not divinely inspired. Modern scholars believe he was the brother of Pope Pius I (A.D. 140–155).

**hesperorn** "Long he stood [ . . . ] until the monkeys no longer feared him . . . and the hesperorn fluttered to her nest" (I, chap. 21, 189).
*History:* a prehistoric fish-eating ostrich.

**Hesperus** a celestial object (presumably Skuld) in the night sky of Urth (II, chap. 17, 151).
*History:* the Latin form of Greek Hesperos, "the Evening Star," a term for the planet Venus seen in the evening. Originally it was paired with Phosphorus, Venus seen in the morning, until Pythagoras realized that the two were a single object.

**hetaerae** those who participate in extramarital sex, or members of a communal marriage (II, chap. 24, 242).
*Greek:* a plural of "hetaera," a female companion, a mistress, a concubine; a courtesan, a harlot.

**heteroclite** deviating from the ordinary rule or standard; irregular, exceptional, abnormal, anomalous, eccentric (v, chap. 48, 337). Said of persons and things.

**Hethor** sailor-lover of Agia. Hethor seems to have recently arrived on Urth since the clothes he sells to Agia at the rag shop, while ancient in design, are "not far from new" (III, chap. 15, 119). At Agia's urging he follows Severian from Nessus to the mountains beyond Thrax and uses three exotic creatures drawn from SPECULA (notule, slug, and salamander) in attempts to kill him. He summons the pteriopes for Agia's rescue of Severian from Ascian evzones, and the worm of white fire for Agia's rescue of Severian from the Ascian camp. Perhaps as a reflection of his mirror magic, Hethor's monologues use a number of terms related to eyes and seeing, giving this lexicon both ABACINATION and SCOPOLAGNA.

Hethor is often seen as a gray figure (I, chap. 30, 257; I, chap. 34, 290), perhaps a reference to the purple-gray bloom of the plant heather, but certainly a clue to his great antiquity: Agia says his name isn't really Hethor, but a much older one (III, chap. 15, 120). He once served on the *Quasar* (I, chap. 30, 257), which may be another name for the *Fortunate Cloud,* the ship on which Jonas served (III, chap. 15, 119). In Severian's dream, Hethor mentions recognizable constellations (Aquarius, Pisces, and Aries [IV, chap. 4, 35]) suggesting that Hethor comes from our time, the Age of Myth. Hethor and Jonas are characters from the First Empire period of Posthistory, in the Age of the Monarch.

Before Severian learns that Hethor's pets are from magic mirrors (IV, chap. 30, 240), he wonders how Hethor could be carting heavy monsters all around the countryside (III, chap. 22,

180). A reader might consider a cart to be required for magic mirrors, since the only case seen in *The Book of the New Sun* is the solid and heavy-seeming installation in the Presence Chamber (I, chap. 20, 183–86; II, chap. 18, 167–68). But Hethor's magic mirrors are almost certainly scraps of mirror sail from Tzadkiel's ship or one just like it: in his more lucid monologue, within the corridors of Time, he speaks of "our demon-haunted mirror sails" (IV, chap. 4, 35).

*History:* Saint Ethor or Hethor was a monk-priest who died circa 870 when Danes raided Chertsey Abbey in Surrey.

*Commentary:* he speaks at times "a gobbling singsong" (I, chap. 35, 293), suggesting an East Asian language. Hethor's true name may very well be KIM LEE SOONG.

There is a curious mention of Hethor when Severian is aboard Tzadkiel's ship, a case that may be more than just a simple comparison. Severian, captured by jibers who force him to watch a motion picture clip of himself, is then told by "a little man with dirty gray hair like Hethor's" that he must imitate the clip or they will kill him (V, chap. 13, 90). It is an odd time to be suddenly invoking Hethor. A very confusing moment, highly charged, quickly gone, never examined. And yet, because of the time-bending characteristics of the starship's travel beyond Briah, it could very well be Hethor (a younger and non-stuttering Hethor) he sees: in fact, this is probably the simplest solution. Following this thread, we can suppose that Hethor was a jiber on Tzadkiel's ship, and that he was rounded up with all the other jibers in order to be memory-wiped and landed as colonists on Ushas in S.R. 50. Somehow he avoided the memory erasure and escaped from the prisoner transport in such a way that he arrived in Nessus in I P.S.

while the ship crashed about two hundred years earlier, creating both Jonas and the KIM LEE SOONG GROUP.

Since Jonas is paired with Hethor in mysterious ways, and as Jonas has elements of the Wandering Jew to his character, so Hethor has elements of another legendary figure who is paired with the Wandering Jew: the captain of the *Flying Dutchman*. Both Hethor and Jonas are living representatives of the First Empire, and as such, they may reveal through their attitudes the reasons for its fall.

**hetman** there are five hetmans in the text.

- Zambdas is hetman of Murene.
- Bregwyn is hetman of Vici.
- The unnamed hetman of Gurgustii (v, chap. 29, 206).
- The unnamed hetman of the stone town in the Age of Myth (v, chap. 49, 348).
- The unnamed young hetman of stone town in Age of Myth (v, chap. 50, 351).

**hetrochthnous** a misspelling of heterochthonous, meaning "not indigenous: foreign, naturalized; not formed in the place where it now occurs: transplanted" (v, chap. 10, 73).

**hexaemeron** the six days of the creation (II, chap. 9, 68).

**Hierarch** "You Hierarchs are magicians," (v, chap. 20, 142). A Hierarch is the human-like larva (or offspring) of a HIEROGRAMMATE (v, chap. 19, 138). Venant and Apheta are both Hierarchs. Additional citations: I, chap. 27, 236; v, chap. 21, 154.

*History:* priest of high rank; angel of high rank. Literally, "Holy Lord."

**Hierodule** one belonging to a race created by the HIEROGRAMMATES of the higher universe, YESOD (II, chap. 25, 237; III, chap. 33). Ossipago, Barbatus, and Famulimus are members of this group, though Ossipago is actually a robot. Their living quarters on Tzadkiel's ship are icy cold and seemingly underwater, with mottled slabs of stone-like furniture (V, chap. 5, 34). They live only twenty years (III, chap. 33, 265).

Other Hierodules in the text include the Cumaean, the officer of the watch on the tender (V, chap. 27, 190), and probably Father Inire.

*Greek:* holy slave.

**Hierogrammate** in YESOD, the beings created by the Hieros, the men of the previous universe (V, chap. 19, 138). They rule BRIAH through the HIERODULES, whom they shaped. Tzadkiel is a Hierogrammate.

*History:* a sacred scribe, one of a lower order of the Egyptian priesthood; a writer of sacred records, specifically of hieroglyphics.

**hieromonach** a monk who is also a priest (III, chap. 1, 8). Present at executions in the Commonwealth.

*History:* from the Eastern Church.

**hierophant** an official expounder of sacred mysteries or religious ceremonies, especially in ancient Greece; an initiating or presiding priest (I, chap. 8, 79). Also the name of a Tarot card: see TAROT AND THE BOOK OF THE NEW SUN.

**Hieros** the men of the previous manvantara (universe), creators of the Hierogrammates (V, chap. 21, 151). See also INCREATE.

**Hierro** an android sailor on Tzadkiel's ship.
*Onomastics:* not a name, it is the word "iron" (Spanish).

**Hildegrin** a Vodalarius, first encountered exhuming a DEAD WOMAN IN THE NECROPOLIS (I, chap. 1, 13). He is a big man, first referred to as an arctother (I, chap. 1, 14) but professionally referred to as a badger because of his digging (I, chap. 23, 205). He is the person who halts the escape of Agilus at the Sanguinary Field (I, chap. 27, 239; I, chap. 28, 245; II, chap. 31, 286). He is ultimately killed by Apu-Punchau in their encounter at the stone town (II, chap. 31, 294).
*History:* Saint Hildegrin (died 827) is remembered for evangelization of the Saxons.

**hipparch** the commander of a xenagie of cavalry: about 500 mounted soldiers (I, chap. 17, 156). See MILITARY ORGANIZATION.

**History of Urth** the history of Urth seems to be divided into four phases: the Age of Myth, the Age of the Monarch, the Age of the Autarch, and the Age of Ushas.

It is difficult to determine the duration of each age from hints in the text, and the difficulty is compounded by certain sleights that lead some readers into incorrect assumptions. For example, many readers interpret the sun's dying condition as a sign of stellar evolution and believe that the Age of the Autarch must lie billions of years in the future (yet this is clearly not the case since the sun is not dying of natural causes). Other readers see the time frame in geological terms and feel Urth must be several million years in the future because the "league-high" cliff near Casdoe's cabin seems to show fossils of a technological age. A few readers have tried to use Lune's orbit as a gauge (since it is said that while the Moon is currently moving away from Earth, at a certain point in the distant future it will come closer), but Lune's situation is a production of engineering rather than evolution.

One million years seems to be the outer limit, since Wolfe has written, "Imagine then what the situation will be in Severian's time for the scholar heirs of a sequence of civilizations that may be over a million years old" (*Plan[e]t Engineering,* 6). To put this into perspective, we ourselves are heirs to a mere 6,000 years of historical civilization, with threads going back 30,000 years to Cro-Magnon cave art, traces stretching 300,000 years since the emergence of *Homo sapiens,* and perhaps the faintest of whispers across a million years since the time of *Homo erectus.* Going by this, then, Urth must be about a million years in our future, three times longer than our species has been around.

One measuring stick that Wolfe uses is the precession of the equinox, which is the shifting of the zodiac through the seasons, a cycle that takes 26,000 years to complete. The position of the stars with regard to the seasons in the Commonwealth seems the same as in Earth's southern hemisphere today, suggesting that the minimum span between Earth and Urth is 26,000 years. (Agia's offhand remark about someone "from a position, say, of thirty thousand years ago" (1, chap. 19, 172) is an approximation of this figure.) This makes for a "Great Year" with four "seasons" of

6,500 years each, allowing a progression of seasons rather like the yuga of a MANVANTARA. This makes a lot of sense, and the crippling of the old sun acts as a Winter Solstice, marking the Age of the Autarch as being the "winter" season of the Great Year. In the era of Apu Punchau, Severian seems to see winter stars in the springtime (V, chap. 49, 346), which suggests that the two ages are separated by about 20,000 years.

**The "Great Year" Model**

| Starting Year | Name of Age | Location of Spring Stars |
|---|---|---|
| 27,000 P.S. | (Earth) | in Winter |
| 20,500 P.S. | Myth | in Spring |
| 14,000 P.S. | Monarch | in Summer |
| 7,500 P.S. | (decline) | in Fall |
| 1,000 P.S. | Autarch | in Winter |
| 5,500 S.R. | (Green Man?) | in Spring |

Another model which was favored in the first edition of this Lexicon is the "100k" model. This timespan is almost four times larger than the "Great Year" Model.

**The "100k" Model**

| Starting Year | Name of Age | Notes |
|---|---|---|
| 97,500 P.S. | Myth | Earth/Urth stars match up. |
| 96,000 P.S. | Monarch | A guess. |
| 72,000 P.S. | (decline) | * |
| 1,000 P.S. | Autarch | |

* Decline "over a thousand lifetimes" (III, chap. 6, 52).

*The Age of Myth:* our own Earth is hopelessly lost in the dawn of the Age of Myth, but there are occasional glimpses, in the Botanical Garden's Jungle Section (the missionary Robert, his wife Marie, and the aeroplane), for example, as well as the familiar "Astronaut on the Moon" picture hanging on a wall within the Citadel. Apu-Punchau is a major figure of this age. He leads a group of primitive people along the road to civilization, and is later venerated as a god in a place known as the stone town. If this figure is the same Apu-Punchau who was worshipped by the Incan people, then perhaps the stone town is Cuzco, where the Inca dynasty was established in A.D. 1200, but it seems more likely that he is the god of a new continent raised in the southern hemisphere.

*The Age of the Monarch:* according to legend, a star-faring race (probably Asiatic, if not Korean) left behind its wild half (emotions), sold them to machines, and established the First Empire upon Order alone. The Empire expanded to 1,000 stars, eventually branching out from the Milky Way galaxy to others. Over a period of time the machines built cities and gave out artifacts to entice humanity into savagery, and eventually the machines returned the emotions to man, causing the Empire to collapse. The machines gave each man and woman an aquastor as an advisor, but after a time the machines died and their closest followers dispersed until each was alone, and each wrote down what he had learned. After a long time, an autarch (probably Typhon) who dreamed of a Second Empire gathered up all the writings in newly built Nessus in order to destroy them. But he decided to shelter the writing in case his Second Empire should fail, which it did, and the library of Nessus was established. (This material based on Cyriaca's tale of the Librarians [III, chap. 6]), with details of the early lives of Hethor and Jonas on the continent that sank to form the isles of the Xanthic Lands.) Legends aside, Typhon is the last of the Monarchs, and his conflict with the Conciliator (roughly 1,100 years prior to the reign of Severian) marks the beginning of the belief in the New Sun.

*The Age of the Autarch:* from Ymar the Almost Just to Severian the Great, this thousand-year phase is marked by unceasing warfare between those who wish to enslave the dying planet (Erebus, Abaia, et cetera, by way of Ascia) and those who would liberate it through rebirth. The latter triumph, and Urth is swept clean by the arrival of the New Sun.

*The Age of Ushas:* not much is known about this age. The enemies of the New Sun have been conquered, and the gods Odilo, the Sleeper, Thais, and Pega seem to form a strong foundation for a new world, where eventually the new human race of the green man will arise, at peace with Nature and masters of Time.

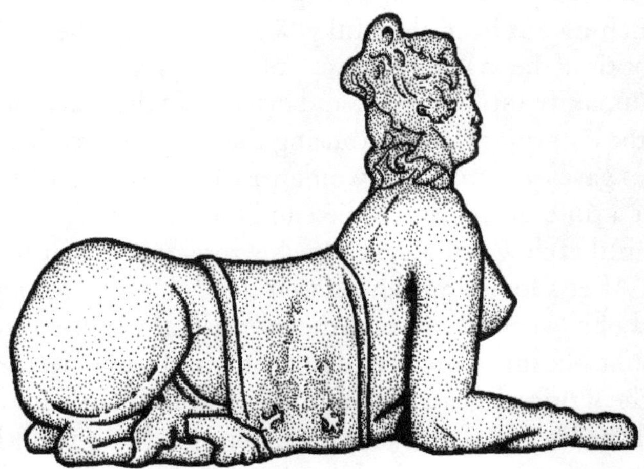

## Fragmentary Timeline of Posthistory

### The Age of Myth

| | |
|---|---|
| | Apu-Punchau lives for 100 years. |

### The Age of the Monarch

| | |
|---|---|
| | Frog founds the Empire (III, chap. 19). |
| | The Empire reaches 1,000 stars (III, chap. 6). |
| | Sinking continent forms Xanthic Lands. |
| | The long decline of the First Empire. |
| | The machine epoch. |
| | The time of the eidolons. |
| | The anchorites. |
| | The androsphinxes. |
| | Second Empire: Era of Typhon and the Conciliator. |
| | Launching of the Whorl. |

### The Age of the Autarch

| | |
|---|---|
| 1,000 P.S. | Autarch Ymar the Almost Just dies. Severian's mausoleum built, Eata's mausoleum built. |
| 1,000–700 | Yellow and Green Empires end their war. First appearance of the Hierodules? |
| 690? | Autarch Maxentius orders execution of Saint Katharine. |
| 350 | *The Book of the Wonders of Urth and Sky* is published (I, chap. 6). |
| 300 | Autarch Sulpicius sets aside books in Library (I, chap. 6). The torturers entertain a guest at Holy Katharine's feast, an event that becomes a part of guild lore (I, chap. 11). |
| 210 | Ship *Fortunate Cloud* crashes on Urth. |
| 100 | The witches complain about the post in the Old Yard, so it is moved into the Matachin Tower (I, chap. 12). |
| 94 | Lomer born. |
| 80 | Ultan born (I, chap. 6). Odilo I born. Sancha born. |

**The Age of the Autarch (continued)**

| | |
|---|---|
| 70 P.S. | Autarch Maruthas closes roads (I, chap. 12). |
| 66 | Scandal in reign of Autarch Appian, leaving Sancha (age fourteen) in disgrace and Lomer (age twenty-eight) sent to the antechamber (III, chap. 15). Odilo (I) serves. |
| 60 | Ultan becomes journeyman curator/librarian. |
| 59 | Sancha leaves the House Absolute (assume twenty-one years old). |
| 50 | Paeon the honey steward dies. Odilo (II) born (II, chap. 19). |
| 50 C. | The villagers of Murene build castle for little Baldanders (III, chap. 31). |
| 50 C. | The door to Severian's mausoleum is opened (V, chap. 47, 335). |
| 45 | Dorcas and her husband open their cloisonné shop (I, chap. 22) in the Oldgate quarter of Nessus (IV, chap. 37). |
| 41 | Dorcas dies. |
| 36 | Gurloes journeyman at age twenty-one, taught by Palaemon. |
| 31 | Palaemon exiled from guild and Winnoc becomes a slave (IV, chap. 12). Master Librarian Gerbold dies, so Ultan becomes master at age fifty (I, chap. 6). Ouen becomes potboy in Oldgate quarter of Nessus (IV, chap. 37). Something happens at Phoenix Throne (II, chap. 24), perhaps the old autarch's trip to Yesod. |
| 24 | Agia and Agilus are born. |
| 23 | Master Ultan goes blind after seven years as master (I, chap. 6). |
| 22 C. | Pia born, Severian born, the old autarch becomes criminal, Catherine in Tower. Gurloes becomes master torturer at around age thirty-five. Ouen buys locket with Dorcas picture from pawnbroker (IV, chap. 37). |
| 19 | Silent man visits the stone town (III, chap. 7). Mother Pyrexia sealed up in her house. |
| 15 P.S. | Odilo (II) begins work at House Absolute. |
| 12 | Chatelaine Sancha returns to the House Absolute. |
| 10 C. | Malrubius dies while Severian is a boy (I, chap. 1). |

| | |
|---|---|
| 9 | Thecla (age thirteen) sees Sancha alive (II, chap. 15). Domnina meets Father Inire (I, chap. 20). |
| 6 | Sancha dies aged seventy-five. Murene villagers burn down Baldanders's castle. |
| 3 | Averns planted in the Garden (spring). |
| 2 P.S. | Severian saves Vodalus (fall); Thecla sent to Matachin Tower (winter); Severian saves Triskele, Severian meets Valeria, Drott and Roche become journeymen, and Severian is taken to Echopraxia (spring). |
| 1 P.S. | Most events of *The Book of the New Sun* (see CALENDAR). |
| 1 S.R. | The Third Battle of Orithyia. Severian becomes autarch. |
| ? | Severian lives in Ascia for a year (V, chap. 51). |
| 5 | Odilo (II) tells tale of "The Cat" (ES, 210). |
| 7 | Eata is convicted of smuggling, escapes from carrack in the Xanthic Lands. |
| 9 | Eata returns to the Commonwealth (V, chap. 46), has adventure of "The Map" (ES, 20). |
| 10 | Severian writes *The Book of the New Sun,* embarks for Yesod. |
| 11 S.R. | Inire's stewardship of the Commonwealth. |
| ?? S.R. | Valeria becomes "autarch," erects cenotaph to Severian, marries Dux Caesidius (V, chap. 46). |
| 49 | Dux Caesidius dies (V, chap. 46), as does an assassin in the House Absolute (V, chap. 41). |
| 50 | Severian returns from Yesod, Valeria dies, deluge comes as the New Sun destroys Urth. Severian meets Odilo (III), Pega, Thais, and his old friend Eata (V, chap. 44–46). |

**The Age Of Ushas**

| | |
|---|---|
| 150 S.R. | Severian arrives in Ushas as the Sleeper awakened, writes *The Urth of the New Sun.* |
| ?? | The time of the Green Man. |

**hobiler** at Orithyia, Severian sees "hobilers on prancing mounts, with bows and arrow cases crossed over their backs" (v, chap. 22, 172).
*History:* a retainer bound to maintain a hobby (a small or middle-sized horse) for military service; a soldier who rides a hobby; a light horseman.

**homunculus** an artificial humanoid of organic origin. See also MANDRAGORA and TALOS; ANDROID and ROBOT.

**hoplite** "I'm Foila, and this is Melito. I was of the Blue Huzzars, he a hoplite" (IV, chap. 5, 40).
*History:* a heavy-armed foot-soldier of ancient Greece.

**Hormisdas** "Any news you have of Abaia's incursions will be fresher than mine . . . Hormisdas has gone into the South" (from "Father Inire's Letter," IV, chap. 35, 288).
*History:* two Hormisdases, one an Italian saint and pope, the other a Persian general. Saint Hormisdas (A.D. 4xx–523) was a pope (A.D. 514–23) who condemned the Monophysites and was father of Silverius. The other Hormisdas was a 4th-century renegade Persian prince (brother of Shapur II) who fled to the Romans. He was a general on Julian the Apostate's invasion of Persia and possibly Julian's candidate for the Persian throne.

**Hounds, the** a constellation near the Hunter (IA, 44). Winter comes when the Hounds chase the Sun south.
*Commentary:* they are probably our Canes Venatici (or Hunting Dogs), lying between Boötes (the Plowman) and Ursa Major (the Great Bear). In our time the Sun goes south across the equator

while in the neighborhood of the Hunting Dogs, just as in the story.

**hours of the day** see WATCHES OF THE DAY.

**House Absolute** the place from which the Autarch rules the Commonwealth. Predating the autarchy, the House Absolute lies underground and is said to have 10,000 corridors, some of which are rumored to reach the Library of the Citadel at Nessus, far to the south. Stairs lead to domes beneath the river, and hatches open onto virgin forest. Within the sprawling, labyrinthine House Absolute are such places as the Antechamber (a "temporary jail" for those who commit crimes within the precinct of the House Absolute), the Hall of Meaning, a hypethral, the Hypogeum Abscititious (built by Valeria), the Hypogeum Amaranthine (the throne room), the Hypogeum Apotropaic (Father Inire's section), the Hypotherm Classis, the Luminary Way, the Presence Chamber, the Road of Air, the Second House, the Vatic Fountain, the Well of Green Chimes, and the Well of Orchids (a place where exultant hostages are kept to ensure the good behavior of their kin). The Green Room is above ground.

**House of Starvation** an Ascian place (IV, chap. 11, 85).

**howdah** a seat to contain two or more persons, usually fitted with a railing and a canopy, erected on the back of an elephant (II, chap. 9, 73).

**huanaco** variant of guanaco, a South American mammal *(Lama guanico)* that is related to the camel, lacks a dorsal hump, resembles a deer in appearance, and has a soft, thick, fawn-colored coat (III, chap. 2, 19).

**hundred** "His hundred was the target of one of those attacks" (IV, chap. 6, 49). A military unit of 100 men, commanded by a lochage. See MILITARY ORGANIZATION.

**Hundred and Two** Conciliator's prisoner number at the hulk (V, chap. 36, 255).

**Hunna** Thecla's maid, tortured early on (I, chap. 3, 29) but not named until much later (IV, chap. 4, 36).
*History:* Saint Hunna (died 679), daughter of an Alsatian duke, married Huno of Hunnawayer and took care of the poor of Strasbourg, even doing their washing.

**Hunter, the** a constellation near the Hounds (IA, 44).
*Commentary:* while our constellation Orion is considered the hunter, in this case it seems to be Boötes (the Ploughman).

**huzzar** a variant of hussar, horseman of Hungarian light cavalry in 15th century (IV, chap. 5, 40).

**hyalite** a colorless variety of opal, occurring in globular concretions (V, chap. 33, 232).

**Hydra** a constellation of Urth, visible during the evening in spring and summer (III, chap. 18, 146).
*Astronomy:* our Hydra, or Water Monster, a spring constellation in the Northern Hemisphere.

**hydraknife** a multibladed throwing dagger from tropical Africa (v, chap. 13, 96).

**hydrargyrum** the "metal heavier than iron, though it flows like water" (I, chap. 14, 129) is quicksilver.

**hyla** a type of large tree toad (II, chap. 23, 210).

**hypethral** a room in the House Absolute which has many plants, and is presumably open to the sky (II, chap. 19, 174).
*Greek:* "hypaethros," open to the sky, uncovered, unroofed; a temple open to the sky.

**Hypogeon** a chthonian name, perhaps an aspect of the Increate, or even the name of the mysterious creature in the depths of the Saltus mine (I, chap. 18, 161).
*History:* "hypogean," subterranean.

**hypogeum** an underground chamber, or a catacomb: burial chamber or series of burial chambers (ES, 210).

**Hypogeum Abscititious** a section of the House Absolute dedicated by Valeria as a memorial to Severian. See ABSCITITIOUS.

**Hypogeum Amaranthine** the throne room of the House Absolute (V, chap. 42, 295).
*Commentary:* although amaranthine is a color word, the allusion to "fadeless, immortal, undying" is probably more pertinent here.

**Hypogeum Apotropaic** Father Inire's section of the House Absolute. It contains the Antechamber, the Presence Chamber, and a picture gallery, as well as a main kitchen and one or two lesser ones. Ouen is the chief steward.

**hypostases** on Urth, the persons whose union constitutes the Increate (I, chap. 6, 67).
*History:* base, foundation; essence, principle, essential principle. Specifically, of the same divine substance, but separate, like the persons of the Christian Trinity. In the early days of Christianity, Wisdom or Sophia was a hypostasis of God. (See CAITANYA.)

**Hypotherm Classis** "There are many isles in that sea. I saw them on a chart in the Hypotherm Classis once" (V, chap. 46, 327).
*Greek:* something like "the glass-roofed meeting place of the council."

# *I*

**Ia** armigette sentenced to be sexually abused in the Matachin Tower (II, chap. 7, 57).
*History:* Saint Ia (died 360) is said to have been a Greek slave in Persia who was tortured and killed during the persecution of King Shapur II.

**Ibar** uhlan of the Seventy-eighth xenagie who meets Severian after Master Ash has disappeared (IV, chap. 18, 142).
*Onomastics:* "yew" (Celtic).
*History:* Saint Ibar (5th century) was probably a follower of Saint Patrick.

**Idas** the male "albino sailor" on Tzadkiel's ship (V, chap. 2, 13), actually a slave of Abaia sent to kill Severian because she was "still small enough to pass as human" (V, chap. 7, 51). This sounds as though she is a juvenile undine.
*Onomastics:* Idas might mean "one from Ida," a mountain range in Phrygia, center of Cybele worship, as well as the scene of the judgment of Paris and the carrying off of Ganymede (Greek).
*Myth:* one of the Argonauts of Greek mythology, a son of Aphareus and brother of Lynceus, who fought with Apollo for the love of Marpessa, daughter of Evenus.
*Commentary:* a further link in the Severian-as-Apollo chain of associations. See TYPHON.

**Ihuaivulu** a constellation appearing on the northern horizon in the summer (II, chap. 29, 275).
*Myth:* (Mapuche) "Ihuaivilu" is a seven-headed fire-monster among the Araucanian Indians of Chile and Argentina. Said to inhabit volcanic neighborhoods. The "vilu" part means *snake.*
*Commentary:* the Mapuche constellations do not appear to include this chthonic creature. (The Pleiades, an obvious candidate, are called "Cajupal.") Their underworld "mapu vilu" (country of snakes) is the land where shamans visit, and the ihuaivilu guards the door. By this reading, ihuaivilu is a type of Cerberus. It just so happens that there is an obsolete constellation for Cerberus, introduced in 1687 by Johannes Hevelius, replacing the branch in the hand of Heracles. Hevelius and all subsequent map makers reproduced it as three snake heads, despite the fact that the Cerberus of myth was a three-headed dog.

**ile** (Greek) a squadron of cavalry (IV, chap. 16, 123).

**imp** there are a few imps within the Urth Cycle. Thecla confesses, "I replaced Josephina's toy imp with the stolen frog" (II, chap. 25, 241) and Father Inire warns, "There's an imp who waits in silvered glass and creeps into the eyes of those who look into it" (I, chap. 20, 182).
*Myth:* a small demon, or by extension, a mischievous child.

**Increate** one of several names for the Ultimate Power (I, chap. 24, 210). Despite appearances to the contrary (the existence of several terms for divine beings, a bewildering number of intermediary beings, and the pantheon at Thrax), the religion of the Commonwealth is monotheistic, with the Increate at its apex.

The term "God" is used only among slaves and the very poor. Other terms for the Ultimate Power include Apeiron, Demiurge, Numen, Pancreator, Panjudicator, Paraclete, and possibly Hypogeon.
*History:* not created, uncreated: said of divine beings or attributes.
*Commentary:* Peter Wright (*Attending Daedelus,* 79–80) asserts that while humans use the term to refer to God, those in Yesod use it to refer to the Hieros (v, chap. 19, 137–38).

**Incusus** a town or village mentioned in Dr. Talos's play, in which an evil portent has been reported (II, chap. 24, 221).
*Latin:* forged, fabricated.

**indanthrene** a shade of blue (II, chap. 1, 8).
*History:* an obsolete English word for a blue dye now known as indanthrone, or Vat Blue 4.

**ingenue** the youngest and prettiest girl in a theatrical troupe (I, chap. 16, 149). The ingenue plays Juliet.

**Inire** an extrasolarian or Hierodule, vizier to countless autarchs since Ymar, Father Inire is the source of many marvels on Urth, among them the specula and the botanical gardens of Nessus (I, chap. 4, 42). He built the SECOND HOUSE for Ymar.
*Onomastics:* "inire" is the infinitive form of "to begin, to enter" (Latin). Related to "initium," which alludes to elements or first principles; auspices, hence the beginning of a reign; and a secret worship. See QUERCINE PENETRALIA; YLEM.
*Commentary:* Robert Borski points out that Inire is described as being like a monkey and is probably even the person acting as

uturucu among the savages guiding Vodalus through the jungle to the Ascian army (*Solar Labyrinth,* 49–52).

**Inn of Lost Loves** an establishment on the path between the living city of Nessus and the Sanguinary Field (I, chap. 25). The law forbids all buildings so near the Wall, so the inn is situated among the limbs of a big tree. The sign shows a weeping woman dragging a bloody sword. A broad stair of rustic wood spirals up the trunk that is twenty-five feet around (suggesting a diameter of roughly eight feet). The chamber used by Severian, Agia, and Dorcas is a circular platform surrounded by pale green foliage, furnished with a canvas chair and a leather couch. It is not known how many such chambers the inn boasts, but there is a bower with a desk and writing supplies. The kitchen seems to be the topmost room of the tree. Abban is the innkeeper, Ouen is the waiter, Trudo is the ostler, KITCHEN GIRL helps the cook, and there is a pot boy to run errands.

**innkeepers** a list of the several innkeepers in Severian's narrative.

- At Nessus, an old man and his wife, where Baldanders and Dr. Talos have stayed for three nights but only paid for the first (I, chap. 15).
- Abban, at the Inn of Lost Loves (I, chap. 25).
- A married man of Saltus (II, chap. 1, 12), who may be a spy for Vodalus (II, chap. 18, 163).
- The mistress of the Duck's Nest in Thrax (III, chap. 3, 28; III, chap. 9, 70), who may be Casdoe's mother, Herais. (But if so, she must have married young, since CASDOE'S FATHER was a friend of Fechin.)

- Kyrin, at the Chowder Pot in Os (v, chap. 30).
- A nameless man of Saltus in Typhon's era (v, chap. 34, 245).

**ironwood** Dr. Talos's walking stick is ironwood, with a gilt-brass knob (I, chap. 15, 144). The zoanthrops use ironwood bludgeons (III, chap. 17, 135).
*History:* a very heavy, hard, tropical wood which, when cast into water, will sink.

**Isangoma** a "native" in the Jungle Garden, talking to the missionaries Robert and Marie (I, chap. 21, 188). The name (sometimes written "isAngoma") is a Zulu name for a diviner. An Isangoma is usually a woman, but a man can be one, too.

**Isid Iooo IoooE** the god in the story "The God and His Man." He seems to be material, in that he can be killed by Maser; but then again, Greek gods were occasionally wounded by the weapons of mortals. He has a starship, and it may be incapable of planetary landings since the transportation of his Man from ship to ground seems to be by way of teleportation. He is probably a thinking engine from the machine epoch of the Age of the Monarch, but this is only a guess.
*Commentary:* the name seems to be a parody of a holy name (for example, the holy unspeakable name "AOUEI" that Robert Graves divines in *The White Goddess).* This may signal that he is a false god, one deserving his fate. The name sounds like a corruption of the sentence "I said, 'Eyou Eyou-Ay,'" the latter part like the dog howling in the night town of James Joyce's *Ulysses.* Or perhaps it is all from the chorus from the nearly unintelligible Kingsman song, "Louie Louie" (1963): "I said, 'Lewie, Lew-

eye . . .'"

**isochronon** "I'm told that the Autarch . . . has an isochronon in his sleeping chamber, a gift from another autarch from beyond the edge of the world . . . this device tells him the watches of the night. When dawn comes, it rouses him" (III, chap. 34, 269). Either a sort of night-watch robot, or more likely, a mechanical clock (high-tech in a world where the wealthy use water-clocks).
*History:* "isochronous" means taking place in or occupying equal times; equal in metrical length; equal in duration, or in intervals of occurrence, as the vibrations of a pendulum.

**Iubar Street** [YEW-bar] a street in Nessus, near the Citadel (I, chap. 6, 57). It is a main thoroughfare with esplanades down the center. It likely runs east and west. It is probably the street that leads to the main gate of the Citadel. The Curators march along this street on their feast day, and in Ultan's memory at least, they are cheered by booksellers and antique dealers.
*Latin:* becoming light, radiance; a heavenly body, especially the sun.

**Ivo** the name of "First Soldier" in the play *Eschatology and Genesis* (II, chap. 24, 219).
*Onomastics:* "yew wood" or "archer's bow" (Germanic; "Yves" is a variant).
*History:* when a skeleton was unearthed in A.D. 1001 near the abbey of Ramsey, a legend grew up which said the body was that of a Persian bishop who had come to England with three companions to live as recluses; he is called Saint Ivo in the narratives.

# J

**jacal** (Mexican Spanish) a crude house or hut in Mexico and southwestern United States with a thatched roof and walls made of upright poles or sticks covered and chinked with mud or clay (III, chap. 2, 17).

**Jader** a poor boy of Thrax (III, chap. 3, 29) whom Severian heals (III, chap. 8, 57).
*Onomastics:* "Jehovah has heard" (Hebrew).
*History:* Saint Jader (died 257) was one of nine bishops of Numidia condemned to servitude in the marble quarries.

**Jader's father** a surly mason (III, chap. 3, 30).

**Jader's sister** close to death as a child, she is healed by the Claw and later becomes the prophetess speaking to Valeria when Severian returns from Yesod (V, chap. 42, 297). Her lines echo those of the prophetess in the play *Eschatology and Genesis* (II, chap. 24, 222–23).

**Jahi** a character in Dr. Talos's play *Eschatology and Genesis* (II, chap. 24, 211).
*Myth:* (Persian) an evil and deceitful druj or female demon in charge of menstruation. In the Avesta she embodied the spirit of whoredom destructive to mankind. She aroused King Mainyu from his long sleep and induced him to pour poison on the body of Gaya Maretan (literally "human life") and caused conflict in

the world (the poison was frost). After Gaya Maretan died, his body made the metal of the world, and eventually Mashya and Mashyoi sprang up from the gold, born in the form of a tree with one stem and fifteen branches. See ASH; MESCHIA; MESCHIANE.

**jazerant** a light coat of armor composed of splints or small plates of metal riveted to each other or to a lining of some strong material, often silk (IV, chap. 32, 266). Also known as "kaza-ghand," it was used in Turkey, Persia, and Arabia from the 11th century onward. While expensive, it must have been quite popular because it was comfortable and attractive. Durable it was not, however, and the cloth soon wore out, especially under conditions of actual warfare.

**jelab** a hooded cloak worn in Morocco (I, chap. 16, 153).

**jennet** a small Spanish horse, or a Spanish light horseman (II, chap. 14, 120).

**jerkin** a close fitting jacket, jersey, or short coat, often made of leather (I, chap. 16, 151).

**jezail** a stellar-level energy rifle, probably more advanced than the arquebus and less advanced than the fusil (IV, chap. 25, 208). *History:* an old type of Afghan gun with a crooked stock. Its original matchlock had a serpentine match holder that operated in a slit of the stock with the trigger underneath. The barrel was very long, usually at least forty-seven inches, with a smooth or rifled bore that was sometimes as large as one inch. Range: 218 to 323 yards.

**jiber** a mutinous sailor or stowaway on Tzadkiel's ship (v, chap. 9, 63). See also CAPTAIN OF THE JIBERS. There are a few notable cases of otherwise unnamed characters.

- The barrel-chested leader of ten or more jibers who capture Severian and try to make him imitate his own recording (v, chap. 12, 88–89). He is likened to an arsinoither. Armed with a gear-wheel mace, he is blasted by Sidero (v, chap. 13, 91).
- A little man with "dirty gray hair like Hethor's" is in the group of ten or more (v, chap. 13, 90).
- The ARCTOTHER-MAN (v, chap. 14, 100–01).

The fate of captured jibers is unknown. They may be used as memory-wiped colonists, or they may be abandoned on "desert island" planets.

**Jolenta** the name given by Dr. Talos to the cafe WAITRESS after he performs the operation that transforms her into an exceedingly beautiful woman (I, chap. 22, 275). Jolenta acts in Dr. Talos's plays and dies in the stone town after he discards her. Jonas falls in love with her at first sight.
*Onomastics:* variant of Jolie "the pretty one" (French).
*History:* Saint Jolenta of Hungary, otherwise known as Helen of Poland (died 1270), was a Dominican nun marked with the stigmata. Helen is linked to beauty following Helen of Troy: when her name is first given in the text, Severian calls her "the most beautiful woman in the world."

**Jonas** an aged wanderer met by Severian at the Gate of Nessus, he turns out to be an android sailor who left Urth in the First Empire period (Age of the Monarch) on a ship named *Fortunate Cloud.* When his ship returned to Urth (perhaps 200 years prior to the reign of Severian), there was no longer a port. The ship made a crash landing, during which Jonas was severely injured. Because there were no other materials at hand, Jonas was repaired with biological material salvaged from an Urth man who had been killed on the ground by the landing. "Jonas" is his post-crash name, a sailor-name implying bad luck at least, if not his direct responsibility for the shipwreck. The crew dispersed, and Jonas wandered alone, searching for them.

It seems that he falls in love at first sight of Jolenta (I, chap. 35, 299), and he feels that she would accept him if he were only whole again. After discovering the descendants of the crew (the KIM LEE SOONG GROUP) living as prisoners in the antechamber of the House Absolute, Jonas is wounded by the young exultants (II, chap. 15). Severian uses the Claw to heal him, and when Jonas wakes up he seems to be the pre-crash Jonas (II, chap. 16, 132). When Jonas makes reference to Lewis Carroll's White Knight (137), it is a big hint that he is about to enter a different world "through the looking glass," which happens when he steps into Father Inire's SPECULA and disappears. Severian believes that Jonas later returned as Miles, a soldier in Orithyia.

*Onomastics:* the name Jonas is a variant of Jonah (Hebrew "dove"), a biblical prophet who was instructed by Jehovah to preach at Nineveh, but willfully took ship in another direction. The Lord sent a mighty tempest that threatened all aboard the ship. Jonah confessed he was the cause of Jehovah's anger, and the sailors reluctantly cast him into the sea, where he was swallowed up by a "great fish." He lived in the belly of the fish for three days and repented, after which he was vomited out onto dry land. He went to Nineveh after Jehovah commanded him again.

*Commentary:* Jonas is a character rich with associations. He is part

Tin Man of Oz; he is part "The Steadfast Tin Soldier," the crippled metal man who loved the doomed paper ballerina; he is also, somehow, part Ahasuerus, the Wandering Jew.

**jonquil** a species of narcissus *(N. jonquilla)* having long linear leaves and spikes of fragrant white and yellow flowers; the rush-leaved daffodil (III, chap. 1, 7).

**Josepha** one of Thecla's friends at the House Absolute. One time Thea and Thecla sewed her doll (I, chap. 10, 99). Another time Thecla and Josepha made up a fishing party and went to the spot where Severian would later resurrect Mineas (II, chap. 13, 113).
*Onomastics:* "Jehovah increases" (Hebrew).
*History:* Josepha of Benignam (A.D. 1625–1696) was born of a poor family near Valencia, Spain. She became a hermit. She was beatified in 1888.

**Josephina** Thecla's friend with a toy imp (II, chap. 25, 241).

**Jovinian** the Master Smith who forged *Terminus Est* (I, chap. 29, 252).
*History:* Saint Jovinian (died c. 300) was a fellow missionary with Saint Peregrinus of Auxerre, and was martyred. Another Jovinian was a 4th-century Milanese monk who denied the virginity of Mary, opposed certain forms of celibacy and asceticism, and maintained the equality of all sins, rewards, and punishments.

**Jurmin** a man of Thrax, friend of the mistress of the Duck's Nest, killed by the salamander (III, chap. 9, 70).

*History:* Saint Jurmin (7th century) was revered in England and his relics were enshrined in Bury Saint Edmunds.

**Jurupari** "a design had been scratched on the filthy stones. It might have been the snarling face of Jurupari, or perhaps a map" (I, chap. 29, 255).
*Myth:* chief god of the Uapes tribe of Brazil, Jurupari was born of a virgin after she drank some "cachari" (native beer). His cult was associated with male initiation rites from which women were excluded. If by accident a woman witnessed even a part of the rite, she was poisoned as a punishment.

**Just Man, The** story told by Loyal to the Group of Seventeen, as interpreted by Foila (IV, chap. 11). It is a tale of how a man wins by simply enduring all and refusing to give up.

**Juturna** an Urth undine (V, chap. 51, 368), whom the apprentice Severian first meets when she rescues him from drowning in the Gyoll (I, chap. 2, 25). She is at least forty cubits (sixty feet) from head to foot, and she can enter the corridors of Time, but her ability at this remains vague.
*Myth:* an ancient Italian spirit of springs and streams, a kindly goddess gifted with prophecy and song, a wife of Janus and mother of Fons, and a goddess who, along with Stata Mater, caused fires to be quenched. According to Monaghan's *Goddesses and Heroines,* Diuturna is another name of Juturna. See FONS.
*Commentary:* at some level, Juturna is a mother figure for Severian. She gives re-birth to him when she rescues him from drowning, the water itself like amniotic fluid. But she is an ambiguous figure, sometimes helping (the re-birthing in volume I,

and giving directions to the Corridors of Time in volume v), sometimes threatening (trying to lure him into the water from the banks of Cephissus in volume II). As she survives the deluge, perhaps she is a good example of a "convert" among the Other People.

*Korsekes*

**Kabbalah** (entry from BORGES; BRIAH; BROOK MADREGOT; GNOSTICISM; HEPTARCH; SEFIROTH) meaning "the received tradition," a collection of works, mostly in Aramaic, dating from early medieval times. Said to be an interpretation of the Pentateuch in the Bible, it is full of mystic theosophical concepts, related to Neo-Platonism and Gnosticism, regarding the nature of the Deity and its relationship to the cosmos and man. The chief assumption of the Kabbalah is that every word and letter has a hidden, mystical meaning which can be learned by the epopt.

**kaberu** African mountain wolf (III, chap. 2, 18).

**kafila** "Vodalus was far to the north, hiding among the frost-pinched forests and raiding kafilas" (I, chap. 10, 100).
*History:* a body of travelers who have banded together for mutual protection.

**Katharine, Holy** patron saint of the Seekers of Truth and Penitence (I, chap. 5, 47).
*Onomastics:* the German form of Catherine ("pure, clean").
*History:* Saint Catherine of Alexandria, patron saint of theologians, philosophers, saddlers, spinsters, students, and rope-makers. According to legend, Catherine was condemned to be executed by order of Maxentius, but as she approached the wheel upon which she was to be broken, the wheel burst apart, or burst into flames, or burst out in roses. Not to be spared, she was subse-

quently beheaded, but she forgave her executioner. Her feast day was November 25 (in the "fading of autumn" in the northern hemisphere, the "fading of spring" in the southern hemisphere) until it was removed from the canon in 1969.

*Myth:* Saint Catherine is one of the most popular saints of all time, despite the fact that she never really existed. One possible key to this spurious saint is to be found in her so-called Catherine Wheel, the wheel of fire on which she was said to have been martyred. At Sinai, the original center of Catherine's cult, the Asiatic Goddess was once portrayed as the Dancer on the Fiery Wheel at the hub of the universe. In the 8th century A.D., a Greek convent of priestess-nuns at Sinai called themselves "kathari," but this name is also akin to the kathakali temple-dancers of India, who performed the Dance of Time in honor of Kali, Goddess of the Karmic Wheel. A group of medieval Gnostics known as Cathari had great reverence for the wheel symbol, and considered Saint Catherine almost as a female counterpart of God. Catholic prelates made efforts to have Saint Catherine eliminated from the canon in the 15th and 16th centuries, after the Cathari were exterminated. (See CAITANYA.)

**kelau** slingers (II, chap. I, II). Light infantry armed with the sling. (Note that they carry incendiary bullets, also known as "shooting stars.") The term is probably Hebrew or Aramaic.

**kelpie** Severian to Barbatus, "Now I see, or think that I see, that you were once inhabitants of lakes and pools, kelpies such as our country folk talk of" (V, chap. 5, 35).

*Myth:* lowland Scottish name of a fabled water-spirit or demon assuming various shapes, but usually appearing in that of a horse;

it is said to haunt lakes and rivers, and to take delight in, or even cause, the drowning of travelers and others.

**kestrel** "you remind me of the old man's kestrel, that sat on a perch for twenty years and then flew off in all directions" (II, chap. 10, 87).
*History:* a common small European falcon *(Falco tinnunculus)* that is noted for its habit of hovering in the air against a wind. It is around a foot long, bluish-gray above in males and reddish-brown in the female.

**khaibit** (aka "shadow woman") a clone of an autarch's concubine, created to serve as bedroom surrogate in the House Absolute (I, chap. 7, 75). Termed "a shadow that is the external soul of its caster" (CD, 238), the chatelaines use such clones to allow them to grow to their exultant stature: the old autarch tells Severian, "They're khaibits, of course, grown from the body cells of exultant women so an exchange of blood will prolong the exultants' youth" (IV, chap. 24, 194); Thecla's khaibit is "somewhat shorter" than Thecla (I, chap. 9, 90); and Ossipago tells Severian, "Growth has its disadvantges, though for your species it is the only method by which youth can be reinstated" (III, chap. 34, 268), which links artificially induced rejuvenation with continued growth.

This hints at the possibility that all exultants use clones, not just the relatively few chatelaines held hostage in the Well of Orchids.

In addition, there seem to be clone soldiers who are multiples of a single individual: first at the Piteous Gate of Nessus, where Severian sees riders whose "faces were more akin than the faces of brothers" (II, chap. 1, 8); and later, while looking at Ascian soldiers, Severian remarks, "not that they all had the same face (as the men in some units of our own army do, who are indeed closer than brothers)" (IV, chap 21, 179). This is a different category of being, but such clone-soldiers may serve the same purpose as the clone-concubines, in rendering service to the autarch without involving the original exultant.

Khaibits in the text include Barbea, Gracia, Thea's khaibit, Thecla's khaibit, and possibly Catherine.
*History:* the ancient Egyptians believed a personality to be made up of a "Ka" (or double), a "Ba" (or soul), and a khaibit (or shadow).

**khan** the khan of Night is across the River Gyoll from the Citadel (I, chap. 2, 27).
*History:* a building (unfurnished) for the accommodation of travelers; a caravansary.

**kheten** an Egyptian pole-axe, according to Stone (I, chap. 16, 151).

**Kim Lee Soong** given as name of earliest ancestor by a group of prisoners in the antechamber of the House Absolute (II, chap. 15, 130).
*Commentary:* Kim Lee Soong is a Korean name, but not linked to any specific persons of the 20th century.

**Kim Lee Soong group** a four-generation family of prisoners in the antechamber of the House Absolute, composed of "several old women, a man of about fifty, another about thirty, three other women, and a flock of children" (II, chap. 15, 129). Included among the children is the girl (very likely Oringa) who talks of "the navigator," a detail that implies the group was from a ship before being imprisoned. The old women claim to be seventh generation prisoners, which would make the children the tenth generation, and with twenty years per generation (the age difference between the two men) this suggests their ancestors were jailed about 200 years earlier.

**kitchen girl** a worker at the Inn of Lost Loves, she is the chief suspect as note-writer, since she was in the room and then fled at the same time as Trudo (I, chap. 28, 247). She brought water and sponge for Dorcas, rags and oil for *Terminus Est;* she got the screen, for which Severian gave her an orichalk (I, chap. 25, 221); she helped Dorcas (I, chap. 25, 223); she ran off, presumably with Trudo (I, chap. 26, 233).

**korsekes** a pyrotechnic pole arm capable of firing one beam forward and two quartering beams, forward left and forward right (IV, chap. 1, 12). "Their range isn't great, but they say they're good for dealing with mass attacks" (IV, chap. 6, 37).
*History:* medieval Italian three-pointed pole arm with a large tassel below the head. In response to the question, Gene Wolfe explains that "It is much like a partizan, with large side blades and a main blade like a cinqueda." Used in the 15th century.

**kraken** probably the giant squid, but emblematic of the malignant, aquatic forces of Abaia and Erebus (I, chap. 6, 60).
*History:* a sea-monster of enormous size, said to have been seen at times off the coast of Norway, thus probably the giant squid.

*Myth:* often associated with Leviathan, the Hebrew name for the Canaanite Lotan, a monstrous primeval serpent or dragon who was slain by Baal. See also CATODON.

**krater** ancient Greek punch bowl (I, chap. 4, 43). At a party or dinner, wine was mixed with water (often at a ratio of 1:4 or 1:5) in the krater by the oldest guest. Only alcoholics drank unmixed wine.

**kronosaur** an aquatic dinosaur with a head nearly eight feet long (V, chap. 32, 228).

**Kyneburga** a name cried out by the Contessa in the play *Eschatology and Genesis* (II, chap. 24, 216). Presumably one of her maids, along with Solange and Lybe.
*History:* there are three Anglo-Saxon saints of the name Cyniburg/Kineburga. One was a Mercian princess (died c. 680), foundress and abbess of the convent of Castor (Northants). Cyniburg of Gloucester was a princess who fled there to escape marriage and took employment as a baker's servant: his jealous wife murdered her. The third Cyniburg, supposedly the first abbess of Gloucester, is possibly a blend of the two.

**Kyrin** innkeeper at the Chowder Pot in Typhon's era (V, chap. 30, 213). He is spooked by the fact that the chrisos Severian gives him has Severian's face, in profile, upon it (214). He investigates the attack of Zamas (V, chap. 31, 218). Severian cures him of alcoholism (V, chap. 32, 225).
*Onomastics:* Curitan from Curran "the hero" (Irish Gaelic).

*History:* Saint Boniface Kyrin (died 660) was bishop of Ross. He may have been a Roman citizen.

*Lictor*

**labyrinth** "The walls were octagonal and painted with labyrinths" (I, chap. 20, 183). A maze of rooms and passages, or just rooms.

**Lactan** a mercenary in Guasacht's unit, one of the two who pass the reins to Severian during his initiation test (IV, chap. 19, 151). (The other one is MESROP.)
*History:* Saint Lactan (died 672) was born near Cork.

**Laetus** Eata's deckhand, who steals the treasure map from him, and murders Syntyche over it (ES, 20).
*Onomastics:* "fat, rich, fertile"; "glad, joyful, happy" (Latin).
*History:* there are three Saints Laetus.

**Lagous** "They crossed the wide valley of the Lagous" (SS, 247). An area in the Green Empire, on the eastern frontier.
*Geography:* the Latin name of a river in Sarmatia Asiatica, or Eastern Sarmatia, a region located between the Black Sea and the Caspian Sea. This suggests that the Green Empire is Eastern Sarmatia, and the Yellow Empire is Western Sarmatia.
*Latin:* (medieval period, British Isles) Lagonus (reason), Laga (law), and/or Lacus (drainage channel).

**lambrequin** "A dead man (he had, I think, been suffocated with a lambrequin, there being those who practice that art) lay at

the corner" (I, chap. 16, 146). This passage suggests that a sort of Thuggee cult exists in Nessus and is well known.
*History:* a scarf or piece of stuff worn over the helmet as a covering.

**lamia** says Agia to Severian, "Do you see rings or earrings? A silver lamia twined about my neck?" (I, chap. 19, 173), suggesting that if she had a lover she would exhibit such jewelry. (The comment recalls Thecla's kraken jewelry with its eyes of cabochon emeralds.) Another young woman who is herself like a lamia is an ALGOPHILIST Severian meets.
*Myth:* a female demon of ancient Greek mythology. Lamias drink blood, are were-snakes, and may appear with a woman's head and a snake body. Lamias play a significant part in Gene Wolfe's *Soldier* series, as well.

**lammergeir** also known as the bearded vulture, the largest European bird of prey (II, chap. 17, 143). It inhabits lofty mountains in South Europe, Asia, and North Africa.

**lancegay** a light lance, occasionally used as a dart (IV, chap. 12, 172). It was carried in place of the war lance in the 14th century; the latter was about fourteen feet long and very heavy.

**Land of Virgins** name of hero's ship in "Tale of the Student and His Son" (II, chap. 17, 147).
*History:* at the beginning of the American Civil War, Union forces scuttled the powerful steam frigate *Merrimack.* She was then raised by the Confederates, converted into an ironclad, and renamed the *Virginia.* When the *Virginia* (aka *Merrimack*) met

the Union ship *Monitor* it was the first engagement between ironclads. *Land of Virgins* is another way of saying *Virginia.*

**lansquenet** mercenary cavalry (I, chap. 16, 151).
*History:* a class of mercenary soldier in the German and other continental armies in the 17th and 18th centuries.

**lantern** an architectural ornament consisting of a small dome lifted on pillars (I, chap. 16, 151).

**lanugo** "I had been as light as lanugo" (V, chap. 31, 221).
*History:* down, either of the face, or of plants.

**larva** in YESOD, the HIERARCH is the larva form of the HIEROGRAMMATE (V, chap. 19, 138). Apheta is a child of the Hierogrammates, a larva, not yet Hierogrammate, nor truly human. Larvae light up when ready to mate (V, chap. 20, 141), a detail which is similar to the "light elves" of Norse mythology, who seem to emit light at times.
*Latin:* a ghost, hobgoblin, specter; also, a mask.
*History:* the newly hatched stage of various animals that differ markedly in the adult form, as a tadpole, for example.

**Last House** a building in or near Orithyia which houses Master Ash (IV, chap. 15, 117). It is a historical research station where each floor exists in a different period of post-historic time, with the lowest floor reaching into the earliest age, that of Severian. It is a type of time machine building. Severian sleeps on the third floor, "many thousands of years" in the future from his time where the world is covered with glaciers (IV, chap. 17, 133). The second floor is only around 150 years in the future (134), where ice wars with the pines and where many people have left for other worlds. For all who do not walk the path correctly, even the lowest story stands in the future. Perhaps it only appears in the dark of the Moon.

**Laurentia of the House of the Harp** a monomachist whose name is shouted at the Sanguinary Field (I, chap. 27, 235), she is almost certainly the woman with the braquemar who splits Agilus's avern (I, chap. 28, 245) after Hildegrin has knocked him down (II, chap. 31, 286). See CADROE OF THE SEVENTEEN STONES and SABAS OF THE PARTED MEADOW.
*Onomastics:* "from the place of the laurel trees" (Latin).
*History:* Saint Laurentia (died 302) was a slave who, along with her mistress (Saint Palatias), was put to death at Fermo, Italy, during the Diocletian persecution.
*Mythology:* (Roman) Acca Laurentia (Etruscan "Lady Mother"), is named as the foster mother of Romulus and Remus, and even as the she-wolf who suckled them (see BONA DEA). As for the harp, it is "equated with the white horse and the mystic ladder. It acts as a bridge between heaven and earth. This is why, in the Norse Edda, heroes express their desire to have a harp buried with them in their grave, so as to facilitate their access to the other world" (Cirlot, *A Dictionary of Symbols,* 139).

**lazaret** a house for the reception of the diseased poor, especially lepers; a hospital, pest-house (I, chap. 16, 150). From Lazarus of the New Testament (Luke 16:20).

**lazaretto** earlier form of lazaret (IV, chap. 51, 364). Note that the word usually refers to a quarantine house or location.

**lazulite** hydrous phosphate of aluminum and magnesium, found in blue monoclinic crystals; also the color of this mineral (II, chap. 1, 8). Sometimes used to mean Lapis Lazuli.

**league** see MEASUREMENT TABLES.

**lechwes** *Kobus leche,* a kind of antelope (I, chap. 25, 220).

**leeks** a food for torturers and their clients (I, chap. 7, 72). "The national food of Wales. They are similar to spring onions, but larger" (CD, 237).

**legion** a large-scale military unit developed by the Roman Republic and Empire, consisting of 5,000 men. This could be made up of ten cohorts, each one having two maniples of antepilani (240 heavy infantry), one maniple of pilani (sixty heavy infantry), one maniple of skimishers (120 light infantry), and one maniple of cavalry (thirty horsemen). See MILITARY ORGANIZATION.

**Lelia** Thecla's friend, a chatelaine with the hairless rats that dance (II, chap. 16, 139).
*Onomastics:* "well spoken" (Greek); a clan name, meaning "lily" (Latin).
*History:* Saint Lelia (6th century?) seems to have been superior of a convent in Munster, Ireland.

**leman** a lover or a sweetheart; a kept woman (I, chap. 7, 76).

**lemures** hostile spirits of the unburied dead, driven from homes in religious observances of early Rome (ES, 211).

**lentils** a food for torturers and their clients (I, chap. 7, 72). "Brown, bean-like seeds. Excellent with leeks. Lentils boiled with ham bone make great soup, too" (CD, 238).

**Leocadia** a chatelaine mentioned by Lomer (II, chap. 15, 125). She engineers the Lomer/Sancha incident to hurt her rival Nympha (ES, 215), and after Sancha dies decades later, a nearly blind Leocadia suffers nightmares of being stalked by Sancha's phantom cat.
*Onomastics:* "clear, shining" (Spanish).
*History:* Saint Leocadia (died 304?), a noble maiden of Toledo, Spain, was tortured during the persecution of Diocletian and died in prison. She is the principal patron of Toledo.
*Commentary:* the name Leocadia means "light, bright" from Greek "lukos," but "leo" evokes the astrological lion of that name, which seems fitting for a story called "The Cat."

**lethe** "For that were you chosen, Severian. You and you alone from many princes. You alone to save your race from lethe" (V, chap. 50, 353).
*Myth:* a river in Hades, the water of which produced, in those who drank it, forgetfulness of the past. Hence, the "waters of oblivion." See PHLEGETHON.

**leveret** a young hare, especially one less than a year old (SS, 254).

**liana** a tropical vine (I, chap. 19, 178).

**lictor** in the Commonwealth the title of the chief subordinate officer of the archon involved with the administration of criminal justice (III, appendix, 300). The lictor supervises the clavigers.
*Latin:* literally, "he who binds"; one who attends the chief Roman magistrates.

**Liege of Leaves** a title of Vodalus, who is also called "Vodalus of the Wood."
*Myth:* in Frazer's *Golden Bough,* "King of the Wood" (Rex Nemorensis) is a title of Virbius, a priest/king/lover of Diana, who was to her what Adonis was to Venus, or Attis to Cybele. The mythical Virbius was represented in historical times at Nemi by a line of priests known as "Kings of the Wood" who regularly perished by the swords of their successors.

**lightning** used as a synonym for electricity. "There's another word for it, but I forget. Anyway, the revolutionary here runs by lightning" (I, chap. 12, 117).
*History:* there is no root-word association between "lightning" and "electricity," the former being akin to "light," and the latter coming from "amber" (which gives off a static charge when rubbed).
*Commentary:* this detail may be either another example of forgotten science (like Severian's knowledge that Urth's rotation is responsible for what we persist in calling "sunrise" and "sunset") or it could be another hint of a long-forgotten Chinese presence, as the thirteen-stroke Chinese character for "Tien" ("lightning"),

an ideogram showing a lightning bolt coming from a rain-heavy cloud, is also used for "electricity."
(For more on the Asian presence in the Urth Cycle, see HISTORY OF URTH: THE AGE OF THE MONARCH; KIM LEE SOONG; and JONAS.)

**linnet** a small Old World songbird, *Acanthis cannabina,* having brownish plumage (I, chap. 2, 21). A similar bird *Carpodacus mexicanus* is found in Western North America.

**lipsanotheca** a shrine or container for holy relics (III, chap. 38, 297).

**litch** variant of *lich:* a body, a corpse (II, chap. 17, 156).

**Liti** the name of Burgundofara's home village, located south of Nessus in the Gyoll delta (V, chap. 29, 203). Burgundofara and Captain Hadelin probably establish their household in Liti during the reign of Typhon. MAXELLINDIS'S UNCLE dies here during the reign of Severian.
*Latin:* "litus," meaning seashore, beach, or coast.

**little Severian** son of Casdoe and Becan, twin of Severa (III, chap. 14, 112). (See FAMILY TREES.) The book his mother read to him (III, chap. 18, 146) was almost certainly Canog's *The Book of the New Sun,* based upon his answer to Severian that the New Sun will "kill Abaia" (chap. 21, 173). After his family is wiped out in separate attacks by the alzabo and the zoanthrops, he is adopted by Severian, who later saves him from the sorcerers. He is blasted near the gold ring on Mount Typhon.

**Little Wolf** a constellation of Urth, found near the Unicorn (III, chap. 18, 146).
*Astronomy:* probably our Canis Minor, located near the Unicorn.

**living statues** harmless, half-living creatures that wander the gardens above the House Absolute (V, chap. 41, 290).

**llanero** [yaw-NAY-row] a cowboy (II, chap. 20, 181).

**Llibio** leader of the Diuturna Islanders (III, chap. 31, 246).
*History:* Saint Llibio (6th century) is the patron saint of Llanllibio on the isle of Anglesey.

**lochage** [LOCK-ij] the commander of a hundred, a unit of 100 men (I, chap. 14, 132).
*History:* leader of a "lochus," a 100-man unit of the army in Sparta and some other Greek states.

**locks (ancient)** do not use keys or combinations, but words of power (II, chap. 18, 166).

**loggia** a gallery or arcade having one or more of its sides open to the air (V, chap. 41, 293).

**Lollian** a friend of Thecla who whirled the firebird during their cruel raid on the antechamber (II, chap. 16, 135).
*History:* Saint Lollian (died 279) was one of the Martyrs of Samosata, Syria.

**Loman** a great historian remembered by Master Ultan (I, chap. 6, 65).
*Onomastics:* "bare" (Irish); "enlightened" (Scottish/Gaelic).
*History:* Saint Loman (died c. 450) was a nephew of Saint Patrick and first bishop of Trim in Meath.

**Lomer** an armiger prisoner in the antechamber (II, chap. 15, 125). Formerly the seneschal of Chatelaine Nympha, his crime was being caught "in flagrante delicto" with the fourteen-year-old Chatelaine Sancha (ES, 214). He would have been executed.
*History:* Saint Lomer (died 593) was a shepherd boy near Chartres, then a priest, then a hermit. He founded the monastery of Corbion and lived to be over a hundred years old.

**Loyal to the Group of Seventeen** an Ascian officer/interpreter who had done something wrong and had to go back into the ranks (IV, chap. 6, 46). As a wounded prisoner of war he is in the lazaret with Foila and the others. He tells the story of "The Just Man" (IV, chap. 11).
*Commentary:* his name may just be his declaration that he is still a loyal Ascian, that he has not switched allegiance. Or it may be one given to him by his superiors as punishment, suggesting his error was one of lacking loyalty, and this case would put his name into the same category as Jonas's, being a badge of shame for his actions.

**lucivee** (French "lynx") the holdout weapon used by Agia, giving Severian his facial scars (IV, chap. 26, 213).

**Lune** the natural satellite of Urth (I, chap. 5, 52). Lune is covered in green forests seeded during the First Empire period of the Age of the Monarch, and is said to be 50,000 leagues (150,000 miles) from Urth (III, chap. 32, 253).
*French:* "the Moon."
*History:* the distance between Earth and the Moon averages 240,000 miles (227,000 miles at closest).
*Commentary:* Gregory Feeley points out that a Moon so close would "exert enormous tides we never see" in the Urth Cycle, that there is no natural reason for the Moon to be closer (orbital ballistics will carry it farther away from the Earth over time), nor is there any reason given for its apparently new position.

Using the formula $T=M/R^3$ (from Gillette's *World-Building),* where T is the tidal force of the Moon on Earth; M is the Mass; and R is the Radius of orbit, we find

$T=1/(0.6)^3$

$T= 1/0.216$

$T= 4.629$

So the tide raised on Urth by Lune is about four and a half times the tide that is raised on Earth by the Moon. Oddly enough, this is about equal to the tides on Sainte Anne/Sainte Croix in Wolfe's non-Urth novel *The Fifth Head of Cerberus* (the meadowmeres on Sainte Anne are swept daily by fifteen-foot tides generated by the twin planet; on Earth the height of the tide in the open ocean averages three feet: the world record for a local average is thirty-three feet in Nova Scotia's Bay of Fundy [Emiliani, *The Scientific Companion,* 241]).

A technical detail more difficult to work around is the fact that a closer orbit would be faster, leading to a lunar period shorter than the twenty-eight days we are told Lune possesses. (The orbital period would be 13.5 days; the month would be 14.02 days.) Then again, this might also fall under the "translation" category, in that readers are told some terms are rendered as approximations.

Or Lune's orbit might be more artificial than natural physics; it might be a powered hovering.

"Has Anybody Seen Junie Moon?" (1999) is a Wolfe story, unrelated to Urth, that describes such a scenario. Here Junie Moon describes a strange theory about antimatter: "current theory says that although antimatter would possess mass just as ordinary matter does, it would be repelled, by the gravitational field of ordinary matter" (SS, 132). This seems similar to the antimatter/antigravity technology used on Urth, described for fliers: "Their lift is supplied by the antimaterial equivalent of iron, held in a penning trap by magnetic fields. Since the anti-iron has a reversed magnetic structure, it is repelled by promagnetism" (IV, chap. 24, 198). Junie goes on to say,

> Our theory says a collision between matter and antimatter should result in a nuclear explosion, but either the theory is mistaken or there's some natural means of circumventing it. Because the White Cow Moon rock was composed of nearly equal parts matter and antimatter. It had to be! The result was rock with a great deal of mass but very little weight, and that's what allows the White Cow Moon to orbit so slowly (133).

Applying this to Lune, we envision vast amounts of antigravity substance on the satellite, allowing constant thrust along a circular track, taking 28 days per lap.

The apparent size (or angular diameter) of Lune from Urth would be about .82°, compared to .52° for the Moon seen from Earth.

The terraforming of the Moon is an intriguing idea. For Lune to be habitable then it must have had its local day "spun up" from twenty-eight days (672 hours) to something between ninety-six and twenty-four hours. There is no indication that Lune is rotating, but it is possible.

In *Terraforming,* Martin Fogg writes, "As a target for terraforming . . . [the Moon's] suitability is next in line after Mars and Venus" (430). Increasing the spin for a shorter Lunar day is estimated to be 1000 times easier than doing the same for Venus.

Loss of atmospheric gas on the Moon is not as bad as one might think. Fogg states that, once an Earthlike atmosphere is in place on the Moon, it would naturally take longer than 100 million years to bleed off. Perhaps the forests of Lune act as a natural canopy to hold atmosphere in as well as pollute it with their waste oxygen.

**Lux dei vitae viam monstrat** a phrase from the Atrium of Time, translated by Valeria as "the beam of the New Sun lights the way of life" (I, chap. 4, 44).
*Latin:* "the light of God shows the road of life."

**Lybe** the name of "the Maid" in the play *Eschatology and Genesis* (II, chap. 24, 216).
*History:* Saint Lybe (died 303) was beheaded at Palmyra, Syria, under Diocletian.

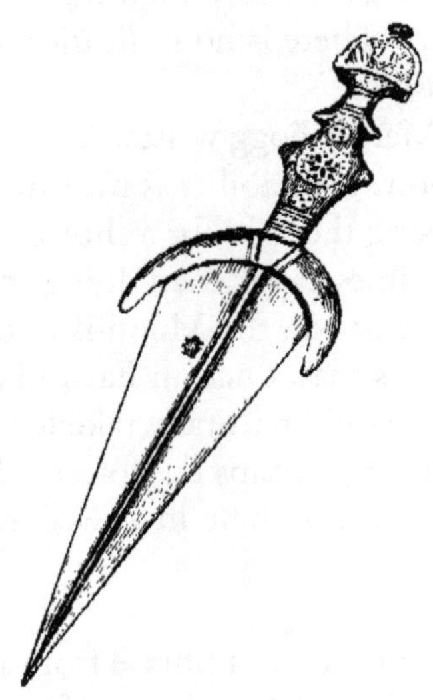

*Misericorde*

**machionations** Agia tells Severian, "When the machionations of the City Wall appear to touch the edge of the solar disc, a trumpet — the first — is sounded on the Sanguinary Field" (I, chap. 26, 228).
*History:* this is a not uncommon garbling of the word "machicolations," the stone balconies projecting from castle walls from which the defenders can drop discouraging substances upon the heads of storming parties.
*Commentary:* it could be a sign that Agia is overstretching her lexicon (what does a rag shop woman know of castle architecture?) in an attempt to impress Severian, or it could be a Freudian slip, since it is very close to "machinations," the exact sort of underhanded scheme that she is leading him into at the dueling grounds, as she has done with men before him. Finally, it could be a rare typo for Wolfe.

**Maden** a shopkeeper of Thrax, in Severian's joke about Maden and Madern (CD, 266).
*Onomastics:* "wet" (Latin).
*History:* another name for Saint Madron (died 545?). He probably passed from Wales to Brittany. He may be the same as Saint Padarn, Saint Madern, or Matronus (Maden, Madern).

**Madern** a shopkeeper of Thrax, in Severian's joke about Maden and Madern (CD, 266).

*History:* another name for Saint Madron (died 545?). See also MADEN.

**Mafalda** an old woman of Os who wept to see Zama alive when she had heard he was dead (V, chap. 32, 228).
*Onomastics:* "strength in battle" (Portuguese form of "Matilda").
*History:* Saint Mafalda (A.D. 1203–1257), daughter of King Sancho of Portugal. She entered a convent and her fortune was used for many construction projects, including a bridge over the Talmeda River.

**Mag** patron saint of the witches (I, chap. 11, 104).
*History:* Mag could be short for "Magdalene," the sacred harlot whose name means "she of the temple-tower." Significant, as the witches live in a tower and seem to have a wanton side to them.
*Myth:* Mag could be short for Magg, also known as Magog, ancient goddess of England honored with chalk-cut effigies. Gog was her consort. Depicted at Wandlebury (near Cambridge) as a four-breasted woman mounted on a horse. Her name may mean "Mother God."

**Magic in the Urth Cycle** there is no "magic" in the Urth Cycle. As Gene Wolfe notes in a magazine interview,

> I view *The Book of the New Sun* as science fantasy — by which I mean a science-fiction story told with the outlook, the flavor of fantasy. There are *no* fantasy elements involved — no "magic" in the fantasy sense. There is time-travel, but that belongs to sf, not fantasy. There are hypnotism,

> sleight of hand, and a few other things, but those belong to the world of reality, if not the world of science (*Thrust* no. 19, winter/spring 1983, 7).

There are four particularly vivid scenes in which magic seems to play a part. First is the group ceremony to contact Apu-Punchau in the stone town at the end of *Claw.* Presided over by the Cumaean, this is the only example of witch activity in the Cycle and could be described as involving interstellar telepathy with a being near Fomalhaut (crossing open space at the speed of thought) and time-warping (done by Apu-Punchau himself). Second is the duel between Severian and Decuman the sorcerer in *Sword.* In this case, the "hypnosis" used in the battle of minds is closer to a kind of psionic power, as it is in the third example, where Typhon projects his worldview into Severian's mind (later in *Sword).* The fourth case involves Ceryx the necromancer in *Urth.* Ceryx has a telekinetic ability (he uses it to break Severian's staff) which may be the method by which he reanimates the dead sailor Zama into a mindless zombie, manipulating the corpse as a puppeteer does a marionette.

**magistrate** "A great many people feel already that the military magistrates are hasty and even capricious. And to be frank, a civil judge would probably have waited a week [rather than only one day before executing the prisoner]" (1, chap. 29, 250).
*History:* a civil officer with power to administer the law, but in the Commonwealth the term would seem to apply to a military judge who hears all cases in his district.

**Magitae** a race or group of people within the Green Empire of EFF.
*History:* the people of Arabia Felix (Yemen), where high coastal mountains receive the moist southwest monsoon winds during the summer. In classical times the name Arabia Felix was applied to a much larger area than present Yemen.

**maid who plays the role of Katharine** the woman who plays the role in the feast every year is "tall and slender, though not so tall nor so slender as Thecla, dark of complexion, dark of eye, raven of hair" (I, chap. II, 106). She appears at every feast for around twenty years and does not seem to change, which strongly suggests that she is travelling through time, presumably by way of the Atrium of Time. She is thought to be Catherine.
*Commentary:* that she is tall means that she is of exultant blood to one degree or another. She may be of an impoverished exultant line that has fallen out of the exultant class, as Severian seems to have thought the likely case over the years. But she also could be a khaibit of a true exultant, or a true exultant who is so young she has not yet reached her full height. The "not so slender" part may point to a waistline altered by motherhood.

**Makar** a soldier who became sick and was permitted to remain behind as his group marched to the front, mentioned in the unsent letter of the DEAD SOLDIER who would later be resurrected as Miles (IV, chap. I, 15).
*Onomastics:* from makarios "blessed" (Greek).
*History:* the relics of Saint Makar (4th century) are in Egypt.

**Malrubius** Master of Apprentices at the Matachin Tower, he died when Severian was a boy (I, chap. I, 17). As an aquastor, Malrubius appears to Severian periodically — when he is drowning (I, chap. 2, 25); just after he is elevated to journeyman (I, chap. II, 110); as he is sleeping at Ctesiphon's Cross (I, chap. 33, 283); while he is battling fever in the lazaret at Orithyia (IV, chap. 4, 34); and just after he becomes autarch (IV, chap. 30, 242).
*History:* Saint Malrubius (died 1040) was an anchorite in Merns, Scotland, martyred by Norwegian invaders.

**Mamas** the thirteen-year-old slave boy of the OLD LEECH, Vodalus's physician (IV, chap. 26, 215). He is used to give blood transfusions to Severian. Seeing the leech and the boy, Severian has a vision of children in flames (216).
*History:* Saint Mamas (died 275?) was a shepherd at Caesarea who suffered martyrdom under Aurelian. Eastern tradition says he died as a boy.

**Mamillian** the old autarch's mammoth (IV, chap. 23, 186).
*History:* Saint Mamillian (died 460) was a Bishop of Palermo, Sicily, said to have been exiled to Tuscany by King Genseric.

**mammoth** the Ice Age ancestor of the elephant, common to Asia, North America, and Europe (IV, chap. 23, 185). Some species were covered with a thick woolly fur. Slightly smaller than modern elephants and weighing four to seven tons, they were hunted to extinction by humans who used the meat, tusks, and hide extensively.

**Manahen** an eclectic dying of a chest wound in the sod house where Severian, Jolenta, and Dorcas visit (II, chap. 29, 276).
*History:* Saint Manahen (1st century), mentioned in the Acts of the Apostles as a foster brother of Herod Antipas and a prophet. He is said to have died at Antioch.

**Manahen's father** the herdsman who jokes that Severian must have borrowed an ox or a cow rather than tame a bull (II, chap. 29, 272). Manahen revives and tells his father to kill Severian as the lictor who will kill all the others. In response Severian has to break the man's arm.

**man-apes** a subterranean race of the Commonwealth (II, chap. 6, 51). They have large eyes and protruding fangs, and they glow with a luminescent mold. Severian's description suggests that they evolved into this form after being trapped underground, rather than being bioengineered (as is the case with the mastiff men and cat women). They guard the mine at Saltus and answer to the autarch, but they also respond to a much larger creature deep in the mine (55).
*Commentary:* the man-apes seem very similar to the subterranean "Morlocks" of Wells's *The Time Machine.*

**manatee** the sea cow, *Trichechus,* one of the origins of the mermaid legend because the breasts of the female are similar to those of human females (I, chap. 22, 197).

**man beasts** "They are man beasts, contrived by the same lost arts that made our destriers faster than the road engines of old.... The Autarch employs them in duties too laborious for men, or

for which men cannot be trusted" (IV, chap. 20, 157). The Wall of Nessus houses military creatures like the mastiff men, and the House Absolute has the cat woman servants.
*Commentary:* Wells's *The Island of Doctor Moreau* comes immediately to mind, but the idea is an ancient one, showing up as the Minotaur on the one hand, and the corollary of Circe's menagerie of men turned into animals (like the zoanthrops of the Commonwealth). Such creatures play a part in other Wolfe stories, including "The Death of Doctor Island and Other Stories," "Sonya, Crane Wesselman, and Kittee," and "The Hero As Werwolf."

**mandragora** "I felt the pale fluid in which the mandragora was immersed had become my own blood-tinged urine" (IV, chap. 35, 282).
*History:* the plant mandrake, the root of which bears an uncanny resemblance to the human form, in miniature.
*Literature:* in conversation with the mandragora, Severian says,

> "If I can do anything for you, tell me what it is."
> *"Break the glass."*
> I hesitated. "Won't you die?"
> *"I have never lived"* (283).

In its answers, the enigmatic creature echoes the immortal sibyl: "For I saw with my own eyes the Sibyl hanging in a jar at Cumae, and when the acolytes said, 'Sibyl, what do you wish?' she replied, 'I wish to die'" (Petronius, *Satyricon,* chap. 48).

That sibyl's story is in Ovid's *Metamorphoses* (book XIV). The mandragora also bears some resemblance to the homunculus of Goethe's *Faust, Part 2* (Act II).
*Commentary:* although Severian calls the homunculus in the Citadel a mandragora, whether it is animal or vegetable in origin

is unclear. Gregory Feeley offers the mandragora as a candidate for Severian's twin. (The search for a twin is prompted by the repetition of Severa/Severian as names for twins. Agia and Agilus are an example of twins with similar names.)

**maned wolf** "and once that giant fox . . . that men call the maned wolf, loped by at dusk on some unguessable errand" (I, chap. 2, 21).
*History: Chrysocyon brachyurus,* also known as the "giant fox," is a rare solitary and nocturnal animal that ranges from Brazil to Argentina.

**maniple** "they seemed the regular tread of a man of purpose, such a one as might, perhaps, command a maniple, or an ile of cavalry" (IV, chap. 16, 123). See MILITARY ORGANIZATION.
*History:* a subdivision of the Roman legion, a unit varying in size by type: numbering 120 men each among the antepilani and light infantry, sixty each among the pilani, and thirty among the cavalry. A manipular legion (509 B.C. to 217 B.C.) would have ten maniples of each type, amounting to 2,400 antepilani, 600 pilani, 1,200 light infantry, and 300 cavalry. In time the maniple was replaced by the cohort.
*Commentary:* because of the context it seems to be a unit of cavalry rather than any of the others. Another point favoring this interpretation is that the infantry maniple would be in some organizational conflict with the hundred (commanded by a lochage), whereas there is no conflict among sizes of cavalry units: maniple fills a niche.

**Mannea** mistress of the Pelerine postulants (IV, chap. 14, 114).

*Onomastics:* region of western Iran, northern Media.
*History:* Saint Mannea (died 287?), wife of Saint Marcellus, a tribune. They were beheaded at Thmuis (a city of Lower Egypt).

**manskin** leather made of human skin (I, chap. 14, 129).

**manvantara** a term Severian uses to mean the life of a universe between Big Bang (or Big Blossom) and the final collapse of matter into itself (V, chap. 19, 137).
*History:* a measure of time in Hindu cosmology, composed of four yuga or ages of the world. These ages devolve, like the four ages of Roman myth, from an Edenic state of happiness to a brutal state of misery.

| Yuga | God years | Man years | Corresponding Western Age |
|---|---|---|---|
| Krita | 4,800 | 1,728,000 | Golden |
| Treta | 3,600 | 1,296,000 | Silver |
| Dvapara | 2,400 | 864,000 | Copper |
| Kali | 1,200 | 432,000 | Iron |

**Map, The** a short story of Urth that first appeared in the anthology *Light Years and Dark* (1984), later collected in ES. Set in the years of Severian's reign before his trip to Yesod, it begins with a treasure hunter named Simulatio who hires Eata and his boat for transportation into the ruins of Nessus. Eata's deck hand Laetus and Laetus's girlfriend Syntyche had robbed Eata the night before.

**Marcellina** an optimate woman sent to the Matachin Tower for the crime of paying bravos to set fire to the house of her fiancé's girlfriend (I, chap. 12, 113). The fiancé was an officer.
*Onomastics:* "dedicated to Mars," Roman god of fertility and later war (Latin).
*History:* Saint Marcellina (died 398?), sister of Saint Ambrose of Milan, she lived a life of great austerity and holiness in Rome.

**Marchfield** "Severian, the king was elected at the Marchfield. Counts were appointed by the kings. That was what they called the dark ages" (II, chap. 16, 137). A place on Urth, perhaps during the Age of the Monarch.
*History:* the ancient Romans had a Field of Mars, but the rites that Jonas describes in the quote above are similar to those of the Frankish State of the early Middle Ages, where the people (free peasant-warriors entitled to political rights) acted jointly with the king at the annual Field of Mars celebration (until circa A.D. 732, at least).

**margay** "His breath is the mist that hides the infant uakaris from the claws of the margay" (I, chap. 21, 190).
*History:* a kind of wild cat, *Felis tigrina.*

**marge** margin (IV, chap. 13, 106).

**margrave** a lord or military governor of a medieval German border province, or a hereditary title of certain princes in the Holy Roman Empire (SS, 249).

**Marie** see ROBERT AND MARIE.

**marmoreal** resembling marble, or made of marble (v, chap. 24, 171).

**Martello** a building near the Matachin Tower (I, chap. 8, 83). A small circular fort with massive walls, containing vaulted rooms for the garrison, and having on the top a platform for one or two guns; usually erected on a coast to prevent the landing of enemies.

**Maruthas** the autarch who closed the roads to travel (I, chap. 13, 125), when Master Palaemon was around twenty years old (perhaps as much as seventy years P.S.). This was done for reasons of security and taxation.
*History:* Saint Maruthas (died 415) was bishop of Maiferkat in Mesopotamia and devoted all of his energy to the reorganization of the church in Persia and eastern Syria.
*Commentary:* a case can be made that Maruthas's reign followed Appian's, but this renders the old autarch nameless. It stems in part from the advanced ages of Palaemon, Malrubius, and the old autarch.

For this alternate timeline we can suppose that Appian was still on the throne in 59 P.S. when Sancha left the House Absolute. We then have Maruthas take the throne and close the roads around 57 P.S. If Palaemon is twenty-one that year, then he is seventy-eight when Severian is exiled.

**Maser** a magical sword in "The God and His Man" (ES, 204).
*History:* the word, like "laser," comes from an acronym: Microwave Amplification by Stimulated Emission of Radiation.

**mastiff** a type of fighting dog bred in the Bear Tower (I, chap. 3, 33).
*History:* a very large, powerful, deep-chested, and smooth-coated dog of old breed used chiefly as a watchdog and guard dog. In medieval times, mastiffs were used as war dogs, outfitted with lances, and trained to attack cavalry horses.

**mastiff man** a man beast guarding the gold in the armored coach that is stuck in the mud (IV, chap. 20, 159).

**Matachin Tower** the torturers' tower in the Citadel complex (I, chap. 2, 20), located behind the Witches' Keep from the Library (I, chap. 5, 51). There are paintings of agonized masks on the tower (53). In the uppermost levels are unseen mouths that sometimes speak to human beings, and to other mouths in other towers and keeps (I, chap. 7, 78).
*History:* matachins are the masked sword dancers of Spanish tradition. Since the members of the torturers' guild wear masks and dance with their executioner's swords on the feast of Holy Katherine, their tower is called the Matachin Tower.

**mate of the Alcyone** ship's first officer with a wife and two babies who, fearing for his life, tells the Conciliator he is willing to kill Captain Hadelin to stop the storm (V, chap. 34, 240). He is in a group that visits the Conciliator at the hulk, where he leaves his dirk for the Conciliator (V, chap. 37, 266): this is the blade which causes Gaudentius's chiliarch to be punished by Typhon (V, chap. 39, 275).

**matelasse** a French dress goods of silk, or silk and wool, having a raised design; also, quilted silk (I, chap. 16, 151).

**matross** a guild in charge of the larger energy canons at the Citadel (I, chap. 5, 48).
*History:* a soldier next in rank below gunner in a train of artillery, who acted as a kind of assistant or mate. Particularly civilians employed to operate artillery. (The word originally meant "sailor," as armed merchant ships were where matrosses learned their gunnery. John Brunner points out that the German word for sailor is still "Matrose.")

**mausoleum** Severian the apprentice has a secret hiding place in the necropolis, a violated mausoleum he considers "his own" (I, chap. 2, 21). Above the door is a bronze blazon showing a fountain and a flying ship, both over a rose. The heavy door is jammed half-shut (I, chap. 12, 114) or three quarters shut (IV, chap. 36, 290), and after the deluge has closed it, Severian speculates that it had been violated a century earlier (V, chap. 47, 335), in essence something like thirty years before his birth.

Inside the crypt are five coffins: two open ones on the floor and three intact ones on a shelf. Sometimes Severian rests in the open ones. There is a single narrow window with one bar. Among funeral brasses is a bronze of "an old exultant" (I, chap. 12, 114) that looks a lot like Severian (I, chap. 2, 22).

Severian assumes his friends have similar secret places (22), which might imply that Eata's is a crypt belonging to an exultant family of the great northern clans, from which Eata borrowed the crest that he drew above his cot. See EATA'S MAUSOLEUM.

When travelers searching for the grave of Cilinia approach apprentice Severian for help, he takes them directly to a mausoleum (*Return to the Whorl,* chap. 19, 391). At first glance it seems this must be "his" mausoleum, and yet from the details given, it probably is not: the crypt has "lots of coffins," most of them not on shelves, and "a lot" are empty. Cilinia's coffin is half-size, so it could not be one of the two open coffins in Severian's hideout.

**mausoleum builder** at some point after writing *The Urth of the New Sun,* Severian must have gone back in time to build the crypt as a message to his younger self. The blazon is clearly such an encrypted communication, alluding to the potent rose symbols of *The Book of the New Sun,* as well as the white fountain and the ship of Tzadkiel, both explicated in URTH.

But the coffins remain a mystery, seeming to tell a story that was not a part of the original design. A single open coffin would at first suggest a grave robbery, but later, after Severian's multiple resurrections, it would obviously point to a resurrection of the mausoleum builder. Two coffins suggest two resurrections, yet who could be the companion of the mausoleum builder? Or was the first opening a robbery and the second an awakening? In any event, the crypt's empty coffins and open door may have a connection to Dorcas's death, which happened about twenty years before Severian's birth, since Severian himself is responsible for setting most of the mysteries in motion. (After all, Dorcas means "gazelle," and Severian is a wolf; and don't forget the Little Red Riding Hood factor.)

**Maxellindis** Eata's girlfriend and shipmate, first met when he is a torturer's apprentice (IV, chap. 37, 307). Her uncle dies at a tavern in Liti, leaving them his boat (V, chap. 46, 326). When Maxellindis and Eata were later caught smuggling, she dove overboard and Eata was captured. He never saw her again. *History:* Saint Maxellindis (died 670?) was born near Cambrai, France. She fled an arranged marriage with Harduin of Solesmes because she had planned to become a nun. Harduin pursued her and stabbed her to death.

**Maxellindis's uncle** a grizzled old moonraker who owns and pilots a two masted smuggling ship on the Gyoll (IV, chap. 37, 299). He tells Severian the strange incident of meeting Trason on the water the night before: he was sailing upriver in a fog and he heard the sweeps of a galleass, illegally passing him in the center of the river (the lane reserved for traffic moving down river). He saw it pass with no running lights. Spooked by this, he called out from time to time and a half-league later his old friend Trason called back, telling him to get away. The mist parted and the moonraker saw Trason's ship, a lugger like his own, loaded with pale soldiers who were tall (tall enough to be exultant bastards but not tall enough to be exultants), and then the mist swallowed everything. The moonraker then heard voices of undines talking to someone with an even deeper voice, in a language he could not understand: the undines spoke, the other answered, the undines spoke, the other answered, and the undines spoke a last time. *Commentary:* the story ends with an apparent conference between an Other Lord and some undines (or perhaps Juturna and some smaller undines). That being the case, it seems possible that the galleass was the Other Lord himself in the "naviscaput" form used by the ogre in "The Tale of the Student and His Son," especially since Severian notes of the giant sea life, "some seemed ships" (I, chap. 15, 140). The mist and the pale soldiers point to Erebus: they may be perischii or slave-soldiers from raids against the Southern Isles.

**Maxentius** autarch who ordered Holy Katharine to be executed (1, chap. 11, 106).
*History:* the Roman emperor (306–12) who ordered Saint Catherine of Alexandria to be executed; as well as a saint (c. 448–c. 515) educated by Saint Severus, who became highly esteemed by Clovis I and by the surrounding population, whom he protected from the invading barbarians.

**meander** "there's a meander coming up" (ES, 23). A circuitous winding or sinuosity of a stream, in this case, a curve on the River Gyoll below Nessus.

**Measurement Tables**

| Linear | Weight |
| --- | --- |
| span = 8 inches | minim = 1/60 drachm |
| cubit = 18 inches | drachm = dram |
| pace = 2.5 feet | = 1/16 oz. (avdp) |
| ell = 5 spans | = 1.772 grams |
| = 40 inches | |
| stride = 5 feet | |
| chain = 100 spans | |
| = 70 feet | |
| league = 3 miles | |

**Monetary**

aes = copper coin, buys an egg
orichalk = brass coin, day's pay for common laborer
asimi = silver coin, buys an optimate's coat
chrisos = gold coin, buys a good mount

**Temporal**

| | |
|---|---|
| chronon | = smallest unit possible |
| time required to say the angelus | = about 1.5 minutes |
| watch | = 1.20 hours |
| | = 1 hour 12 minutes |
| day | = 20 watches |
| week | = 7 days |
| month | = 28 days |
| year | = 13 months |
| pentad | = 5 years |
| saros (modern) | = 18 years |
| chiliad | = 1000 years |
| saros (ancient) | = 3600 years |
| age | = variable period |
| manvantara | = lifespan of a universe |

**Media Pars** a location in or near Orithyia, probably the central section (IV, chap. 18, 143).
*Latin:* media ("middle") pars ("a portion of territory").

**Medoc** a general name for the red wines produced in Medoc, comprising all the best growths of claret (I, chap. 25, 220).

**megatherian** from a book in the Library entitled *Lives of the Seventeen Megatherians,* this term is used to describe a person or creature not unlike the Beast of Revelations (I, chap. 6, 64).
*Greek:* "great beast."

*Commentary:* for those interested in numerology, this is another example in the Urth Cycle of the number seventeen being associated with sinister forces. See GROUP OF SEVENTEEN.

**megathere** [meg-a-THEER] a large creature of the Commonwealth, not uncommon (II, chap. 22, 193).
*History:* a genus of huge herbivorous edentates *(Megatherium)* resembling the sloths, the fossil remains of which are found in the upper tertiary deposits of South America. It had huge claws on its forefeet, was larger than the modern elephant, and was able to reach leaves twenty feet off the ground by rearing up on its hindfeet.

**Melito** the farmer-soldier suitor of Foila (IV, chap. 5, 40). He tells the story of "The Cock, the Angel, and the Eagle" (IV, chap. 9).
*History:* there are two saints, but the appropriate one is Saint Melito (died 320), youngest of the forty soldier-martyrs of Sebaste, Phrygia. He was put to death during the persecution of Licinius. The group had been exposed for three days and nights in a freezing lake; the survivors, including Melito, had their legs and arms broken and were thrown into a furnace.

**Mennas** a journeyman torturer (I, chap. 3, 30).
*History:* Saint Mennas (3rd century), an Egyptian in the Roman army, was tortured and beheaded for his Christianity. His cult spread over the East and he became one of the great warrior saints of the Middle Ages.

**mensal** a place supplying a monthly rent to a religious order or official, particularly if the rent is given in the form of food (I, chap. 18, 163).

**meretrices** plural of meretrix, a prostitute (II, chap. 7, 72).

**merlon** "The merlons were several spans higher than my head, but he [Baldanders] put his hands on them as upon a railing" (III, chap. 35, 276). These merlons are thus eight feet high.
*History:* the solid portion of a crenelated wall between two open spaces.

**Merryn** a witch who appears with the Cumaean at the stone town and participates in the calling of Apu-Punchau (II, chap. 30, 282). She is a strong candidate for being Severian's twin sister, since girls born in the Matachin Tower are given to the witches.
*History:* Saint Modwenna (or Merryn) was possibly a recluse on the island of Andreseey in the Trent river, but the facts of her life are inextricably confused with those of the (male) Irish Monine (died 517?); Modwenna, abbess of Whitby (died 695?); and Modwenna, abbess of Polesworth (died 900?).
*Commentary:* John Clute alludes to Merryn as the most likely candidate for Severian the Great's twin. The search for a twin is prompted by the fact that at two points in the text the name Severian is said to be the male half of a brother/sister pair: first there is little Severian and his sister Severa (III, chap. 14, 98–100); and later, when Ava says "Severian is one of those brother-sister names, isn't it? Do you have a sister?" Severian replies, "I don't know. If I do, she's a witch" (IV, chap. 10, 79). See also MANDRAGORA.

**merychip** a riding mount in the Commonwealth, but only suitable for someone as light as a child (I, chap. 35, 297).
*History: Merychippus* was a small, pony-sized precursor to the modern horse.

**Meschia** a character in Dr. Talos's play *Eschatology and Genesis.*
*Myth:* (Persian) the first man, also known as "Mashya." See JAHI.

**Meschiane** a character in Dr. Talos's play *Eschatology and Genesis.*
*Myth:* (Persian) the first woman, also known as "Mashyoi." See JAHI.

**Mesmin** a man of Saltus, one of two named volunteers who breaks Barnoch's door (II, chap. 2, 16). (The other was Sebald.) They are joined by three unnamed VOLUNTEERS, one of whom is a Vodalarius.
*History:* Saint Memorius (died 451), also known as Mesmin, was a deacon at Troyes, France. According to an unreliable story he was sent with four companions by Saint Lupus to beg Attila to spare the area; all were beheaded.

**Mesrop** a mercenary in Guasacht's unit, who, with Lactan, throws the reins in Severian's face (IV, chap. 19, 151). Also mentioned later on (IV, chap. 21, 166).
*Onomastics:* the creator of the Armenian alphabet, his name remains a mystery.
*History:* Saint Mesrop (died 440) was Armenian.

**metamynodon** the hornless rhinoceros (I, chap. 18, 164). A not-uncommon riding mount in Nessus.

**Midan** huntsman of Thecla's uncle, when she was a girl (IV, chap. 1, 11).
*History:* Saint Midan (died 610?) lived in Anglesey, Wales.

**midinette** a Parisian shopgirl; especially a Parisian seamstress (III, chap. 6, 49).

**Miles** the DEAD SOLDIER, resurrected and renamed by Severian, who gives him a "soldier" name (IV, chap. 6, 46). Severian believes that he in some way incarnates Jonas (IV, chap. 3, 25) because he uses SAILOR TALK like Jonas, even though he has no sailing background (IV, chap. 4, 32), and in his death-dream he saw a face multiplied, that of a girl with red hair (Jolenta).
*Onomastics:* "a soldier" (Latin); "merciful" (Old German).
*Commentary:* there seem to be two souls in that man's body. Jonas's soul was drawn down into the body of the anonymous dead soldier when Severian used the Claw upon the corpse.

## Military Organization

**Military Organization**

| Leader | Unit |
|---|---|
| — | Legion (5,000 men) |
| — | Mora (1,272 men) |
| Chiliarch | Regiment (1,000 men) or a Xenagie of dimarchi |
| — | Cohort (300 to 600 men) |
| Hipparch | Xenagie (500 cavalry) |
| Lochage | Hundred (100 men) |
| Lancer | Bacele (fifty to sixty cavalry) |
| — | Maniple (thirty cavalry) |
| Vingtner | — (twenty infantry) |
| Seraph | Squadron of anpiel |
| — | Ile (ten cavalry) |

**mimalone** a sect of maenads who wore horned headdresses and were more violent than most (IV, chap. 21, 167). The Thracian women of Greek mythology who killed Orpheus for Dionysus were probably mimalones.

**Mineas** an uhlan killed by notules, revived by the Claw (II, chap. 11, 112).
*History:* Saint Minias (died 250) was a soldier, stationed in France, where he spread the faith among his comrades, and where he was martyred under Decius.

**minim** a unit of measurement, one sixtieth of a drachm (I, chap. 3, 29). See MEASUREMENT TABLES.

**Miracles** an attempt to list all the miracles evident in Severian's narrative. Included are some possible resurrections (for example, at the end of *Citadel* Severian wonders if the Claw hadn't restored both Agia and himself after the fiacre crash in *Shadow;* there is also the recurrent notion that somebody drowned in the River Gyoll in his place).

- Severian the apprentice drowned in river, resurrected.
- Triskele resurrected.
- Fiacre crash, Severian and Agia resurrected.
- Flying cross (airplane) in jungle garden.
- Dorcas resurrected.
- Severian killed in duel, resurrected.
- Flying cathedral.
- Water into wine at Saltus inn.
- Light in Saltus mine.
- Man-ape healed.
- Thecla within Severian, resurrected.
- Ulhan Cornet Mineas on the grounds of House Absolute, resurrected.
- Jonas healed/resurrected after whip attack in antechamber.
- Bull on pampas tamed.
- Peasants Manahen and his father healed.
- Manahen's sodhouse grew green.
- Jader and his sister healed.
- Light for salamander.
- Light in Vincula.
- Typhon resurrected.
- Light thrown by Baldanders.
- Miles resurrected/Jonas's soul invades.
- Exultant Emilian in the lazaret healed.
- Severian killed on battlefield, resurrected.
- Mandragora in bottle, resurrected.
- Power outage on Tzadkiel's ship.

- Severian the Great killed by winged thing on Tzadkiel's ship, resurrected.
- Twisted limbs of Herena reshaped.
- Declan healed.
- Zama the zombie resurrected.
- Os cursed.
- Storm called.
- Storm calmed.
- Eskil healed.
- Severian as Conciliator killed by convulsor, resurrected.
- Smilodon tamed.
- Dead assassin resurrected.
- Severian drowned at Deluge, resurrected.
- Severian killed as Apu Punchau, resurrected.

**misericorde** Agia laments that Agilus had pawned her misericorde the week before (I, chap. 25, 226).
*History:* a dagger with a stiff, diamond cross-section or three-sided blade; used to dispatch a man in armor by stabbing through some chink, usually in the armpit. Named "dagger of mercy" because the sight of the uplifted weapon caused the intended victim to surrender.

**mist machine** Baldanders's device, described as a "casket with knobs" (III, chap. 36, 283), is a kind of hologram projector (III, chap. 35, 280). First it generates a white-mist screen, and then it projects lifelike, moving holograms within the mist.

**mitre** the carved mountains wear diadems, tiaras, and mitres (III, chap. 2, 20).

*History:* a tall, pointed hat with peaks in front and back, worn by bishops and some other ecclesiastics, or the ceremonial headdress worn by ancient Jewish high priests.
*Commentary:* diadems denote royalty and tiaras suggest both royalty and religious office, but mitres are exclusively religious symbols. This points to the religious side of the autarch's position in the Commonwealth.

**Modan** a sailor who fights jibers in a group of five including Purn (V, chap. 11, 80). He uses a dirk.
*Onomastics:* a saga name (Norse).
*History:* Saint Modan (died 550) is believed to have been a Scottish monk.

**Moira** Greek term for one's personal fate, destiny (I, chap. 14, 129); also appears in "moiraic women" (III, chap. 6, 54). A sacred lottery: luck as an instrument of the INCREATE.

**monach** a monk (I, chap. 18, 163).

**monstrance** a receptacle used for the exhibition of relics, or of a host (III, chap. 26, 210).

**montane** pertaining to or living in mountains (III, chap. 18, 144).

**mora** see MILITARY ORGANIZATION (IV, chap. 1, 12).
*History:* one of the divisions of the Spartan Army. There were originally six, each composed of around 1,272 men: 576 infantry, sixty cavalry, and one slave (helot) for each man to carry baggage.

**Morwenna** a woman of Saltus executed by Severian for the murder of her husband Stachys and her son Chad (II, chap. 1, 7). They seem to have died of a fever-inducing poison (7). Severian imagines her motives as being "because she recalled a time in which she was free and, perhaps, virginal" (IV, chap. 2, 20). She was chained by the water's edge the night before her execution, as was custom, and since she was not stoned or raped, Severian thinks she is greatly feared (II, chap. 4, 32). She manages to poison her accuser Eusebia after her own death. She is the only woman Severian executed (IV, chap. 37, 298). Her father had been a drover (II, chap. 1, 9).
*Onomastics:* "sea wave," "maiden" (Welsh).
*History:* Saint Morwenna (5th century) holy woman of Cornwall, England, she is often confused with other saints of the same name, or with such Irish saints as the 6th-century hermit Moninne.
*Commentary:* there is a parallel between Morwenna and "Mother Pyrexia," whose nickname means "fever," and who was executed (perhaps by burning) in Saltus eighteen years earlier.

**moth** in the gardens above the House Absolute, there is a species of giant moth with wings "as long as a man's arms" which seems capable of vocal communication among themselves, in voices nearly too high for human hearing (II, chap. 27, 256). For another example of apparently intelligent animals, see RAT.

**Mount Typhon** the first of the mountain-statues, carved by order of the Monarch Typhon, and apparently intended to be his mausoleum. The statue is that of a seated ruler, facing west. In the lap of the statue are a few buildings, including the round house (III, chap. 23, 191), and the giant robots that had carved the statue (III, chap. 23, 189). The thumb is 100 paces (250 feet) long (III, chap. 23, 187), and there is a golden ring on the left hand (III, chap. 24, 195), protected by powerful energy weapons. The hollow head chamber is as big as a ballroom (III, chap. 26, 208), and the eye-windows are 100 paces (250 feet) apart, 10 cubits (15 feet) wide. Transportation from the cursed city at the lap of the statue to the head chamber is by a flier-like shuttle that travels through tunnels.

**mountains** the immovable idols of Urth (or the Commonwealth, at least) were carved during a period beginning with Monarch Typhon and ending with some unknown autarch (III, chap. 2, 20). All the mountains of the Commonwealth are so carved.

**mucid** "the mist . . . was as mucid as any specter" (V, chap. 49, 343). Moldy, from Latin "mucidus," musty.

**muni** a sage (I, chap. 17, 158).

**Murene** the name of the village on the shore of Lake Diuturna (III, chap. 32, 258).
*History:* (variant of "muraena") in early use applied vaguely as the name of a kind of eel mentioned by ancient writers.

**mutton** "Ah, the torturers get mutton — that's the difference" (I, chap. 7, 72). The flesh of a full-grown sheep.
*Commentary:* Byfield's wonderful lexicon, *The Book of Weird* (also known as *The Glass Harmonica* [1973]), speaks to this: "Torturers

reek of mutton, rust, and cold sweat" (entry on "Torture"), a line that may sound familiar. If not, recall the passage where the chiliarch admonishes Petronax to use his nose if he can't use his head in determining that Severian is a real torturer and not an armiger in costume. The chiliarch then describes the odors that entered the room with Severian as "Rusting iron, cold sweat, putrescent blood" (I, chap. 14, 135).

**myrmidon** from Father Inire's letter: "the Chatelaine Thea . . . at first attempted to gain control of those myrmidons who were about him [Vodalus] at his death" (IV, chap. 35, 287).
*History:* a blindly loyal though unscrupulous faction, from the Greek word for "ant," the name of a group that fought on the side of the Greeks at Troy.

**myrrhic** "from [the avern] there drifted a myrrhic perfume" (I, chap. 24, 217). Resembling myrrh, an aromatic resin formerly used in embalming. "The gold, frankincense, and myrrh brought to Jesus by the magi symbolized his kingship, divinity, and death" (CD, 245).

**myste** one initiated into mysteries (I, chap. I, 11).

**Mysteries of the Urth Cycle** as we read and re-read the narrative of Severian (and various satellite works), we should keep an eye out for answers to the following questions, some of them resembling "What song did the sirens sing?" and "What was the alias of Heracles at this obscure period of his life?"

- Who is Severian's mother?
- Who is Severian's father? (Too easy?)

- Who is Severian's sister?
- Who is buried in Severian's mausoleum?
- Who (or what) is the intelligence in the depths of the mine at Saltus?
- What is the answer to the riddle of Apu-Punchau, i.e., how was the sunrise delayed during the long dance? (Too easy?)
- Are the Matachin and Witches' Towers somehow related to Jachin and Boaz (pillars at the entrance to the Temple of Solomon)?
- What is Hethor's real name?
- What is the relation between Jonas and Miles?
- Given that Burgundofara leaves Hadelin and returns to the ship of Tzadkiel, did they even marry? If so, then perhaps they had children before she left. Because she is from Liti, and Maxellindis's uncle dies in Liti, might there be a bloodline connection between Burgundofara and Maxellindis?
- Is Maxellindis transformed by nixies into an undine, perhaps even Juturna?
- What was the commotion at the gate of Nessus (end of book 1) all about? (This is one of the largest gaps in the narrative.)
- What is so sinister about the number seventeen, such that we have the "Group of Seventeen" in Ascia and the book lives of the *Lives of the Seventeen Megatherians* in the Library?
- What were the names of the journeymen Master Gurloes had sent in search of the House Absolute (1, chap. 8, 68), and whatever became of them?

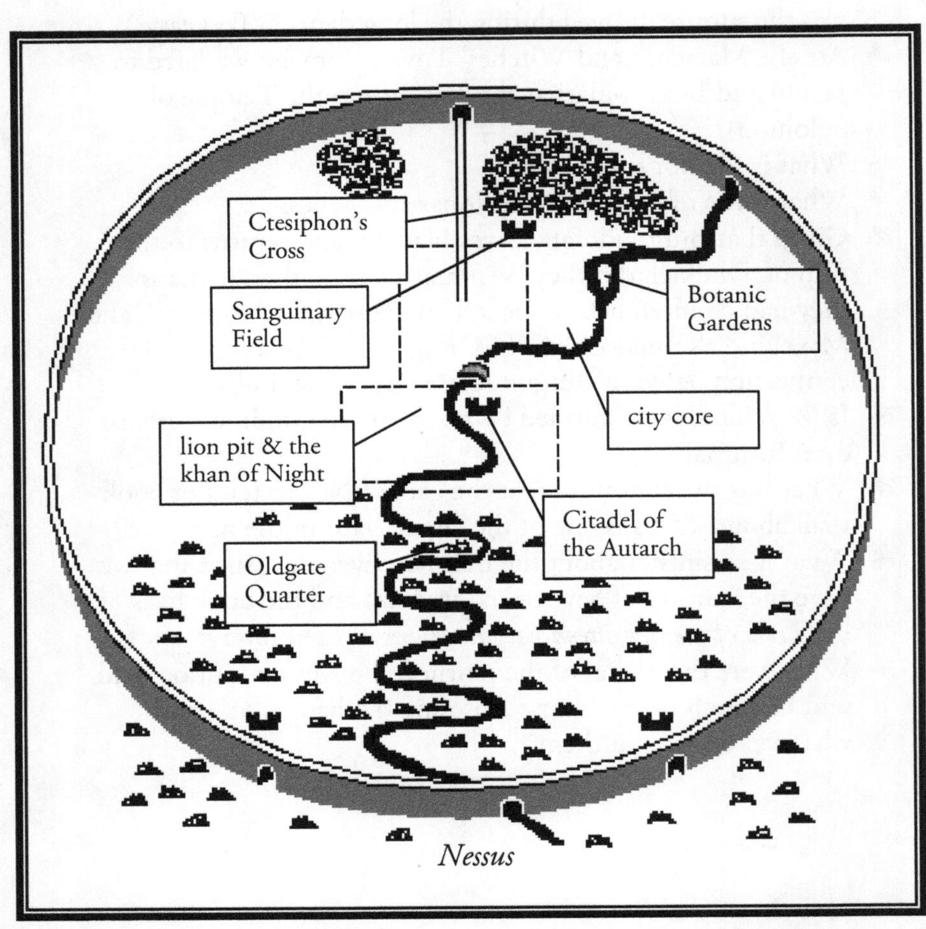
Ctesiphon's Cross
Sanguinary Field
Botanic Gardens
city core
lion pit & the khan of Night
Citadel of the Autarch
Oldgate Quarter
*Nessus*

**nacker** one who buys the bodies of dead horses and other dead animals (IV, chap. 18, 141). Also spelled "knacker."

**naiad** a river nymph (IV, chap. 21, 167).

**Naked One** "For so he had been taught by the Naked One, who was also called the Savage, or Squanto" (III, chap. 19, 156). The teacher of the animal-people in "The Tale of the Boy Called Frog."
*Literature:* this role is played by Baloo the brown bear in Kipling's Jungle Books.
*History:* Squanto or Tisquantum (died 1622) was a North American Indian of the Pawtuxet tribe. From at least 1615 to 1619, he lived in England. In 1621 he acted as interpreter in concluding a treaty between the Pilgrim settlers and Massasoit (chief of the Wampanoag tribe). Squanto became friendly with the Plymouth colonists, aiding them particularly in their planting and fishing. He died of smallpox.

**narrow lands** "I remember your red hair and high color. Far to the south, in the narrow lands, the savages paint a fire spirit much like you" (I, chap. 9, 88). The area in the Commonwealth far to the south, analogous to the tapering area of southern South America.

**narthex** "It was written on cream-colored parchment, the finest I had then seen, and bore the narthex sigil of the order stamped in gold" (IV, chap. 15, 117).
*History:* an old church portico, of a crucifix shape.

**Natrium** an old name for sodium (III, title of chap. 30, 239; III, chap. 35, 277). The active ingredient for the power bullets used by the shore people of Lake Diuturna against the islanders.

**naviscaput** the nameless monster in "The Tale of the Student and His Son," which has a ship for a head disguising a massive body below water (II, chap. 17, 146). Reviewing the story while a prisoner in the ziggurat, Severian notes this bears a certain resemblance to Erebus and Abaia, but he sees it as an author's invention (IV, chap. 26, 218). Nevertheless, the lightless galleass seen by Maxillindis's uncle may have been a naviscaput.
*Latin:* navis (ship) + caput (head).
*Myth:* this creature takes on the combined roles of Minos/Daedalus/Minotaur in the Theseus thread of the story: Minos as king of the island, Daedalus as inventor of the labyrinth to hide the monster in, and Minotaur as the monster himself. As "Wind" to Night's "Nox," he might be "Boreas."
*Commentary:* Gregory Feeley points to the non-Urth story "A Solar Labyrinth" (*Storeys from the Old Hotel)* as an explicit example of a character being a combination of Minos/Daedalus/Minotaur in a Wolfe tale.

**Nennoc** a woman of Halvard's story, "The Two Sealers." She is from the big isle (in the Southern Isles), the woman whom

Gundulf of Glacies fell in love with and wanted to marry, even though she was a widow with one child (IV, chap. 7, 58).
*History:* Saint Nennoc (died 467?) was a daughter of Brychan of Brecknock. She is said to have followed Saint Germanus from England to France and to have become abbess in Armorica.

**nenuphar** a water lily with a wide, blue flower (I, chap. 2, 24).

**Nessus** the name of the major city of the Commonwealth, so called because the river Gyoll, which passes through it, is poisoned. Nessus is surrounded by a circular metal wall that is very tall (see WALL OF NESSUS). There are at least three gates to Nessus, named Sorrowing (south-southwest?), Praise (south-southeast?), and Piteous (north). The inhabited part of the city is divided into various quarters: the Algedonic Quarter and Cobbler's Common are two examples. The southern part of Nessus lies in ruins, largely uninhabited and forgotten. Oldgate is a ruinous district near the river on the west bank (IV, chap. 37, 304). Near the center of the sprawling megalopolis lies the Citadel of the Autarch, situated on the northern edge of the Algedonic Quarter.

Nessus is said to have been moving up the Gyoll for chiliads. Its original location may have been in the vicinity of Liti. At one point the Ascians laid waste to Nessus (IV, chap. 24, 196), but this must have occurred early in the Age of the Autarch.
*Myth:* (Greek) the centaur who was killed by Heracles, yet had his revenge by killing Heracles with a poisoned shirt.
*Greek:* the word might be a corruption of "neossos" (young bird or animal).

**New Year's Day** a mid-summer celebration in the Commonwealth (IV, chap. 18, 142). Since the Commonwealth is located in the southern hemisphere, this date corresponds to the middle of winter in the northern hemisphere, which would be sometime in February.

**newel post** the pillar forming the center from which the steps of a winding stair radiate (II, chap. 19, 171).

**Nicarete** an armigette (II, appendix, 298) who had volunteered to stay in the antechamber (II, chap. 15, 125). She is an old woman with white hair but she wears it "flowing about her shoulders as young women do" (126), suggesting that she entered as a young woman.
*History:* Saint Nicarete was a virgin and supporter of Saint John Chrysostom. A native of Nicomedia, she took care of John Chrysostom when he was ill and shared in his exile from the imperial capital.

**nidorous** having the odor of burnt fat (I, chap. 18, 163).

**Night** a goddess-like being in "The Tale of the Student and His Son" who was forcefully married to the nameless naviscaput (II, chap. 17, 151). The daughter of this union is Noctua. Additionally, a statue of Night stands atop the khan on the west bank of the Gyoll opposite the Citadel (I, chap. 2, 27).
*Myth:* (Greek) *Nox*, a primeval goddess personifying night. The Orphic creation myth has Night courted by the Wind resulting in the birth of Eros, a god of love. Hesiod's later philosophical creation myth in *Theogony* has the union of Erebus and Nox

producing Doom, Old Age, Death, Murder, Continence, Sleep (Hypnos; male), Dreams, Discord, Misery, Vexation, Nemesis (female), Joy, Friendship, Pity, the Three Fates, and the three Hesperides.
*Commentary:* her role in the Theseus thread of "The Student and His Son" would seem to be that of Pasiphae (wife of Minos, mother of Ariadne).

**nigrescent** in the necropolis "the dark death roses came into bloom . . . nigrescent purple flecked with scarlet" (I, chap. 10, 99). Of a blackish hue or color.

**Nilammon** "Now there's trees enough on it to hide Nilammon, as the saw goes" (I, chap. 52).
*History:* Saint Nilamon (with one M) in the 4th century hid from an Egyptian mob that wanted to proclaim him bishop. He was eventually found, dead, in his cell.
*Commentary:* within the context of the scene, the name seems at first to be a corruption of "Neil Armstrong," the first man on the Moon, similar to the case later where "kimleesoong" is revealed to be "Kim Lee Soong."

**nixie** probably a term for a small undine, as Eata says of his lost love "maybe a nixie pulled her down" (V, chap. 46, 327).
*Myth:* (Norse) water-sprites who live in rivers and lakes. Considered malignant in some areas, harmless and friendly in others.

**noctilucent** of or relating to marine phosphorescence, from *Noctiluca,* a species of phosphorus (II, chap. 6, 51).

**Noctua** the daughter of Night and the naviscaput (II, chap. 17, 148), the princess whom the hero saves in "The Tale of the Student and His Son."
*Latin:* owl.
*Myth:* judging by her role in the story she may be Nemesis or a female Hypnos. For list of Night's children, see NIGHT.
*Commentary:* Wolfe writes, "The original Erebus . . . was the god of darkness and the husband of Nox, the goddess of night. (And thus the stepfather, if you like, of our Princess Noctua)" (CD, 252). This refutes the idea that Erebus and the naviscaput are one and the same, putting the naviscaput in the role of the Wind to Night, an out of wedlock affair leading to birth. The owl is a symbol of Athena (patron of Athens, the city paying tribute to the Minotaur in the Theseus story), but Theseus is said to have been aided by Aphrodite, and in any case, Noctua's role in "The Student and His Son" is more akin to that of Ariadne.

Within the larger frame of Severian's life, her role is played by Juturna.

**nocturne** a musical piece that evokes night; in this case a song that postulant Ava is scheduled to play on a summer's eve, presumably to mark the arrival of night (IV, chap. 10, 76). See AUBADE.

**Nod** a character in Dr. Talos's play *Eschatology and Genesis.*
*Myth:* (Hebrew) one of the Nephilim, the giants inhabiting prehistoric Canaan. Said to be the offspring of "sons of God" (perhaps angels) and human women, the Nephilim might have been recent descendants of hominids (akin to "Big Foot" and Yeti) and wives stolen from human settlements. According to one

tradition they supplied wives to Adam's sons. The Land of Nod, refuge of Cain, was located somewhere east of Eden. See the article "Onomastics, the Study of Names" in *Castle of Days.*

**Nones** "Then come into my presence chamber tomorrow a little after Nones" (I, chap. 20, 182). Noon, the period of mid-day, as Wolfe writes, "prayers said at noon (which takes its name from them)" (CD, 244). See WATCHES OF THE DAY.
*History:* the word originally applied to the ninth hour of the Roman day, which would be around 3 P.M., but over time it shifted backward into mid-day, our noon.

**notule** creatures used on an alien world for ritual murders, so called by sailors because they usually come after dark (II, chap. 11, 101). They are attracted to heat, but seem to be able to distinguish between life heat and other forms of heat. They kill by smothering a victim, then feed off of the body heat.
*Commentary:* the notule seems to be a night or darkness elemental. On Earth "noctule" is a large red bat (*Nyctalus noctula)* common to Eurasia (from "Nottola," Italian for bat or owl; and "noctua," Latin for night owl). But "notule" is also French for a brief note (or perhaps "an abstract"), which makes a kind of nightmare sense for this weird creature.

**noyade** the execution of persons by drowning, as practiced by Carrier at Nantes in 1794 (III, chap. 29, 235).

**Numen** "That night my nephew went to the Numen, the Proud One, and slit the throat of a young oreodont" (I, chap. 21, 189).

*History:* deity, divinity; divine or presiding power or spirit. See INCREATE.

**nurse** the middle-aged Pelerine who tends Severian at the lazaret in Orithyia (IV, chap. 8, 60–65). Miles tells her about his conversation with Severian involving the Claw; the nurse confronts Severian; the nurse later tells the postulant Ava, who comes to visit him. She may very well be Einhildis, the Pelerine friend who wrote the letter to Cyriaca.

**Nympha** Lomer's former employer, a chatelaine (II, chap. 15, 125). She successfully worked to lift his death sentence, so he was sent to the antechamber (ES, 215).
*Onomastics:* bride (Greek).
*History:* Saint Nympha (4th century) remains an uncertain figure. Legend says she was martyred at Porto, Italy.

# O

**Oannes** the fish god of the "floating islands" folk of Lake Diuturna (III, chap. 31, 251). The Sleeper, a god of Ushas, is said to be a kind of Oannes (V, chap. 51, 367).
*Myth:* Babylonian god, half-man, half-fish, from Akkadian Ea (and ultimately the Sumerian god Enki). In the beginning of time, when people lived in a lawless manner like beasts, Ea ("lord of the house of water") appeared from the sea, and he instructed humankind in handicrafts, farming, letters, laws, architecture, and magic. After a day of instruction Ea retired to the sea, from which he made only three other appearances over a period of thousands of years. (One of these appearances was to warn Utnapishtim, the "Babylonian Noah," about the coming deluge.)

**Och** (entry from SOLAR SYSTEM TABLE) occultic angel who governs the sun, Och is also governor of twenty-eight of the 196 Olympian Provinces in which Heaven is divided. He is a mineralogist and a prince of alchemy.

**odalisque** a female slave or concubine in an Eastern harem, especially in the seraglio of the Sultan of Turkey (II, chap. 8, 72).

**Odilo the Steward** any one of a long line of stewards in the House Absolute, three generations of which appear in the Urth Cycle. The earliest Odilo is mentioned in "The Cat" (ES, 210). The second Odilo encountered Severian in the House Absolute (II, chap. 19, 171) and later wrote "The Cat." The third Odilo

survived the deluge and became the god of learning on Ushas (v, chap. 51, 367).
*Onomastics:* "fortunate or prosperous in battle" (Old German).
*History:* tenth-century Abbot of Cluny who established All Souls' Day (so it is fitting that an Odilo tells the ghost story of "The Cat" on Halloween). He was in office for fifty-four years, and died at the age of eighty-six.

**Odo** a journeyman torturer (I, chap. 3, 30).
*Onomastics:* variant of "Otto" meaning "wealth" (Old German).
*History:* Saint Odo (A.D. 801–880) was a soldier who entered the Benedictines and taught the sons of Charles Martel.

**oillet** an aperture or loophole for observation; a spy-hole (v, chap. 41, 291).

**Olaguer** "Any news you have of Abaia's incursions will be fresher than mine . . . but Olaguer may be able to inform you" (from "Father Inire's Letter," IV, chap. 35, 288). An important general or minister in the House Absolute.
*History:* also known as Saint Ollegarius (A.D. 1060–1137), he was born in Barcelona, Spain. He supported the new Knights Templar, preached a crusade against the Moors in Spain, and rebuilt much of the property they had destroyed.

**old autarch** first appearing as the manager of the echopraxia near the Citadel, he was the first autarch to visit Yesod since Ymar, and his name is probably Appian. His physical features: "short, white hair, wide but rounded brow, eyes like windows" (I, chap. 9, 87); "short, white hair . . . rounded brow . . . face . . .

plump woman of forty" (II, chap. 20, 181); blue eyes (IV, chap. 24, 192). Previously a servant in House Absolute (IV, chap. 25, 206); connection to bees (IV, chap. 29, 237); possible childhood in Famulorum (V, chap. 40, 284). In the corridors of Time he has the animal aspect of a bull (IV, chap. 23, 189–90), or more specifically, an ox.

**old leech** the physician of the Vodalarii (IV, chap. 26, 214). He owns the boy Mamas and treats Severian at the jungle ziggurat.

**old sun** the primary star of Urth is a big, red, dim star. This condition is impossible according to science and nature as we know them: it is, rather, the lurid, swollen sun of pulp science fiction covers, tracing all the way back to *The Time Machine* by H. G. Wells.

A character of *In Green's Jungle* finds that the old sun is so large that "when I stretched forth my arm, my hand could not cover it all" (chap. 21, 313). The width of a fist held at arm's length is a standard field measure of 10°. Since the old sun cannot be completely covered with an outstretched hand, this implies that its apparent size, or angular diameter, is greater than 10° but less than 20°, averaging 15°.

So the equation $S = 57.3 \times D/R$ (where S is angular diameter, D is diameter of star, and R is distance from star) is expressed as $15° = 57.3 \times D/149{,}600{,}000$ km. Solving for D gives a diameter of 39.16 million kilometers, nearly forty times the size of our Sun's diameter of 1.39 million kilometers, yet fears that the planet Mercury has been swallowed by the swollen star prove to be groundless, since that planet orbits at 57.9 million km.

Urth rotates at 15° per hour, so it would take one hour from the moment when the horizon touches the disc of the sun to when the horizon completely covers the disc.

The old sun is not dying of natural causes. The mistaken notion that it has naturally evolved over billions of years into its swollen red state has tripped up many readers. Rather than evolution it was ASTEROENGINEERING, or stellar engineering: through intent or accident somebody put a black hole into the old sun, which caused its dying condition.

This is established at two points in the text. The first is a line from a holy book, read before an execution, addressing the Increate, "You, the hero who will destroy the black worm that devours the sun" (II, chap. 4, 33). The second is a line from the play *Eschatology and Genesis,* where the Prophet says to the Autarch, "Yet even you must know that cancer eats the heart of the old sun. At its center, matter falls in upon itself, as though there were there a pit without bottom, whose top surrounds it" (II, chap. 24, 222).

Typhon supplies further technical details in the following passage.

> It was a period of great confusion as well. My astronomers had told me that this sun's activity would decay slowly. Far too slowly, in fact, for the change to be noticeable in a human lifetime. They were wrong. The heat of the world declined by nearly two parts in a thousand over a few years, then stabilized. Crops failed, and there were famines and riots (III, chap. 25, 206).

The fact of the old sun's unnatural condition and the short period of its development together provide another example of the "collapsing scale" used so often in Severian's Narrative: where, in this case, something that implies billions of years of natural evolution is revealed to have happened in just a few years.

**Old Woman Whose Rolling Pin Is the Sun, The** a short story of Urth, collected in IA. It is a tale told by a man to his grand daughter Becca, explaining the nature of the cosmos: how the movement of the constellations signal changes in the seasons, and how the Old Woman (Nature, Fauna, or Bona Dea) constantly creates the physical world while her unnamed husband constantly consumes it. The story makes reference to "our longfather," a culture hero who went to the stars. The constellations and celestial bodies mentioned are Cor Caroli, the Great Bear, the Harp, the Hounds (named Asterion and Chara), the Hunter, La Supra, Skuld (IA, 44), the Spiral Nebula, and the Swan (identified in this case as Cygnus, not Sagittarius: see SWAN). The goat of Capricorn (also called "Stonebuck") is ridden by a child, and while the child is benign, the goat itself is dangerous.

> Him too you may meet in wood or field, most often at noon, they say. . . . Flee any goat, or any man with a goat's feet and horns. If you see the print of his cloven hoof beside water, turn away. And whether you see him on earth or in the sky, know that he brings heat and storm (45).

*Myth:* since Christmas falls in the sign of Capricorn, the child riding the goat is clearly the newly born Christ child effortlessly

subduing Satan, a creature that nevertheless remains dangerous. The detail about appearing at noon alludes to Pan, the goat-legged nature god of Arcadia, who would send the sudden fear we call "panic" if he was disturbed during his noon nap. The warning about heat and storm evokes Typhon in his aspect of Set, god of desert storms.
*Commentary:* Wolfe has a few stories that deal explicitly with the zodiac ("At the Point of Capricorn" and "To the Dark Tower Came"), but this one seems tied to the Urth Cycle by a few points, the most obvious being the name "Skuld" for the planet Venus, another being the reference to Fauna, who appears in a story in the brown book. The "longfather" may be another avatar of the New Sun, or a later name for the Sleeper god of Ushas. The astronomy of the story shows that it is taking place in the northern hemisphere, and that the stars are in the same positions that they are today, so the story is probably set relatively early in the history of Ushas.

**omophagist** an eater of raw flesh (1, chap. 8, 85). Inhabitants of the abandoned districts of Nessus are afraid to call attention to themselves by lighting fires, hence this term for them.
*Myth:* omophagia ("eating-into-the-Belly") is an ancient Greek ritual of holy communion by eating the flesh of sacrificial victims, human or animal, so there is also a hint of cannibalism in the word. Practiced by the MIMALONES, among others.

**onegar** a misspelling (CD, 243) of onager, the wild ass (1, chap. 18, 162).

**onomastics** the study of names. These are the naming conventions found within the Urth Cycle: Ascians are presumably labeled with phrases of Correct Thought (Loyal to the Group of Seventeen); people of the Commonwealth are named after saints (Dorcas, Eata, Fechin), or after mythological figures (Typhon, Talos) if they are allied with the Other People; in rare cases, people of the Commonwealth have professional names (Mother Pyrexia, a witch; Jonas, a sailor cursed: his Old Testament name also pre-dates that of the saints, pointing to his great antiquity); the Other People (Abaia, Erebus, and Juturna) and the Hierodules (Ossipago, Barbatus, and Famulimus) are named after mythological figures, non-Olympians and Olympians respectively; Hierarchs (Venant and Apheta) have obscure star names; Hierogrammates (Tzadkiel) are named after archangels; and the big androids that are hollow are named "iron" in modern Earth languages (there are no names given in the text for any of the small silver androids). Villages and towns have Latin names usually based on local terrain (Saltus, Pascua, Os) and cities have Greek names (Nessus, Thrax). See "Onomastics" (CD).

**ophicleid** a musical wind instrument of powerful tone, a development of the ancient "serpent," consisting of a conical brass tube bent double, with keys, usually eleven in number, forming the bass or alto to the key bugle (I, chap. 3, 33).

**Ophiel** (entry from SOLAR SYSTEM TABLE) one of the seven Olympian Spirits, he rules Mercury and his name appears on the Necromantic Bell of Girardius, which is rung to summon the dead.

**optimate** the social class of wealthy traders, below armiger and above the commonality (I, chap. 2, 20). Probably what we too easily call "middle class." Optimates in the text include Ava, Dorcas, Marcellina, and possibly Simulatio.

**oread** "the young woman's face, immobile as an oread's in a picture, gave me no clue" (II, chap. 30, 282).
*Myth:* (Greek) a nymph of mountains and grottoes.

**oreodont** [o-REE-o-dont] a plant-eating prehistoric animal about the size of a sheep (I, chap. 21, 189).

**oribi** a small, brownish African antelope, *Ourebia ourebia* (CD, 268).

**orichalk** the large brass coin of the Commonwealth, which is a day's pay for a common laborer (I, chap. 3, 31). See MEASUREMENT TABLES.

**oriflamme** a banner that is golden, bright, or conspicuous like the Oriflamme (banner) of Saint Denis (I, chap. 17, 158).

**Oringa** a name given in passing (V, chap. 41, 291), almost certainly the name of the little girl prisoner in the antechamber who warns Severian about taking the scarf left behind by the tormentors (II, chap. 16, 134). This girl is probably a member of the Kim Lee Soong group, not only because of her young age, but because she speaks of the funeral of the navigator: "When the navigator was buried there were black wagons and people in black clothes walking" (II, chap. 16, 134).

*History:* Oringa of the Cross (died 1310) was a Tuscan serving woman who, in spite of the fact that she passed most of her life in domestic service, founded a convent.

**Orithyia** a northern district of the Commonwealth, frontline of the Ascian War at the beginning of Severian's reign, and perhaps as much as twenty-two days' walking distance from Lake Diuturna. The pass of Orithyia is probably the strategic chokepoint that drew all the fighting, and the so-called springs of Gyoll are located here (III, chap. 12, 90). See THIRD BATTLE OF ORITHYIA.
*Myth:* (Greek) Oreithyia ("she who rages on the mountains"), daughter of Erechthous and Praxithea (King and Queen of Athens), was ravished by Boreas (the north wind). She became his wife and bore him twin sons and two daughters. (Boreas has serpent tails for feet, not unlike Abraxas.)

**orpiment** a bright yellow mineral substance used as a pigment called King's Yellow (IV, chap. 24, 191).

**Os** a town on the River Gyoll, at the mouth of the Fluminis, one day by boat downstream to Nessus (V, chap. 29, 206). To reach Thrax from Os by boat would require at least seven days, traveling upstream (V, chap. 32, 227–28).
*Latin:* "mouth"; hence, "opening," "source."

**Osela** a golden bird on a goldsmith's sign a few streets away from the Cygnet Inn of Nessus (ES, 33).
*History:* from a medal of a bird ordered by the doge (elected chief magistrate in the former republics of Venice and Genoa) as a

substitute for real birds usually presented to nobles on New Year's Day.

**ossifrage** the "bone breaker" bird of prey (II, chap. 17, 143), either (1) the Lammergeyer or Geir Eagle, or (2) the Osprey or fish-hawk.

**Ossipago** of the group Ossipago, Barbatus, and Famulimus, three creatures traveling backward through time in order to trace the history of the New Sun (III, chap. 33, 262). Ossipago is a short and stout automaton, a gruff former nursemaid for the two young Hierodules.
*Myth:* (Greek) Ossipago (one of Hera's titles) nurtured children's bones and kept them from breaking.

**ostiary** "that has charge of the door," a person assigned to guard a door (V, chap. 25, 179).

**ostler** a stableboy (I, chap. 26, 230).

**Other People** "We're the Other People, the folk of the Great Lords who dwell in the sea and underground" (V, chap. 7, 52). A broad group of creatures, from nixies to undines and beyond to mountain-sized beings like Abaia, as well as the man-apes and the large, unseen chthonic creature they flee to. The fact that Idas is a juvenile undine points to the possibility that the pandours on Trason's boat are the same. In the undine dream, Severian sees "great shapes — things hundreds of times larger than a man. Some seemed ships, and some clouds; one was a living head without a body; one had a hundred heads" (I, chap. 15, 140).

There is also a connection between the undines, who claim to be able to swim through space, and the Hierogrammates, who do swim through space.
*Myth:* merfolk, trolls, and similar legendary creatures.
*Commentary:* just as the devils of Christian theology are seen as "fallen angels" who rebelled against God and were cast down, it is probable that the Enemies of the New Sun are similarly disgraced denizens of Yesod. Another parallel can be found in the Islamic milieu of *The Arabian Nights,* where jinn (genies) are only evil if unconverted, but if brought around to the faith, they become angelic intermediaries between God and Man.

**oubliette** [OO-blee-ET] the subterranean levels of the Matachin Tower (I, chap. 3, 29).
*History:* literally, "a place of forgetting." A dungeon entered from above.

**Ouen** a middle-aged waiter at the Inn of Lost Loves (I, chap. 25, 221; I, chap. 26, 230; IV, chap. 37, 303–8). He tries to leave a note for Dorcas, who looks like the picture of his mother he has in a locket. See also ABBAN, TRUDO, and KITCHEN GIRL.
*Onomastics:* Welsh variant of Eugene, "wellborn" (Greek).
*History:* Saint Ouen (A.D. 610–684), son of Saint Authaire, founded the abbey of Rebais, became bishop of Rouen (641), and died near Paris. Saint Ouen is associated with deafness. Owen Tudor (died 1461) married the king's widow, Catherine of Valois, and founded the Tudor dynasty (Henry VII was his grandson).
*Commentary:* this character turns out to be the son of Dorcas and the father of Severian. Clute favors the Tudor allusion, especially because of the Ouen/Catherine pairing, and he notes, "the Tu-

dors, whose badge — like Severian's — is a Rose" (*Strokes,* 170). This notion is strengthened by the fact that when Ouen's name is first mentioned, it is shouted alongside that of another employee, Trudo, whose name is an anagram of "Tudor."

# P

**pace** see MEASUREMENT TABLES.

**pacho** (Spanish) toothed clubs from Mexico, Peru, et cetera (III, chap. 30, 242).

**paduasoy** a strong corded or grosgrain silk fabric, much worn in the 18th century by both sexes, of which Poult-De-Soie is the modern representative (I, chap. 16, 151).

**Paeon** honey steward of the House Absolute (circa 50 P.S.), he appears as an aquastor in visits to the old autarch, telling him that Severian will be the next autarch (IV, chap. 25, 207).
*Myth:* (Greek) Paeon (or "Paean") is a god identified with Apollo in his capacity as healer.
*History:* Saint Justinus, also known as Paeon, was martyred at Rome.

**pagne** "You will know your true love by her red pagne" (I, chap. 25, 223). Agia here makes a rude joke.
*History:* a loincloth, or a short petticoat, worn by uncivilized races, or retained by the more civilized as a part of their costume.

**Palaemon** the master torturer in charge of education during Severian's apprenticeship. He wears a "protruding optical device" (possibly a pair of spectacles, but more likely a cybernetic prosthetic) that permits him to see (I, chap. 1, 18). The guild has shrunk to two masters and less than twenty journeymen by the time of Severian. Palaemon taught Gurloes until Gurloes became journeyman, which must have been around 36 P.S. Palaemon then did something against his guild for which he was exiled. He may have even been demoted to journeyman during that time. The length of his exile is uncertain but it seems to have beeen at least twelve years between 35 P.S. to 21 P.S. The location of his exile appears to be down the river near the sea, which would be around Liti. Somehow he returned, and it seems he brought *Terminus Est* with him.

*Onomastics:* "wrestler" (Greek). (See PANTOCRATOR.)

*History:* Saint Palaemon was one of the earliest Egyptian hermits, closely associated with Pachomius in organizing the hermits on cenobitical lines.

*Myth:* (Greek) a marine deity connected with Poseidon, and identified by the Romans with Portunus (god of harbors). He was originally Melicertes, son of Ino, and became a marine god together with his mother when she cast herself with him into the sea. Ino became Leucothea, the White Goddess. There is another tradition according to Robert Graves: "At first, Heracles was called Alcaeus, or Palaemon" and he received the name Heracles from the Pythoness ("The Birth of Heracles" in *The Greek Myths*).

*Commentary:* Palaemon's name forms a cryptic link not only to the Other People (as a mythological name), but also to the Enemies of the New Sun (Abaia, his undines, and the codeword "pelagic" are all marine oriented). This could be an important clue as to the nature of his crime against the guild. (Leucothea plays a large part in the *Soldier* series and *There Are Doors.*)

The question remains as to how Palaemon could have been a journeyman (according to Winnoc) when exiled. Perhaps he was stripped of his master rank, and later when he returned to the tower (with *Terminus Est,* it seems), he was reinstated as a master. His story may be the original solution to "The Feast of Saint Catherine."

**palatinate** the territory or district under the rule or jurisdiction of a palatine or count-palatine, a lord having sovereign power over a province (I, chap. 18, 164). In the Middle Ages Hungary, Poland, and Lithuania (to name a few) were palatinates.
*Commentary:* the territory implies a corresponding rank of earl-palatine, palatine, count-palatine, or palsgrave.

**palfrenier** a groom (I, chap. 8, 84).

**palinode** "how strange it was that they should have been so brave when they faced a horror, but such cowards when confronted by the palinode of fate" (V, chap. 31, 219).
*History:* an ode or song in which the author retracts something said in a former poem; hence, generally a recantation.

**palmer** a pilgrim wearing palm leaves as proof of a holy visit (I, chap. 17, 160).

**Pancreator** Creator of All, a title or aspect of the INCREATE (II, chap. 3, 24).
*Myth:* a partial list of creator gods drawn from world mythology would include Allah, Ahura-Mazda, Amen, Brahma, El, Elohim, Ptah, and Quetzalcoatl.

**pandours** super-soldiers inside the Wall at the Piteous Gate (I, chap. 35, 299), also used for the strangely pale soldiers seen on Trason's boat (IV, chap. 37, 301).
*History:* "soldiers of unusual size and strength, originally recruited from private guards, gamekeepers, and the like" (CD, 249).

**Panjudicator** Judge of All, another title or aspect of the INCREATE (I, chap. 31, 264).
*Myth:* to show the spectrum of deities of judgment, justice, and law, here are a few figures drawn from world mythology: Marduk, Nemesis, Osiris, Shamash, Themis, Yama, and Zeus. (Of this group, Marduk, Osiris, and Shamash are noteworthy as they are also solar gods.)

**panoply** a magnificent array (II, chap. 9, 79).

**pantheon** a temple consecrated to all the gods (III, chap. 1, 9).

**pantocrator** "enameled pictures of ascetic pantocrators and hypostases with black halos" (I, chap. 6, 67). Images found in the green book.
*History:* "those who have mastered the physical. Also, incarnations of the Pancreator. Those fit for spiritual and philosophical 'wrestling.' Originally, the word designated what we would call all-around athletes; but its figurative meanings have overwhelmed its literal one" (CD, 237).
*Commentary:* this term also figures in the *Soldier* series, which is about ancient Greece, after all.

**paphian** pertaining to love; especially pertaining to, or devoted to, unlawful sexual indulgence; belonging to the class of prostitutes (I, chap. 9, 91). From Greek Paphos, ancient city of Cyprus that was the center of Aphrodite worship.

**Paraclete** in the Commonwealth, a name or aspect of the INCREATE (II, chap. 24, 217).
*Myth:* a title of the Holy Spirit; properly "an advocate, one called upon for assistance, and intercessor" but often taken as equal to "comforter."

**paracoita** the female partner in sexual intercourse (I, chap. 30, 257). (The male partner is the paracoitus.)

**Paralian** the name of a group or race living in the northern, presumably coastal region of the Commonwealth (IV, chap. 35, 288).
*History:* a dweller by the sea.

**paramour** a lover, of either sex, especially in an adulterous relationship, or (archaic) a sweetheart (I, chap. 10, 98).

**pardal** "Isn't there a story about a hunter's daughter who was blessed by a pardal, so that beads of jet fell from her mouth when she spoke?" (III, chap. 10, 78).
*History:* another name for the panther or leopard; more commonly identified with the leopard when this was supposed to be distinct from the panther.

**pardine limers** leopard-spotted hounds hunted on the leash so that they will not overtake the peccaries (wild pigs) before the hunters do (I, chap. 10, 98).

**par-terre** a flat garden, as opposed to a landscaped one, and particularly a garden (or garden-like area) in which large potted plants, statues, and the like stand on a floor or pavement (I, chap. 16, 151).

**Pascua** "When my grandmother was young, there was a villa in my country so remote that no one ever came there. It belonged to an armiger, a feudatory of the Liege of Pascua" (IV, chap. 13, 100). The name of a Commonwealth town or province on the pampas.
*Latin:* a pasture. Note that Commonwealth towns and villages are often named after the local terrain.

**paterissa** "And so I trudged along under stars brightened by the wind, no longer a torturer in the eyes of the few who passed me, but only a somberly clad traveler who shouldered a dark paterissa" (I, chap. 14, 131).
*History:* a staff topped by a cross.

**Patizithes** Prince of Vert (in EFF) who seduces the child traveling with Father Thyme (SS, 249). She becomes pregnant with a son who she names Barrus.
*History:* in the ancient Middle East, a Median magus who was left in charge of Cambyses's household when the latter went on his campaign against Egypt. Patizithes plotted revolt against Cambyses and carried it out in 525 B.C. by setting his brother Gaumata

on the throne under the name of Smerdis. In 521 B.C. Darius killed Gaumata and founded the Persian Empire.

**pavonine** of or pertaining to, resembling, or characteristic of a peacock (I, chap. 16, 152).

**peccary** a wild pig that is small but very aggressive (I, chap. 7, 72). It can be found in herds as large as twenty or thirty members.

**Pega** the armigette Pelagia's servant (V, chap. 44, 312), she claims she had been a soubrette (a lady's maid, or perhaps a saucy maid) but Odillo says she was an ancilla (a handmaid). One of the few survivors of the deluge, she is later deified as the day goddess of Ushas (V, chap. 51, 367).
*Onomastics:* "pega" is a word for the figurehead of a ship (Phoenician).
*History:* Saint Pega (died 719), sister of Saint Guthlac, was reputed to have cured a man of blindness.

**Pelagia** an armigette at the House Absolute, employer of Pega, who died in the deluge (V, chap. 44, 312).
*Onomastics:* "from the sea" (Greek).
*History:* there are three saints Pelagia, but the most historical one seems to be Pelagia of Antioch (died 311), a martyred virgin who was a disciple of Saint Lucian of Antioch. She was greatly praised by Saint John Chrysostom.
*Commentary:* Robert Borski feels her name is so close to "pelagic" that she must be an agent of Abaia (*Solar Labyrinth,* 16). He also wonders about the close similarity between the names "Pelagia" and "Pega."

**pelagic** a term used as a codeword among the Vodalarii as an allusion to Abaia (II, chap. 11, 97). The fact that Thecla uses it points to her own divided loyalties (I, chap. 10, 97).
*History:* of or pertaining to the open or high sea, as distinguished from the shallow water near the coast; oceanic.

**pele tower** a tower-house, like a small keep, in or near the marches of Scotland (III, chap. 33, 260). The barmkin is an enclosure subsidiary to a pele.

**Pelerine** a member of the group of monials that has the Claw of the Conciliator (I, chap. 18, 167). The name comes from the short, red cape that is part of their habit. This cape is scarlet silk, with tassels along the fringe, and it might be attached to the scarlet hood worn by all the monials or at least the domnicellae.

It is "a rather aristocratic order" (IV, chap. 10, 77) of armigettes and exultants. "Occasionally an optimate's daughter . . . is admitted, when the optimate has been a longtime friend of the the order," but Ava is one of only three (77).

Pelerines in the text include Ava (postulant), possibly Catherine (who left after vows), Cyriaca (who left before vows), Domnicellae, Einhildis, Epicharis, a historian (see Winnoc), Mannea, and NURSE.
*History:* a mantle or cape worn by women, from the feminine form of Pilgrim's mantle or cape in French. Made of fur or cloth, it is close-fitting, usually waist-length in back and having long ends in front like a tippet.
*Commentary:* the domnicellae's garment is something like a red riding hood.

**pelisses** long fur cloaks; similar cloaks of cloth trimmed with fur (I, chap. 35, 297). Mentioned erroneously by Jolenta when she is trying to remember the word "pelerines."

**peltast** a type of soldier in Nessus (I, chap. 14, 132). The peltasts carry transparent shields and blazing spears, and they guard the bridge that connects the living city with the semi-ruinous Algedonic Quarter.
*History:* a kind of foot soldier, between heavy-armed and light-armed, furnished with a pelta (or light shield) and a short spear or javelin.

**pelycosaur** "sail reptile," the earliest known mammal-like reptiles, from the Permian period (I, chap. 23, 206). The sail-fin dinosaurs.
*Commentary:* the reptile Severian sees in the Jungle Garden (I, chap. 20, 181) may in fact be only a kind of iguana.

**penetralia** from a Vodalus related password "quercine penetralia" (II, chap 11, 97). The innermost parts of a building; the inner sanctum.

**pentad** a period of five years (III, chap. 6, 50).

**pentadactyl** Severian's name for the Ascian air-striding machines (IV, chap. 21, 167).
*Greek:* "having five fingers or toes."

**peon** "A hairy figure rose . . . and cut them down as a peon hews a tree" (IV, chap. 22, 182). A sub-class of the peasantry.

*History:* a day-laborer in Spanish America; (Mexico) a debtor held in servitude by his creditor until his debts are worked off.

**peregrine** a typical species of falcon *(Falco peregrinus)* of very wide distribution and held in the greatest esteem for hawking since ancient times (III, chap. 28, 223).

**perfume** there are at least three noteworthy examples of perfume used in *The Book of the New Sun.* Foremost is Thecla's scent, used by herself and her khaibit, which is that of a burning rose. Then there is the scented scarf left behind by the tormentors in the antechamber (II, chap. 16, 134). Finally there is the musk of Abdiesus.

**peri** [PEE-ree] in Persian mythology, one of a race of superhuman beings, originally represented as of evil or malevolent character, but subsequently as good genii, fairies, or angels, endowed with grace and beauty (IV, chap. 3, 27).

**peridot** a name of the chrysolite; a jeweler's term for the variety of chrysolite called Olivine (III, chap. 4, 40).

**perischii** [pear-ISH-ih-eye] variant of "Periscii," a legendary people dwelling within the polar circles, whose shadows revolve around them as the sun moves around the heavens on a summer day (III, chap. 5, 46).
*Commentary:* Erebus's antarctic people must be known by this name.

**peryton** the name of a constellation that to Severian looks like a sort of fantastic pterodactyl (III, chap. 13, 101).
*History:* any creature (animal, demon, et cetera) that flies with batlike wings.
*Myth:* in *The Book of Imaginary Beings,* Borges reports the Sibyl of Erythraea prophecy that Rome would finally be destroyed by the perytons. A peryton is said to be half deer and half bird, with the head and legs of a deer. Instead of casting its own shadow, it casts the shadow of a man.
*Astronomy:* possibly our constellation Phoenix (visible in the southern hemisphere) or, less likely, our Pegasus.

**Pestis** what some people called the town of "The Tale of the Town That Forgot Fauna" (V, chap. 33, 232).
*Latin:* ruin, pest.

**petasos** a type of hat worn by men in the audience of the play at the House Absolute (II, chap. 25, 238). A variant of "petasus," a low-crowned broad-brimmed hat worn by the ancient Greeks, and frequently represented as worn by the god Hermes or Mercury.

**Petronax** a peltast at the bridge in Nessus who fails to believe that Severian is a torturer until Severian uses a grip on him (I, chap. 14, 135).
*History:* Saint Petronax (died 747) is known as the second founder of Montecassino.

**Petronax's lochage** a commander keeping the peace at the bridge in Nessus, he quickly realizes that Severian is a real torturer rather than an armiger in costume (I, chap. 14, 132). (See also commentary for MUTTON.)

**Phaleg** the Hierodule name for the planet Verthandi (IV, chap. 31, 247).
*Occult:* the governing spirit of planet Mars, often called the Warlord. Of the 196 Olympic Provinces, Phaleg has dominion over thirty-five.

**pharmacon** a medicine, drug, or poison (I, chap. 6, 65).

**phenocod** [FEEN-ah-code] an animal that skulks around battlefields in Orithyia (IV, chap. 23, 185).
*History:* from "phenacodus," a prehistoric carnivorous mammal about the size of a goat, being 5.5 feet in length from head to base of tail. Fore and hind feet have five digits ending in small hoofs. Adapted to moving in forests and on soft ground, but performance on the plains would have been inferior to that of a gazelle or donkey. Late Paleocene to middle Eocene in North America and Europe.

**philomath** a lover of learning; a student, especially of mathematics, natural philosophy, and the like; formerly popularly applied to an astrologer or prognosticator (II, chap. 14, 125).

**philonoist** a searcher for knowledge (III, chap. 16, 126).

**philosophist** one who is a lover of sophistry (III, chap. 38, 295).

**Phlegethon** "Who in Phlegethon are you?" (I, chap. 23, 203).

*Myth:* a fabled river of fire, one of the five rivers of Hades.
*Literature:* in Dante's *Inferno,* Phlegethon runs as a river of boiling blood through the seventh circle, inhabited by violent souls of tyrants and warmongers like Attila and Alexander the Great. Centaurs guard the bathers, and it is Nessus (significantly) who carries Dante and Virgil across the river.

**Phocas** mentioned by Lomer as the reason he came to the House Absolute, since his mistress Nympha wanted to review the accounts of her estate "while she attended the rites of the philomath Phocas" (II, chap. 15, 125).
*History:* Saint Phocas (died 117) was the bishop of Sinope on the Black Sea, put to death during the reign of Trajan; Saint Phocas the Gardener (died 303), native of Sinope, was beheaded during Diocletian's persecution.

**phoebad** [FEE-bad] one possessed by a spirit of divination, traditionally Phoebus or Apollo (III, chap. 38, 295).

**Phoenix** one of the symbols of the Autarch; for example, his throne is called "the Phoenix Throne."
*Myth:* the Egyptian myth of "benu," a cyclical and deathless bird, was elaborated upon by the ancient Greeks and Romans and is widespread. The Chinese Phoenix (male "Feng" and female "Huang") in prehistoric times visited the gardens and palaces of virtuous emperors as a visible token of celestial favor. Feng lives in the sun, and together with Huang forms the emblem of everlasting love.

**phororhacos** a misspelling of *Phorusrhacos* [FOR-russ-HOCK-us], a genus of gigantic flightless birds from the Miocene period of Patagonia (II, chap. 10, 88).

**phrontiserion** "Probably the old phrontiserion has interceded for her erring child, eh?" (V, chap. 37, 264).
*History:* one who is in charge of a phrontistery: a place for thinking or studying; a "thinking-shop."

**Phul** (entry from SOLAR SYSTEM TABLE) lord of the moon and seven of the Olympian Provinces; "Supreme Lord of the Waters" is one of his titles.

**physician at the hulk** this man gives a "rational" explanation for the Conciliator surviving a hit from the convulsor (V, chap. 36, 258). (In Typhon's era the Matachin Tower is simply called "the hulk.")

**Pia** a woman of Lake Diuturna's floating isles who is "precisely the same age" as Severian (III, chap. 28, 229). When Severian first meets her she is a slave of Zambdas, hetman of Murene. He frees her when he escapes.
*Onomastics:* "pious" (Italian).
*History:* Saint Pia (2nd century) was in a group put to death in Numidia, Africa.

**Piaton** Typhon's head was grafted onto this slave, who has a heroic physique (III, chap. 25, 202). The idea was that after Typhon's head took over all functions, Piaton's head would be removed. Piaton lacks vocal cords, but he mouths the words "Kill me" to Severian, providing the trick that gets the job done. *History:* Saint Piaton (died 286?), born in Benevento, Italy, was sent to Gaul and was probably slain at Tournai during the persecution of Maximian.

**Pietist** one who hopes to achieve direct contact with the Increate; a follower of a 17th-century religious movement originating in Germany that stressed informal meetings, Bible study, and personal religious experience (I, chap. 20, 180).

**pika** any of several small, tailless, harelike mammals of the genus *Ochotona,* of the mountains of North America and Eurasia (V, chap. 4, 25). Also called "cony."

**pilani** experienced Roman soldiers, drawn up in the third rank, behind the two ranks of antepilani (IV, chap. 35, 288). Also known as "triari."

**pilaster** a rectangular column set into a wall (I, chap. 18, 165).

**pilete** a simple pole of wood tipped with iron, not enhanced by pyrotechnology, as a hastarus is (II, chap. 2, 17). A pike, according to Stone.

**pinakotheken** [PINE-uh-ko-THEE-ken] a place for the keeping and exhibition of pictures and other works of art; a picture gallery (I, chap. 5, 49). *Mrs. Byrne's Dictionary* gives *pinacotheca* for the singular, and pinakotheken seems to be the plural form (art galleries). Ultimately the word comes from Greek.

**Pinian** Zama's employer, the man owning the boat (v, chap. 31, 222). Zama had been boarding at Pinian's house.
*History:* Saint Pinian, a missionary of Saint Patrick, became a patron saint of Cornish tin miners.

**piquenaires** pikemen (II, chap. 24, 215).

**Piteous Gate** the northern gate to the city of Nessus. Mystery surrounds the incident at the gate closing *The Shadow of the Torturer.* There is a security alert ahead of Severian's group, triggered by one of Hethor's pets or something unrelated to visible events of *The Book of the New Sun.*

**planteration** using food as a torment (III, chap. 4, 36).

**platybelodon** on Urth, used as a beast of burden by the Ascians (IV, chap. 29, 231).
*History:* an elephant-sized shovel-tusker mammal. Short and broad tusks were presumably used to dig up the soil for edible roots. From Asia during the Pliocene.

**pleasance** a secluded garden or landscaped area, or (archaic) "pleasure" or "a source of pleasure" (I, chap. 20, 184).
*Commentary:* uttered by Father Inire, this word was also the middle name of Alice Liddell, Lewis Carroll's muse for the Alice novels. Carroll put a poem before *Through the Looking Glass* and another one after it: the name "Pleasance" appears in both. Father Inire's two passions seem to be mirrors and little girls: his interest in his child friends is a little frightening in its intensity (Domnina

is never sure whether or not she's returned to the world she left through Father Inire's looking glass).

**pochette** "a pochette was knocked from the table and broken" (ES, 214).
*History:* a handbag.

**pointille** the result of a painting technique characterized by the application of paint in small dots that blend together when seen from a distance (V, chap. 38, 271).

**pomegranate** tree bearing a fruit of the same name, said fruit being large, red, seedy berries about the size of an apple (I, chap. 16, 151). Severian later eats a pomegranate fruit for breakfast at Ctesiphon's Cross (I, chap. 34, 287).

**pommander ball** (misspelling or variant of pomander ball) a case or box for holding pomander, a mixture of aromatic substances formerly worn as protection against odor and infection (II, chap. 19, 173).

**popul vuh** "all the things people have said were The Secret after they had . . . studied the *popul vuh* of the magicians" (I, chap. 32, 272).
*History:* (meaning "what is written on leaves" or "book of the community") sacred book of the ancient Quiche Maya Indians of Guatemala. It is divided into four parts: the first deals with the creation of the world, the second and third are concerned with the heroes of the Indians, and the last gives myths of cult origins, accounts of tribal wars, and records of historic rulers.

**Porter, Brother** the man responsible for guarding the Corpse Door at the Matachin Tower (I, chap. 2, 19). According to Wolfe he is a regular torturer of the guild who does not actually do any torturing. The Brother Porter of Typhon's era uses a carnificial sword (V, chap. 36, 256). (See also AYBERT, BROTHER; COOK, BROTHER; and CORBINIAN, BROTHER.)

**portico** a porch or walkway with a roof supported by columns, often leading to the entrance of a building (I, chap. 9, 87).

**portreeve** a bailiff having broad powers (I, chap. 29, 249). "Here the civilian official who assists the chiliarch by keeping order among the civilians present in the military compound, and in conducting the trials of civilian offenders arrested by his troops" (CD, 247). The one in question is attached to the fortress occupied by the Xenagie of the Blue Dimarchi when Severian visits. He is an imposing man with a high, white forehead like the belly of a pitcher.
*History:* the ruler or chief officer of a town or borough.

**potboy** a boy or young man employed by a tavern to carry pots of ale or beer to the customers. The text has a few notable cases.

- the "dirty boy" at the Inn of Lost Loves (I, chap. 26, 231), who tells of Trudo and the KITCHEN GIRL (233), is probably a potboy.
- Ouen had been a potboy starting at age ten (IV, chap. 37, 304).
- a potboy at the Chowder Inn of Typhon's era helps Declan and Harena (V, chap. 33, 237).

**power boat** exclusively maintained and used by the military in the reign of Typhon, this class of high-tech vehicle vanishes from the face of Urth long before the reign of Severian (v, chap. 35, 249).

**Prehistoric Eras** in order to put the post-historic Urth (see HISTORY OF URTH) into perspective, it is helpful to reference a timeline of pre-history.

| Era | Years Ago | Life Forms |
|---|---|---|
| Precambrian | 4,000 to 600 million | Algae |
| Paleozoic | 600 to 225 million | Early animals |
| Mesozoic | 225 to 65 million | Dinosaurs |
| Cenozoic | 65 million to present | Mammals |

The Mesozoic Era ended with a major die-off called the Cretaceous-Tertiary (KT) extinction, probably caused by a meteor strike. Approximately half of all genera became extinct, including all of the non-avian dinosaurs. Many of the creatures described in this lexicon come from the Cenozoic Era which followed, so a more detailed look at this period is in order.

**Epochs of the Cenozoic**

| Epoch | Years Ago | Life Forms | Endpoint |
|---|---|---|---|
| Paleocene | 65 to 56 million | barylambda<br>coryphodon<br>diatryma | No extinction. |
| Eocene | 56 to 34 million | basilosaur<br>oreodont | The Grande Coupure, a major extinction due to a meteor impact. |
| Oligocene | 34 to 23 million | arsinoither<br>baluchither<br>metamynodon | No extinction. |
| Miocene | 23 to 5.3 million | phorusrhacos<br>trilophodon | No extinction. |
| Pliocene | 5.3 to 1.8 million | aelurodon<br>merychip<br>platybelodon<br>thylacosmil | A major extinction, possibly due to supernovas. |
| Pleistocene | 1.8 million to 11,550 | arctother<br>cathartidae<br>cynocephalus<br>glyptodon<br>(humans)<br>mammoth<br>megather<br>smilodon<br>teratornis | The last Ice Age. |

**Preceptress** the title Isangoma uses for Marie in the Jungle Garden, from "preceptor," a teacher, instructor (1, chap. 21, 188).

**primesong** the song sung at Prime, the first hour of the day, at 6 A.M. or sunrise (ES, 29). See WATCHES OF THE DAY.

**Prisca, Prefect** a figure universally hated as a sadistic leader of the jailers (prototype of the torturers) during the reign of Typhon (v, chap. 36, 258). Her crime is apparently that of acting as judge and executioner, rather than simply being an impartial tool of judicial sentencing. She is one of the few people killed by the Conciliator.
*Onomastics:* "ancient, venerable" (Latin).
*History:* Saint Prisca was a 3rd-century virgin martyr (died 270?) venerated from ancient times (the Prisca Acts was important to the early church). A church on the Aventine in Rome is dedicated in her honor, but nothing authentic is known of her.

**prisoners** an entry to list the inhabitants of the four prisons found in Severian's narrative.

ANTECHAMBER PRISONERS

- Kim Lee Soong group.
- Lomer.
- Nicarete.
- Oringa.

HULK PRISONERS

- Canog.
- Hundred and Two.

MATACHIN TOWER PRISONERS

- Catherine.
- Furniture woman, who makes furniture from children (IV, chap. 34, 274–75).
- Hunna.

- The insane one (I, chap. 7, 78).
- Marcellina.
- Prisoner in Thecla's cell, who spins a contradictory account about his conviction involving his wife, his mother-in-law, his sister-in-law, and some gold (IV, chap. 34, 273–74). Robert Borski speculates this man is Trudo.
- Thecla.

VINCULA PRISONERS
- Maden.
- Madern.

**Prophetess** a role in Dr. Talos's play, *Eschatology and Genesis* (II, chap. 2, 13). This role is played in real life at the Deluge of House Absolute by JADER'S SISTER (V, chap. 2, 13).

**proscenium** the wall that separates a theatrical stage from the seating area, including the arch over the stage (I, chap. 16, 149). The arch is often highly decorated.

**Proust, Marcel** one of Wolfe's favorite authors. In Proust's monumental *Remembrance of Things Past* we find stages of love for the Duchess (seemly mirrored by Severian's stages with Thecla), social climbing (like Pip in *Great Expectations,* which is in contrast to Claudius of *I, Claudius),* and a certain richness of narrative texture.

A few suggestive quotes (from Moncrieff & Kilmartin translation, Vintage edition).

ALIENS AMONG US

"Albertine had deceived me as to her profoundest humanity, the fact that she did not belong to ordinary humanity, but to an alien race which moves among it, hides itself among it and never merges with it" (*The Fugitive,* 537).

THECLA AS ALBERTINE

"Sometimes . . . I felt that the Albertine of long ago, invisible to my eyes, was nevertheless enclosed within me as in the *Piombi* of an inner Venice, the tight lid of which some incident occasionally lifted to give me a glimpse of the past.

"Thus for instance one evening a letter from my stockbroker reopened for me for an instant the gates of the prison in which Albertine dwelt within me, alive, but so remote, so profoundly buried that she remained inaccessible to me" (*The Fugitive,* 654).

[Receiving a telegram while still coming to grips with Albertine's sudden death] "I opened it as soon as I was in my room, and, glancing through the message which was filled with inaccurately transmitted words, managed nevertheless to make out: 'My dear friend, you think me dead, forgive me, I am quite alive, I long to see you, talk about marriage, when do you return? Affectionately. Albertine'" (*The Fugitive,* 656).

MULTIVERSE AS VANILLA BEAN

"Like so many creatures of the animal and vegetable kingdoms, like the plant which would produce vanilla but, because in its structure the male organ is separated by a partition from the female, remains sterile unless the hummingbirds or certain tiny bees convey the pollen from one to the other, or man fertilises them by artificial means" (*Cities of the Plain*, 650).

**pseudothyrum** (Latin) a secret door (III, chap. 6, 54).

**psychopomp** "It's like encountering a psychopomp" (I, chap. 17, 155).
*History:* a conductor of souls to the place of the dead.

**pteriope** Agia says to Severian, "and in the end you will come into my hands again, as you did when our pteriopes took you from the evzones" (IV, chap. 30, 241). Vodalus's forces are augmented by several of these white flying monsters, with hands three times human size and beaks like scimitars (IV, chap. 25, 211), drawn from the mirrors by Hethor the thaumaturgist. Severian recognizes the thing as one from his dream when he shared a bed with Baldanders (I, chap. 15, 139), but in that dream he was riding rather than being carried (i.e., it was Agia's point of view). The monster may be a leathery Harpy: "Her beak was of an ibis, her face the face of a hag; on her head was a miter of bone" (140). The headdress part sounds like the antlers of the PERYTONS.
*History:* "those able to fly from birth," usually applied to pterosaurs on the assumption that the young received no care from their parents.

**purlieu** the parts about the border of any place; the outskirts (V, chap. 2, 10).

**Purn** a blond sailor on Tzadkiel's ship (V, chap. 2, 13). At first it seems he is not from Urth, but that he probably visited when

Lune was still white (v, chap. 4, 27). Idas says Purn is from Urth (v, chap. 7, 53). Later Purn admits he signed on from the era of Severian's reign in order to kill Severian (v, chap. 12, 84).
*Commentary:* "Purn" is probably a nickname form of a longer name, just as "Gunnie" is derived from "Burgundofara," and "Zak" from "Tzadkiel."

**pursuivant** an assistant to a herald (I, chap. 7, 78). A messenger with some limited authority to negotiate.

**pylon** a pyramidal or conical marker (I, chap. 19, 174).

**Pyrexia** a woman of Saltus sealed in her house for a season eighteen years prior to the reign of Severian (II, chap. 2, 17). She had changed into something very strange when the house was opened, a nocturnal creature, and was quickly killed (with fire, it seems).
*Commentary:* Pyrexia means "Fever." Mother Pyrexia is not really her name; it is what the people called her. The alcalde does not remember her real name. There is a weird connection between Mother Pyrexia and MORWENNA.

**pyrolater** a fire worshipper (v, chap. 44, 310).

**pyx** the Host case or ciborium, or a ship's binnacle: the non-magnetic stand that the compass rests upon (III, chap. 38, 297).

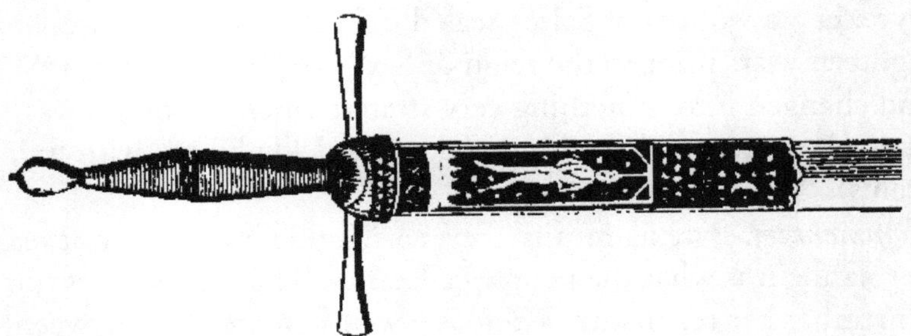

*Quillions*

**quadrille** "Now the Autarch can't play quadrille with five hundred women" (I, chap. 7, 75). A card game played by four persons with forty cards, the eights, nines, and tens of the ordinary pack being discarded. Here used as a euphemism for sexual congress.

**quaesitor** an official who signals the carnifex to begin his task (I, chap. 14, 129).
*Latin:* investigator, inquirer, especially judicial.

**Quartillosa** a famous male artist, long dead by Severian's time (I, chap. 5, 51).
*History:* Saint Quartillosa (died 259) was put to death with her husband, son, and others during the persecution of Solon.

**Quasar** a ship that Hethor served on (I, chap. 30, 257).
*History:* the word was coined by astronomers in the 1960s to name a class of "quasi-stellar radio sources" that had been discovered. A quasar can release energy in levels equal to the output of hundreds of galaxies combined, and it does this as a single point source. Quasars are often found to be moving at relativistic speeds.
*Commentary:* Wolfe is slyly suggesting that quasars are starships. Quasar, like Maser, is one of the more modern words in the Urth Cycle.

**quercine penetralia** a Vodalus related password, the (perhaps secret) name of the Vodalarii forest (II, chap. 11, 97). "Quercine" is from the Latin "quercus," meaning oak. Thus the password probably means something like "the oaken inner sanctum." Oak is a sacred tree for many thunder gods and is host to the parasite mistletoe that was venerated by the Druids.

**Quiesco** a town or village in the Commonwealth, located on Gyoll between Saltus and the House Absolute (II, chap. 13, 112). It takes a few days of sailing upstream, both day and night, to get from Saltus to Quiesco.
*Latin:* "I rest," from "quiescere," to rest; to be at peace; to sleep; to cease (from action).

**quillions** the arms of a simple cross guard on a blade weapon (I, chap. 31, 264).

**Racho** an armiger first encountered by Severian in the picture gallery of the Citadel (I, chap. 5, 50), and later the passenger patron of the fiacre against whom Agia and Severian race (I, chap. 18, 164), a trial that ends in the destruction of the altar of the Pelerines.
*Onomastics:* variant of Horace, from Horatius, a Roman family name which may be related to "hora" (time). (Making the fiacre contest a "race against time"?)
*History:* Saint Racho of Autun (died 660), also known as Ragnobert, was the first bishop of Autun, France.
*Commentary:* Robert Borski speculates that Racho is the absent husband of Cyriaca (*Solar Labyrinth,* 94). An argument against this intriguing idea is that a week before Severian meets Cyriaca alone at the party, Cyriaca and her husband had appeared in court at Thrax to charge a peon with theft (III, chap. 5, 44). Cyriaca had first seen Severian there, in his role as lictor, and presumably Severian would have recognized Racho, or, failing that, have heard the name spoken in the course of the trial.

**Racho's armiger companion** someone who seems to be telling Racho about the necropolis grave-robbing episode of chapter one (I, chap. 5, 49). He does not recognize Severian's clothing, but Racho does. He gives Severian directions on how to get to the library, directions that Rudesind scoffs at.

**Racho's female companion** a woman in the fiacre with Racho (I, chap. 18, 164). Agia claims she is a prostitute who has been riding in the carriage for half the night. (See FIACRE for the connection between prostitution and carriage.)

**raddle** to beat, thrash (II, chap. 24, 226).

**ransieur** this pyrotechnic pole arm used on Urth by the Ascian army probably fires one beam forward and two quartering beams to either side, like a korseke (IV, chap. 28, 230).
*History:* a 16th- and 17th-century staff weapon with a three-pronged head comprising a long double-edged spike flanked by two short upcurved blades. Also known as "rawcon."

**rat** the rats of the Library of Nessus seem to be intelligent, as they have a written language and are capable of a crude architecture (I, chap. 6, 58). Perhaps the rat's heightened brainpower is an effect of the erudite nature of its environment.

**rebec** variant of "rebeck," a musical instrument (I, chap. 11, 106).

**Reechy** the nickname of Ymar during his time as an apprentice jailer (V, chap. 38, 268). He says, "It means I stink." The word, meaning "smoky, squalid, dirty, rancid," was used by Shakespeare. Reechy offers Severian coins to buy extra food, but Severian is reluctant to take them, so Reechy throws them down (V, chap. 37, 261). This action is later codified as the method by which torturers are paid: see CHILIARCH OF THE XENAGIE OF THE BLUE DIMARCHI.

**refulgence** splendor, brightness, radiance (IV, chap. 21, 165).

**Religion** there is a hint that belief in a personal cycle of incarnations is not unusual in the Commonwealth, as Master Gurloes says, "Doubtless I had aquired merit in a previous life, as I hope I have in this one" (I, chap. 7, 76).

**remontado** "the remontados burning their own homes and setting their eyes upon the mountains" (III, chap. 5, 42).
*History:* someone who has fled to the mountains; a person who has renounced civilization.

**rheostat** "There were cables to be wound from one part of the examination room to another, rheostats and magnetic amplifiers to be adjusted" (I, chap. 12, 116).
*History:* a variable resistor used to control the flow of current in an electrical circuit, like a dimmer switch on a lamp.

**ridotto** an entertainment or social assembly consisting of music and dancing (III, chap. 5, 42).

**Robert and Marie** these missionaries, apparently from the 20th century (Severian sees what appears to be a propeller-driven airplane), are glimpsed in the Botanical Gardens of Nessus (I, chap. 21, 188–92) and later referred to as "the woman and her brother" (II, chap. 31, 294).
*Commentary:* since Robert recalls art school in Paris, it seems we should know him. Some have guessed that he is Robert Louis Stevenson, but RLS wasn't a missionary and his expatriate experience was in the South Pacific rather than the Jungle Garden's

blend of East Indies (based on the tree *caesalipinia sappan*, found in Indonesia) and African rainforest (based on TOKOLOSHE).

Robert Borski points out that there is also a link to Wolfe's non-Urth novel *Peace,* which has minor characters Reverend Carl Lorn and his wife Emerald, or "Em" for short. The Lorns hope to become missionaries: as Em herself explains it, "The South Seas is what I'd like . . . but Carl, he wants Africa" (104). Paris is mentioned, and Em says "I've never been there . . . I'd like to go someday and so would Carl" (98), forming an obvious resonance with Robert.

**robot** "'Why you're all three just robots!' (You must understand that . . . there had been a strong Czech influence on this planet)" (CD, 272). The word "robot" is not used on Urth, where "android" is used for mechanical men, and "homunculus" designates an artificial man of organic origin.
*History:* from *robata*, a Czech word meaning "forced labor" that first appeared in Capek's play *R.U.R.* (1921; trans. 1923), but the robots in question were artificial men of organic origin, not the mechanical men that the term has since come to mean.

**Roche** [ROCK] an apprentice torturer, boyhood friend of Severian (I, chap. 1, 9). He has red hair, which links him to fire in the text (I, chap. 9, 88; III, chap. 28, 231). He is elevated to journeyman the year before Severian, suggesting that he is one year older. He takes Severian to the House Azure.
*Onomastics:* "rest" (German/Italian).
*History:* there are two Saints Roche: one (died 1337) was a citizen of Montpelier in France who devoted his life to helping the plague-stricken, and the other was a martyr of Paraguay.

**rood** "There were pretty things in the window. Trays and boxes, and a rood" (I, chap. 23, 204). One of Dorcas's first recovered memories, later on this is revealed to be about the cloisonné shop she ran with her husband, and it shows the types of things they sold.
*History:* a cross.
*Commentary:* based on this passage, Gregory Feeley suspects that Dorcas's family made crucifixes for the Pelerines.

**rosolio** a sweet Mediterranean liqueur of brandy and raisins, or a sour black currant wine mentioned in Thackeray's *The Great Haggarty Diamond* (III, chap. 4, 38).

**rotunda** a circular building, hall, or room, especially one with a dome (I, chap. 16, 151).

**roundsman** one who makes rounds of inspection, a patrol man (I, chap. 14, 132).

**Rudesind** the picture-cleaning curator of the pinakotheken in the Citadel (I, chap. 5, 51). He is roughly eighty-five years old when Severian first meets him: "I was just a boy . . . seventy years ago" (IV, chap. 35, 285).

Rudesind mentions that he has cleaned the Astronaut on the Moon painting on three occasions: the first time as an apprentice just learning to clean, the second after the birth of his second daughter, when his wife was still alive, and the third on the day that Severian meets him.

As a youth he was an artist and he once modeled for a portrait by Fechin (II, chap. 20, 179–80). Rudesind is looking for this

portrait, in a situation that seems hauntingly similar to the quest of Dorcas's husband. Twice he has cleaned it.
*History:* Saint Rudesind (A.D. 907–977) was born of a noble family in Spanish Galacia, and he became bishop of Mondonedo at the age of eighteen.

# S

**Sabaoth** mentioned in "The Boy Who Hooked the Sun" (SS, 217).
*Hebrew:* Lord of Hosts.

**sabarcane** "with the [staff's] head removed it had formed a sabarcane for shooting poisoned darts" (III, chap. 22, 181).
*French:* a blowgun.

**Sabas of the Parted Meadow** another monomachist at the Sanguinary Field (I, chap. 27, 235). See also LAURENTIA OF THE HOUSE OF THE HARP and CADROE OF THE SEVENTEEN STONES.
*Onomastics:* "elderly man," or "born on Saturday."
*History:* Saint Sabas (died 272), said to have been a Goth serving as an officer in Rome, was put to death there with seventy other Christians during the persecution of Aurelian.

**sabretache** [SA-bur-TAHSH] a leather satchel suspended on the left side by long straps from the sword belt of a cavalry officer (I, chap. 5, 48).

**sacar** a type of energy cannon in the artillery of the autarch (IV, chap. 15, 118).
*History:* an old form of cannon smaller than a demi-culverin, formerly much employed in sieges and on ships. Also known as "saker."

**saffian** a leather made from goatskin or sheepskin and tanned with sumac (I, chap. 6, 67). It is often dyed in bright colors, typically red or yellow.

**saffian book** one of the four books Thecla requested: "as large as the top of a small table, a cubit in width and a scant ell in height; from the arms impressed upon its saffian cover, I supposed it to be the history of some old noble family" (I, chap. 6, 67). Wolfe writes it is "almost certainly a history of Thecla's own family, its wide pages occupied by genealogical charts" (PE, 9).

**sagum** a Roman soldier's cape, fastened and draped at the right shoulder (SS, 260).

**sailor** in the Age of the Autarch, those sailors who steer ships among the stars are often (but not always) automatons (see ANDROID), and they share most of the skills of water sailors. Nonmetallic sailors include captain of the *Samru*, captain of the tender, Eata, Gunnie, Hadelin, Hethor, Idas, Maxellindis, Maxellindis's uncle, Purn, and Trason.

**sailor, brawny** the unnamed fellow who mans the aft boat hook of the *Alcyone* (V, chap. 34, 245) and later becomes a follower of the Conciliator.

**sailor talk** Wolfe's sailors pepper their talk with joking tag phrases, a device often termed "Wellerism" after the cockney character Sam Weller in the *Pickwick Papers* by Charles Dickens. The pattern is usually to begin with the punchline and then work back into the lead-up. This quirk evolved among the androids because they tried to humanize their metallic appearances with these ribald jokes (IV, chap. 6, 52). The human sailors then caught the habit from them. Here then, by way of example, are the sayings of Jonas and other sailors.

- "I don't know what was wrong, but believe me, their departure was impressive and unmistakable — that's what the bear said, you know, about the picknickers" (I, chap. 35, 297).
- "You have understood me better than I wanted, as the man said when he looked into the mirror" (I, chap. 35, 300). Meaning *You're a rogue and I'm no better.*
- "You know what the octopus remarked when he got out of the mermaid's kelp bed: 'I'm not impugning your skill — quite the opposite. But you look as if you could use a little cheering up'" (II, chap. 5, 41).
- "'Still, it's a terrible way to earn a living.' That's what the thorn-bush said to the shrike, you know" (II, chap. 5, 42).
- "I'm going to tell you what all housewives sooner or later tell their husbands: 'Before you ask more questions, think about whether you really want to know the answers'" (II, chap. 8, 68).
- "That's something that's always welcome . . . like the misfortunes of an older brother" (II, chap. 10, 85).
- "Both of them look like they outvalue either of us, though, as the sailor told the surgeon who took off his legs" (II, chap. 12, 102).
- "'They would not obey us, and the world is better off without them anyway,' as the butcher's wife told him when she cut away his manhood" (II, chap. 13, 110).

**sailor talk**

- "I lost it somewhere along the way. That's what the jaguar said, who had promised to guide the goat" (IV, chap. 4, 32).
- "I think you'll make it — that's what the thrush sang while the lynx chased the hare around the bay tree" (IV, chap. 6, 47).
- "I lost it somewhere along the way. That was the basket's story, that had been filled with water" (IV, chap. 6, 52).
- "We'll both be glad of the company, like the undertaker remarked to the ghost" (IV, chap. 37, 299).
- "Eyes? I never heard of 'um, no more than a crow in a court" (IV, chap. 37, 299).
- "I'll tell you what I saw myself, like the carpenter did when he had the shutter up" (IV, chap. 37, 299).
- "Pray for them that's comin' down . . . like the ox said when he fell out of the riggin'" (IV, chap. 37, 301).
- "A knife wouldn't have scratched him — that's what the whoremaster said when the sailor came" (V, chap. 3, 18).
- "That's what makes the ship go, as the skipper said when they asked about the wench" (V, chap. 4, 26).
- "You know more than me, like the hog told the butcher" (V, chap. 11, 81). The sailor is obliquely calling Severian a torturer, a butcher of men, signalling that he knows Severian's hidden identity as the target/reason for the shipwide mutiny.
- "And foller your nose. That's what the monkey told the elephant" (V, chap. 11, 81).
- "You weren't hurt, and no harm done, as the viper told the sow" (V, chap. 11, 83).
- "That's what boys are like, like the skipper said when he showed his daughter" (V, chap. 46, 325).

- ☙ "We can only hope, that's like the frog said when he seen the stork. But his mouth was dry, and he couldn't quite get the word out" (v, chap. 46, 328).
- ☙ "Why, I never thought about it . . . Which is what the dog said when they asked why they shouldn't cut off his tail" (CD, 272).
- ☙ "I've not thought of it either, and that was what the diplomat said just before war broke out. At least, that was it as well as they could recall afterward" (CD, 272).
- ☙ "Why that's perfectly true, ma'am . . . Which is what the skipper told the strumpet when she asked if he wasn't usin' his wooden leg" (CD, 272).
- ☙ "But the devil take me — which is what the Irishman said, that didn't have time to say wife" (CD, 273).

**salamander** the monster Severian encounters in Thrax is a creature from the mirrors (III, chap. 9, 71). Normally low and squat, it can rear up and expand itself to attack, somewhat analogous to the hooded cobra, though in appearance the attacking salamander looks more like a suddenly blooming rose. It uses intense heat as its weapon.
*Myth:* a small dragon that lives in fire. Just as the phoenix was used as an argument by theologians to prove the resurrection of the flesh, so was the salamander cited as proof that bodies can live in fire.
*Commentary:* the fire elemental of Urth. See NOTULE; PTERIOPE; SLUG; WORM OF WHITE FIRE.

**salpinx** [SAL-pinks] one of the "common words" that Master Gurloes mispronounces (I, chap. 7, 78); see also BORDEREAU and URTICATE.
*History:* an ancient Greek trumpet.
*Anatomy:* the supposedly trumpet-shaped Eustachian tubes (connecting inner ear to throat) and Fallopian tubes (connecting ovaries to uterus).

**salsify** a biennial composite plant, the purple goat's beard, indigenous to Great Britain and Europe, producing an esculent root (V, chap. 5, 31).

**Saltus** the name of a village on the river Gyoll roughly ten leagues north of Nessus. Near the village is an ancient mine that was begun during the reign of Typhon, on the advice of a HATIF (II, chap. 1, 7). The mine is to the north-east; Vodalus's wood is to the north, which one reaches after passing over the mine-trailings (II, chap. 9).
*Latin:* narrow wooded valley.

**Samru** the ship that carries Severian from the sea shore to Nessus (IV, chap. 32).
*Myth:* an alternative name for Sinurqh, the bird of immortality in Persian myth. A third name is Akra, and the creature may be akin to the Roc.

**sanbenito** "As I was about to answer her question, a couple strolled by our alcove, the man robed in a sanbenito, the woman dressed as a midinette" (III, chap. 6, 49).

*History:* under the Spanish Inquisition, a penitential garment of yellow cloth, resembling a monk's sleeveless robe in shape, ornamented with a red Saint Andrew's cross before and behind, worn by a confessed and penitent heretic; also, a similar garment of a black color ornamented with flames, devils, and other devices worn by an impenitent confessed heretic at an auto-da-fé.

**Sancha** the young exultant caught with Lomer, later married to Fors, finally returned to House Absolute as the Dowager of Fors (II, chap. 15, 125; "The Cat," ES, 210–17). When Sancha was seven years old she became a pupil of Father Inire and gained an invisible familiar. At age thirteen or fourteen she was caught undressing Lomer (twenty-eight years old), a scandal which marked her for life. When she came of age (at twenty-one years of age) she received a villa in the south and married the heir of Fors. Later in life she returned to the House Absolute and died there, probably in her seventies.
*Onomastics:* "holy" (Spanish).
*History:* Saint Sancha (A.D. 1180?–1229), daughter of King Sancho I of Portugal.
*Commentary:* there seems to be a pattern of seven years (Sancha at age seven, fourteen, twenty-one, possibly seventy).

**Sancha's cat** the mysterious pet turned familiar ("The Cat," ES, 210–17). When Sancha first meets Father Inire he gives her a toy. The next time he sees her she still has the toy, and since she asks for a story rather than a new toy, she becomes his pupil. Inire takes her to the Presence Chamber and she tosses her gray cat into the magic mirrors, scattering it to the edge of Briah. Inire promises to retrieve the pet, and soon thereafter it becomes known that

Sancha is "attended by some fey thing" in the form of a phantom cat (214). When Sancha dies, a tiny doll materializes, seemingly made of flesh and blood, and a pawprint appears on her death-bed's counterpane. Odilo has the doll buried with Sancha and sends the counterpane to Leocadia, giving her nightmares. *Commentary:* what was the toy Inire gave her? A strong case can be made that it was the cat, or it could be the mysterious doll. What is the relationship between the doll and the cat? The doll may be a tiny homunculus made by Inire to anchor the disembodied spirit of the cat, analogous to the way that Jonas's ghost becomes attached to Miles.

**Sanguinary Field** the dueling arena of Nessus (I, chap. 17, 157), located "in the far northwestern part of the city, within easy sight of the Wall" (IV, chap. 10, 76), i.e., northwest of the built, living section. It is "between a residential enclave of city armigers and the barracks and stables of the Xenagie of the Blue Dimarchi" (I, chap. 27, 234). The Inn of Lost Loves is nearby, presumably near the southeast margin. Ava comes from this part of Nessus, and she is present at Severian's duel. Also present are CADROE OF THE SEVENTEEN STONES, LAURENTIA OF THE HOUSE OF THE HARP, and SABAS OF THE PARTED MEADOW.
*History:* "sanguinary" means attended by bloodshed; characterized by slaughter; bloody.

**sannyasin** a wandering mendicant Hindu ascetic; a holy man; monk; specifically one belonging to a Brahman or Jain order comprising men in the fourth ashrama (IV, chap. 31, 253).

**sarcin** from Latin "sarcina," a load, pack (V, chap. 28, 196).

**sardonyx** a variety of onyx or stratified chalcedony having white layers alternating with one or more strata of sard (I, chap. 16, 151).

**saros** the Babylonian name for the number 3,600, and hence for a period of 3,600 years. In modern times, the term was adopted by astronomers as the name of the cycle of eighteen years and ten and two-thirds days, in which solar and lunar eclipses repeat themselves. Both meanings apply to Urth: the ancient sense ("the decades of a saros would not be long enough for me to write all they meant to the ragged apprentice boy I was" [I, chap. 2, 21]) as well as the modern sense ("There is such a one in the stone town, and once or twice in each saros one of those he has called to him will sup with us" [III, chap. 7, 61]).

**sateen** a cotton or woolen fabric with a glossy surface like that of satin (I, chap. 12, 112).

**savages** three native guides of Vodalus in the jungle (IV, chap. 28, 228). Two are young men who might be brothers or even twins; the third is an old man who always wears a mask and carries a crooked staff surmounted with the dried head of a monkey. This man is said to be an UTURUNCU.

**Savitar** (also Savitri) a Hindu king of heaven and god of active power (IV, chap. 35, 287). Savitri is the principle of movement which causes all things to move and work. He makes the sun shine, the winds blow, the plants grow, and the tides ebb and flow. He rides in a chariot of gold pulled by white horses.

**schiavoni** in the Commonwealth, a word seemingly synonymous with "mercenary" (IV, chap. 19, 148).
*History:* Italian term meaning "Slavonic" for a sword with a distinctive basket hilt, peculiar to the Slavonian corps, mercenary bodyguards to the Doge until the end of the Venetian Republic in 1797.

**scopolagna** [skoh-poh-LAG-nuh] a word used by Hethor in talking to Severian about his shipboard lovedoll: "Wh-wh-where is she now, my own scopolagna, my poppet? Let h-h-hooks be buried in the hands that took her!" (I, chap. 30, 257). Meaning "A woman whose appearance others find stimulating in the extreme" (CD, 247).
*History: Mrs. Byrne's Dictionary* gives scopolagnia [skoh-poh-LAG-nih-uh] as "the pleasure gained from voyeurism." So the word could be a coinage by Hethor.

**scorpion** "They had scorpions and voulges — I could see the heads of them stickin' over the crests of their helmets" (IV, chap. 37, 301).
*History:* in Europe, a halberd with a very deep and narrow blade (Stone).

**Scylla** [SIL-la] one of the major enemies of the New Sun, in league with ABAIA, ARIOCH, and EREBUS (II, chap. 4, 33).
*Myth:* ("she who rends") a half-human sea-monster of Greek myth, located in the Straits of Messina, that snatched and devoured men from passing ships; usually paired with Charybdis.

**Sebald** a man of Saltus, one of the two named volunteers (with Mesmin) who batter down Barnoch's door (II, chap. 2, 16). *History:* Saint Sebald (died 770?), patron of Nuremberg, Bavaria.

**Second House** the palace-within-a-palace at the House Absolute, a secret place of narrow passages with padded ladder-like steps and cramped chambers.

**secret house** same as Second House, but should not have been capitalized, according to Wolfe (V, chap. 5, 32).

**Sefiroth** plural of sefira, a divine emanation through which God manifested His existence in the creation of the universe (V, chap. 39, 281). In the Kabbalah, there are ten holy successive sefiroth: Kether (crown), Chokmah (wisdom), Binah (understanding), Chesed (mercy), Geburah (strength), Tiphereth (beauty), Netzach (victory), Hod (splendor), Yesod (foundation), and Malkuth (kingdom). See YESOD.

**self-reflexive moments** "I have noticed that in books this sort of stalemate never seems to occur" (III, chap. 3, 30); "Had you been with me then, reader, and insisted I walk farther with you, I think I would have taken your life" (V, chap. 49, 344).

**seneschal** a bailiff, steward, or majordomo of a great medieval lord or king representing the lord in, for example, the feudal courts, in the management of his estate, and in the superintendence of feasts and domestic ceremonies (ES, 214).

**sennet** the trumpet flourish used to cue an actor. Title of chapter (I, chap. 26, 227).

**Septentrion Guard** the elite corps guarding the northern frontier of the Commonwealth (I, chap. 18, 161). They seem to be, or have a reputation of being, a "barbarian" group, as Agilus says to Severian: "Agia and I wore the gaudy armor of a barbarian — you wore his heart" (I, chap. 29, 253). Judging from the one example of armor, their symbol would seem to be a chimera, their tinct gold (I, chap. 17, 156). Speaking of that armor, it is either fake costumery or more likely it is authentic, the property of a previous victim in their deadly scam.
*Astronomy:* Septentrion is the constellation of the Great Bear.

**seraph** on Urth, the seraphim are commanders of the anpiels (IV, chap. 20, 164).
*Myth:* one of the seraphim, the highest rank of the nine orders of angels.

**sere** dry, withered (II, chap. 24, 227).

**Serenus** Latin meaning "serene," this is the name Severian uses for the planet Jupiter (V, chap. 1, 6). See SOLAR SYSTEM TABLE.

**sergeant at the vincula** claviger who tells his boss, Severian, about the recent fire-murders (two killings two nights earlier, three more the night before) in Thrax (III, chap. 4, 37–38).

**Seven Orders of Transcendence** mentioned in passing with regard to the advanced spiritual tutoring of Severian the Great (IV, chap. 28, 228), they may correspond to the Alchemical Levels.

| The Orders | Alchemical Levels (and their meaning) |
| --- | --- |
| Aspiration | Calcination (death of the profane) |
| Integration | Petrification (separation of destroyed remains) |
| — | Solution (purification of matter) |
| — | Distillation (rain of purified matter) |
| — | Conjunction (joining opposites) |
| Assurance | Sublimation (suffering mystic detachment) |
| Assimilation | Congelation (binding paradoxes) |

**Severa** lost daughter of Casdoe and Becan, sister-twin of little Severian; the first of the family to be eaten by the alzabo (III, chap. 14, 111).
*History:* Saint Severa (died 750?) was abbess of the Benedictine convent of Oehren at Treves, France.
*Commentary:* in the Commonwealth Severa/Severian are well-known names for twins.

**several** whenever Severian writes "several" he means "three."

**Severian** the narrator of *The Book of the New Sun* and *The Urth of the New Sun,* a man who is by turns torturer, lictor, soldier, and autarch, to name a few (I, chap. 1, 1). When he leaves the Citadel as a journeyman torturer,

> He is 6'1", and weighs 175 pounds. He is pale, with dark eyes, dark straight hair, and good teeth. His face is long and rather bony: high, square

> forehead, moderately high cheek-bones; strong chin. He is muscular; his hands are a little larger than average (*Thrust* no. 19, 8).

In sharp contrast, when he returns to the Citadel six months later he walks with a limp, he has a disfiguring scar on his face, and he is autarch, one who will be known as both Severian the Great and Severian the Lame. Grandson of Dorcas and the Charon-like boatman, son of Catherine and Ouen. See FAMILY TREES.
*History:* there are five Saint Severians: early martyrs Severian and Aquila, a husband and wife killed in Julia Caesarea of Mauritania (date unknown); (died 452) a bishop of Scythopolis (Bethsan) in Galilee who was murdered by Eutychian heretics with connivance of the empress Eudocia; (died 303) one of the martyrs at Nicomedia; (died 320) an Armenian senator who openly professed his Christianity and was torn with rakes until he died; and one of the Four Crowned Martyrs. Outside of the church, "Severian" refers either to a member of an Encratite or Gnostic sect of the 2nd century that condemned marriage and other social practices, or to a follower of Severus, the Monophysite patriarch of Antioch (early 5th century). These histories aside, his name is one of Severity, the opposite of Mercy.
*Commentary:* the suggestion of a "first Severian" who preceeds the Severian of the narrative begins in the following quote.

> Two things are clear to me. The first is that I am not the first Severian. Those who walk the corridors of Time saw him gain the Phoenix Throne, and thus it was that the Autarch, having been told of me, smiled in the House Azure, and

the undine thrust me up when it seemed I must drown. (Yet surely the first Severian did not; something had already begun to reshape my life.) Let me guess now, though it is only a guess, at the story of that first Severian.

He too was reared by the torturers, I think. He too was sent forth to Thrax. He too fled Thrax, and though he did not carry the Claw of the Conciliator, he must have been drawn to the fighting in the north — no doubt he hoped to escape the archon by hiding himself among the army. How he encountered the Autarch there I cannot say; but encounter him he did, and so, even as I, he (who in the final sense was and is myself) became Autarch in turn and sailed beyond the candles of night. Then those who walk the corridors walked back to the time he was young, and my own story — as I have given here in so many pages — began.

The second thing is this. He was not returned to his own time but became himself a walker of the corridors. I know now the identity of the man called the Head of Day, and why Hildegrin, who was too near, perished when we met, and why the witches fled. I know too in whose mausoleum I tarried as a child, that little building of stone with its rose, its fountain, and its flying ship all graven. I have disturbed my own tomb, and now I go to lie in it (IV, ch. 38).

Using this as a starting point, let us follow further.

Severian One: proto-Severian, Severian the Cruel. In this "alternate history" version of Severian's narrative, Severian goes to Thrax, then to the War; he gains the throne, goes to Yesod, and returns; all as per the quote above.

Severian One had no Thecla, and certainly no Dorcas. (Possibly his crime against the guild was killing a prostitute at the House Azure.) He was sent to Thrax at the request of the Archon of Thrax. Somehow from there he was drawn to the war (as Severian Two muses about Severian One). And his killing of the autarch was more Oedipal in nature (it was Severian Two's involvement with Vodalus which first brought Severian's autarch-hating elements to the surface, and then, as he was treated badly by Vodalus and treated well by the Autarch, his alliances shifted so that Severian Two's murder of the Autarch was not something he wanted to do but was ordered to do).

Severian Two: the narrator of *The Book of the New Sun*, the optimized version of Severian One. He plays in the mausoleum (of Severian Seven or Eight) gets the Claw of the Conciliator (i.e., Severian Three); meets Apu Punchau (Severian Six); goes to Thrax; meets Typhon; meets Ash; gains the throne; gets on ship bound for Yesod; is mentored by Gunnie; creates the Claw of the Conciliator (Severian Three); and dies on the ship (v, ch. 6), whereupon the narrative moves to Severian Four.

The drowning; the dog Triskele (Severian's first resurrection; exercises in mercy and compassion; the exercises in loss, searching, and letting go. As Valeria says, having loved the dog, you can now love another creature); Thecla's four books. These are the first milestones warping Severian One into Severian Two.

Severian Three: the Claw of the Conciliator. A rose thorn covered with blood cells of Severian Two (v, ch. 6). Independent, but possibly has memories of Severian Four's penitence in Yesod: this becomes the miracle worker (or "miracle allower").

Severian Four: Avatar of Change, the Conciliator. He wakes up on the ship of Tzadkiel; goes to Yesod; creates the white fountain (Severian Five, a significant trigger point); mentors Burgundofara; returns to Urth as the Conciliator; gives the Claw to soldiers; goes to the Deluge; dies in the Deluge (at which point the narrative essence moves to Severian Six).

Severian Five: the white fountain. Linked to Severian the narrator; might best be considered "son of Severian Four and Apheta" (pun intended). Enters new phase (not so closely bound to Severian) when it merges with the Old Sun to create the New Sun.

Severian Six: Avatar of Culture, Apu-Punchau. Stripped of his ability to resurrect and heal others, he goes back in time as far as he can; teaches civilization to the autochthons; is murdered when he tries to leave; becomes independent of Severian the Narrator (a significant trigger point); has a later career as the vivimancer at the stone town where he eventually wrestles Hildegrin the badger.

Severian Seven: the Sleeper God of Ushas. Narrator of *The Urth of the New Sun*. Presumably he still has the ability to walk the corridors of time and will somehow or another end up becoming the mausoleum builder.

Severian Eight: the Mausoleum Builder. At the very least he builds the mausoleum in the necropolis early in the Age of the Autarch and is present at the miracle of Holy Katharine during the reign of Autarch Maxentius. (See MAUSOLEUM.) He probably does more. He might be the hatiff who tells the elders of Saltus about the buried city. He probably kills Dorcas when she dies the first time.

**servitrix** a female personal servant (I, chap. 20, 182).

**shah mat** (Arabic, "the king is dead") the game of chess, or an early version of chess, or a chess-like game, from the phrase meaning "checkmate" (in chess), from Persian "shah," meaning king (V, chap. 19, 135).

**shallop** a usually two-masted ship with lugsails, or a small open boat propelled by oars or sails and used chiefly in shallow waters (ES, 26).

**shaman** the religious leader at the town in the Age of Myth (V, chap. 49, 347).

**shewbread** bread displayed upon an altar (I, chap. 11, 110).

**shotel** a sickle weapon used at the Battle of Orithyia by the dwarf-ridden tall men of Ascia (IV, chap. 22, 181).

*History:* Ethiopian sickle-shaped, double-edged weapon. Length thirty inches from base of hilt to point, and up to thirty-nine inches measured along curve. Its shape allows it to strike around shields. Stone calls it an "extremely awkward weapon" and says the Ethiopians have no idea of fencing.

**Sidero** an android sailor on Tzadkiel's ship. His name means "iron" according to Ossipago (v, chap. 2, 13). Sidero pushes Severian off the ledge. Later he is damaged and loses his right arm (v, chap. 8, 58). Severian climbs inside him and they are together when Severian is killed by the dragon in the air shaft.
*Onomastics:* not a name, it is the word "iron" (Greek).
*Myth:* (Greek) Sidero is the stepmother of Tyro, who in turn is mother to the city-founding twins Neleus and Pelias. Sidero was killed by Pelias in a temple of Hera. Robert Graves translates the name as "starry."
*Commentary:* although Jonas was formerly a silver class android and Sidero is an iron class android (large enough to serve as a suit of armor), still there is a symmetry between them both losing an arm (Jonas loses his left arm, Sidero loses his right arm).

**Sieur** a term of address applied to men of armiger (or higher) rank. The OED lists two forms of this word, both "alien, not naturalized" to English. The first is an archaic word related to the French "monsieur" and used as a courtesy title or form of address; the second is a South African word related to the Dutch "sinjeur" (lord, master) but ultimately assimilated into the first word, used as a respectful form of address to a superior; master, "sir." In a cited example from 1812, the Hottentots addressed their master as Baas (i.e., Boss) while the slaves addressed him as Sieur.

**Signal Street** a street in Oldgate, on the west bank of the River Gyoll (I, chap. 22, 199).

**sikinnis** (Greek) a picture of nymphs and satyrs (III, chap. 6, 50).

**Silva** "Thecla had heard once or twice when the court went to hunt near Silva" (IV, chap. 23, 184). A town or village, presumably located in or near a forest.
*Latin:* a wood or forest.

**simar** a woman's dress consisting of two long strips of linen or cotton that cover the wearer from neck to ankle but leave an opening at each side from ankle to arm (I, chap. 29, 249). See also CYMAR.

**simples** single ingredients that would later be compounded into medicines (I, chap. 1, 11). Usually herbs of various kinds.

**Simulatio** the treasure-hunter who hires Eata for transport the day after Eata has been robbed of his own treasure map (ES, 22). He claims to have sailed on a lake to the north, which may be an allusion to Lake Diuturna (22). He recalls the mountain meads of his father's estate (28), but since he is not as tall as an exultant, he is likely an armiger. He supposes his map to date from starfaring days (31) and he claims to have found it between the pages of an old book (34). He stays at the Cygnet, and Eata, after saving his life, tells him about the goldsmith's shop at the sign of the Osela.
*Latin:* assumed appearance, pretense, feint.

*Commentary:* his name may be an obvious pseudonym, suggested by the Latin meaning and Eata's reaction. Robert Borski thinks it the name of a male clone, which is interesting and appropriate to the Latin, but the character does not seem tall enough for an exultant.

**Sirius** a star in the night sky of Urth (II, chap. 17, 151).
*History:* the brightest star in the sky, it is also known as the Dog Star. Located in the constellation of Canis Major.

**sisal** the name of a port in Yucatan, used attributively with fiber, grass, hemp, to designate the prepared fiber for use in rope making (V, chap. 2, 15).

**Sith** "Sith, called by the ignorant Kronos, son of Uranus" (SS, 217). A god in the story "The Boy Who Hooked the Sun."

**six-legged machine** used as a beast of burden by the Ascian Army (IV, chap. 29, 231).

**skewbald** irregular markings on animals, especially horses, of white and brown or red, or some similar color (III, chap. 2, 20). Distinct from piebald (white with black), which is sometimes inexactly used for it.

**Skuld** the planet corresponding to our Venus (II, chap. 10, 83). Terraformed in the First Empire. See HISTORY OF URTH; SOLAR SYSTEM TABLE.
*Myth:* (Norse) the Norn representing the Future.

**slavery in the Commonwealth** a slave may be brought as a slave from foreign lands and can be sold; prisoners of war are slaves of the autarch, and he can sell them (many Ascians have become rowers on the upper rivers in this manner); and a person can sell himself into slavery (IV, chap. 12, 94).

**Sleeper's priest** in Ushas, possibly a descendant of Odilo (V, chap. 51, 366–68). Or he just preserves the man's mannerisms.

**slug** brought to Urth by Hethor's mirrors, the slug is a large, black creature, as heavy as several men or a destrier. It has black or dark green blood and attacks with an acid touch (III, chap. 22, 176). It first appears in the antechamber of the House Absolute (II, chap. 18), hunting for Severian, but it doesn't find him until much later, at the arboreal village of the sorcerers (III, chap. 21). If Hethor used a monster at the Piteous Gate of Nessus, it may have been this one.
*Commentary:* the slug is an elemental, apparently a hybrid of earth and water. See ANPIEL; MAN-APE; NOTULE; PTERIOPE; SALAMANDER; UNDINE.

**smilodon** [SMY-low-don] a kind of sabertooth tiger (I, chap. 4, 43). Smilodons roam the pampas of the Commonwealth, and the Atrium of Time has statues of them.

**Solange** a name cried out by the contessa in the play *Eschatology and Genesis* (II, chap. 24, 216).
*Onomastics:* "dignified," "rare jewel," "solitary" (French).

*History:* Saint Solange (died c. 880), a poor shepherdess of the neighborhood of Bourges, was brutally murdered by the local lord for resisting his attempts on her chastity.

**"solar panels"** black plates "that drink the sun" are used by Dr. Talos to power his theatrical machinery (II, chap. 23, 204).

## Solar System Table

| English | Urth | Hierodule |
|---|---|---|
| Sun | old sun | Och* |
| Mercury | Abaddon? | Ophiel* |
| Venus | Skuld | Hagith* |
| Earth | Urth | — |
| Moon | Lune | Phul* |
| Mars | Verthandi | Phaleg |
| Jupiter | Serenus | Bethor |
| Saturn | — | Aratron |
| Uranus | — | — |
| Neptune | — | — |
| Pluto | Dis | — |

* not mentioned in the Urth Cycle, but fitting the pattern of the Seven Olympic Spirits.

**sommelier** a servant under the wine steward; a barman or wine waiter (III, chap. 6, 53).

**soubrette** a maidservant or lady's maid; or a "saucy maid" in the tradition of French theater (I, chap. 20, 182; V, chap. 44, 312). It is first mentioned regarding a set of paper dolls that includes "soubrettes, columbines, coryphees, harlequinas, figurantes, and so on" which seems like a theatrical cast of saucy maids, pretty ladies, prima ballerinas, clownettes, and female extras. So when Odillo chides Pega for calling herself a soubrette rather than an ancilla, one wonders if he thinks she is either trying to claim a higher station (where a soubrette is above an ancilla) or being frivilous (where soubrettes only exist on the stage).

**spado** a eunuch (V, chap. 13, 94).

**spadone** one of the names of the two-handed fighting sword of the Middle Ages (II, chap. 19, 173).

**spadroon** an 18th- to 19th-century sword much lighter than a broadsword and made to both cut and thrust (II, chap. 11, 92). A German sword used as an officer's weapon.

**spahis** (Persian) a Turkish horseman (II, chap. 26, 245).

**span** see MEASUREMENT TABLES.

**spatha** Greek meaning "broad blade," a broad two-edged sword, apparently used as a cavalry weapon in the Commonwealth (III, chap. 2, 40).
*History:* the long sword of the Roman cavalry, the plural is "spathae."

**specie** coins (I, chap. 34, 289).

**specula** magical or scientific mirrors, the place where the flagae originate (I, chap. 20, 181). The shape called "The Fish" is the least important and most common of the inhabitants of specula,

whereas the Woman Butterfly that Severian glimpses in the Book of Mirrors is a more advanced creature, perhaps a Hierogrammate.
*Myth:* the fauna of mirrors is a Chinese notion that goes back to the legendary times of the Yellow Emperor. Originally the world of mirrors and the world of men were not divided, nor were they identical, and one could freely travel between the two. For reasons unknown, the mirror people invaded the earth one night, but after a terrible war the Yellow Emperor was able to triumph over them. He imprisoned them in their mirrors and forced them to slavishly repeat all the actions of men. However, they will one day break loose again.

> The first to awaken will be the Fish. . . . Later on, other shapes will begin to stir. . . . They will break through the barriers of glass or metal and this time will not be defeated. Side by side with these mirror creatures, the creatures of water will join the battle (Borges, *The Book of Imaginary Beings,* 68).

*Commentary:* this passage from Borges seems to be a thumbnail sketch for the background of the Urth Cycle.

**spelaeae** cave-dwelling creatures (II, chap. 31, 292).

**spiracle** a well-like section that descends several decks in Tzadkiel's ship (V, chap. 9, 66).
*History:* a breathing hole, airhole, or vent.

**Spring Wind** son of Early Summer, father of Fish and Frog, Spring Wind is an accomplished agriculturist and a peerless soldier in "The Tale of the Boy Called Frog" (III, chap. 19, 147).
*Myth:* (Roman) the god Mars (the month of March, named after him, is a spring month renowned for wind) is perhaps too often associated with the bellicose Ares (Greek god of war). Mars was originally an agricultural god (his planet is red because he was the flayed god) who, over time, became a soldier god.

**squab** young pigeon or young rabbit (I, chap. 32, 278).

**Stachys** Morwenna's husband, whom she killed (II, chap. 1, 7). He was quite a bit older than she (II, chap. 4, 32), making theirs a May-December wedding. They had a farm. Stachys chose to marry Morwenna instead of Eusebia, possibly because Eusebia was past her child-bearing years.
*Onomastics:* "spike or ear of corn" (Biblical).
*History:* Saint Stachys, Disciple of the Seventy Apostles, was appointed by the Apostle Saint Andrew as first bishop of Constantinople.

**starost** an exultant title (I, chap. 7, 71). It seems low level when compared with the hereditary power of the northern clans, but Thecla seems to be counting on this individual named Egino.
*History:* in Russia and Poland, one whose estate is his for life only and cannot be deeded to his heirs.

**stele** an upright slab bearing sculptured designs or inscriptions (I, chap. 1, 12). Sometimes loosely applied to any prepared surface, such as the face of a building or a rock, that is covered with an inscription.

**stephane** a kind of diadem or coronet, represented in statuary as worn by the goddess Hera and other deities; also worn by military commanders (IV, chap. 33, 266).

**steward on Tzadkiel's ship** first seen waking Severian to meet Ossipago, Barbatus, and Famulimus (V, chap. 5, 31), he is shortly thereafter killed by Purn with Gunnie's assistance (V, chap. 6, 38; chap. 10, 76). Severian's attempt to resurrect the man causes the shipwide power outage.

**stone town** an ancient ruin located in the arid lands between the House Absolute and Thrax (II, chap. 29, 274). It is a magical area which seems to draw travelers in, stepping into (or "bending") their path if they try to go around. This is the town that Apu Punchau visited and made his capital in the Age of Myth. His house is located here and his spirit is the vivimancer that draws people.

After Jolenta dies, Severian and Dorcas spend the night in the hut of a man and his aged mother. The man tells them that adventurers have been known to comb the ruins, looking for treasure. The woman tells of their last guest, a silent man with a staff, who had come perhaps eighteen years earlier (III, chap. 7, 61).

**stride** see MEASUREMENT TABLES.

**stuns'ls** studding sails. Sails extended from the sides of a square sail, as by lashing additional spars to the yard (I, chap. 35, 293).

**Sulpicius** an autarch whose reign ended 300 years prior to that of Severian the Great, he has a special bookcase at the center of the library set aside for him (I, chap. 6, 59).
*History:* there are four saints of this name.

**sumpter** "The chiliarch . . . had solved the problem by ordering that the body should be pulled behind a baggage sumpter" (I, chap. 31, 265).
*History:* an animal (less often, a person) used to carry supplies.

**supercargo** one of the shipboard positions that Hethor claims to have held (I, chap. 35, 293). "A clerk put aboard a vessel by a shipper to attend to his shipment" (CD, 249).

**surtout** a man's greatcoat or overcoat (I, chap. 16, 151).

**Surya** the most distinct of several Hindu sun gods (IV, chap. 35, 287). Also, in Hindu demonology, a good angel or genie.

**sutler** one who follows an army or lives in a garrison town and sells provisions to the soldiers (IV, chap. 20, 158).

**Swan** a constellation of Urth, apparently the ZODIAC sign of Thecla's birth (IV, chap. 23, 190).
*Astronomy:* our constellation Cygnus is the Swan, but it is far from the zodiac (and not likely to become part of the zodiac).

*Commentary:* since it is highly unlikely that Cygnus would enter the zodiac, this suggests an alien zodiac from a nearby star system, where a different inclination of orbit to the ecliptic would give a different zodiac from that seen on Urth, though of course from among the same constellations. Or it could be a different name for one of our zodiac constellations: "Dupuis said [Sagittarius] was shown in [ancient] Egypt as an Ibis or Swan" (Allen, *Star Names,* 353).

Charles François Dupuis (1742–1809) was a French scientific writer and politician in Revolutionary France. His published views on Upper Egypt being the source of all science and religion seems to have spurred Napoleon into invading that country. This seems relevant to the Franco-Egyptian details about Nessus.

**sweepsmen** rowers using long oars (sweeps) that require them to stand (1, chap. 14, 131).

**sylph** originally a spirit of the air, "sylph" has come to mean a beautiful, slender girl (1, chap. 16, 149).
*Commentary:* for air spirits see ANPIEL, NOTULE, and PTERIOPE.

**Syntyche** Laetus's girlfriend (ES, 20). Laetus, after stealing the treasure map from Eata with her help, treacherously kills her. Simulatio finds her corpse in the midnight Gyoll (27).
*Onomastics:* "that speaks or discourses" (Biblical).
*History:* Saint Syntyche (1st century) was a female member of the church of Philippi, described by Saint Paul as his fellow laborer in the gospel and as one whose name is in the Book of Life.

*Thyacine*

# *T*

**taffrail** "The captain pointed over the taffrail" (v, chap. 27, 195). The rail at the stern of a ship.

**Talarican** an exultant of Nessus whose madness manifested itself as an obsession with the lowest aspects of human existence (I, chap. 14, 134).
*History:* Saint Talarican was a 6th (?) century bishop, probably Pictish, in whose honor various Scottish churches were dedicated.
*Commentary:* David Langford reports that Talarican's statistical interest seems akin to journalist Henry Mayhew's *London Labor and the London Poor* (1851), but he could find no matching material in Mayhew's sections on acrobats and scavengers.

**Tale of a Man Who Sold His Shadow** Master Ash says "In a fable made in the earliest morning of our race, a man sold his shadow and found himself driven out everywhere he went. No one would believe that he was human." When asked if the man ever regained his shadow, he answers, "No. But for a time he traveled with a man who had no reflection" (IV, chap. 16, 125–26).

**Tale of the Boy Called Frog** a story in the brown book, about a culture hero named Frog who is raised by wolves and eventually founds an empire, perhaps the First Empire (III, chap. 19). See HISTORY OF URTH.
*Myth:* (Roman) the tale parallels the legend of Romulus and Remus.

*Literature:* the tale draws from Kipling's short story "Mowgli's Brothers."
*History:* the tale seems to commemorate the Plymouth Pilgrims and the first Thanksgiving (1621).

**Tale of the Student and His Son** a story from the brown book, about a hero who journeys to an island, kills a sea monster, and rescues a princess (II, chap. 17).
*Myth:* (Greek) much like the myth of Theseus and the Minotaur.
*History:* the battle between the "Land of Virgins" and the naviscaput echoes the battle between the Merrimack and the Monitor (9 March 1862).
*Commentary:* there is also an allusive pun turning the stalwart "Theseus" into a student's "thesis."

**tall woman** the autochthon woman who gives Severian a loin cloth, food, and water upon his first arrival at the town in the Age of Myth (V, chap. 49, 346).

**tallman riders** among the Ascian forces at the Third Battle of Orithyia is a strange cavalry of dwarfs riding on the shoulders of tall men who are blinded (IV, chap. 22, 180–82).
*Commentary:* the image appeared in Wolfe's *The Fifth Head of Cerberus,* where small humanoids blind humans and ride on their shoulders. This is the nightmarish stuff of fairytales, a perversion of the phrase "We are like dwarfs on the shoulders of giants, so that we can see more than they, and things at a greater distance, not by virtue of any sharpness of sight on our part, or any physical distinction, but because we are carried high and raised up by their giant size" in *Metalogicon* (1159) by Bernard of Chartres.

**Talos** a slight and spry playwright, surgeon, and scientist (I, chap. 14, 142). His face is described by Severian as being like a fox mask (I, chap. 16, 148), and his fiery red hair accents his fox-like character. Dr. Talos is Baldanders's creation, and his almost magical operations transform a rather ordinary waitress into the goddess-like Jolenta.
*Myth:* Talos was the miraculous bronze (or brass) man who defended Crete for King Minos by hurling stones or fire at strangers, or by scorching them in his red-hot clasp.

**tambour** a small drum (I, chap. 21, 192).

**Tanco** a soldier of Typhon-era Urth and friend of Eskil (V, chap. 35, 251).
*History:* Saint Tanco (died 808) was an Irish monk who eventually became the See of Werden before being killed by a pagan mob whose savage customs he had denounced.

**Tarentine** the name of a race or a group in a part of the Commonwealth (IV, chap. 35, 288).
*History:* of or pertaining to Taranto, a city in the heel of Italy, established by Greek colonists in 700 B.C. It was the only colony of Sparta. They named it "Taras" after the son of the Sea God Poseidon and the local nymph Satyrion. Another source claims Herakles founded it.

**tarn** a small mountain lake (III, chap. 13, 104).

**Tarnung** a magic cloak of invisibility in "The God and His Man" (ES, 204).
*German:* camouflage.

**Tarot and The Book of the New Sun** it is clear that Wolfe is familiar with the Tarot deck, since his most famous poem, "The Computer Iterates the Greater Trumps," is all about his interpretation of the twenty-two cards of the Major Arcana. (The poem won the Rhysling Award, and is collected in both *Plan[e]t Engineering* and *For Rosemary.*) The following diagram attempts to link characters and events with cards from the Major Arcana.

| Tarot Card | Character | Details |
|---|---|---|
| The Fool | Severian | The dog (Triskele), the traveler's staff, the rose (the Claw), the cliff (near Casdoe's cabin). |
| The Magician | Vodalus | |
| The High Priestess | Catherine | Her role as Holy Katharine in the feast day mystery; her role as a pelerine. |
| The Empress | Thecla | |
| The Emperor | The old autarch | |
| The Hierophant | The Domnicellae | |
| The Lovers | Severian & Dorcas | Eden imagery. |
| The Chariot | The fiacre race | |
| The Hermit | Master Ash | |
| Death | Severian | Robert, Agia, and Dr. Talos each call him "Death." |
| The Devil | Typhon | Typhon's temptation of Severian. |
| The Tower | Baldanders | Baldanders floating down in the fight at the bailey. |
| The Star | The white fountain | |
| Judgment | The Deluge | |
| The World | Ushas | |

**Tchataka** "Tchataka, who opens its mouth to the sky and drinks wisdom with the dew" (ss, 217). Some sort of magical bird from "The Boy Who Hooked the Sun."

**tea seller at Saltus fair** she tells Severian about the miracle of the flying cathedral, and she also points him toward the Green Man (II, chap. 3, 23–25).

**technology levels** Wolfe describes three levels of technology in the Urth Cycle, from low to high: "smith" level, "Urth" level, and "stellar" level.

Smith-level technology is represented by swords, knives, axes, and pikes (piletes), as they might have been forged by any skilled metalworker of Medieval/Renaissance times. These appear to be easily obtained by the common citizen and to represent the technological ability of the society as a whole.

The Urth level of technology is represented by pyrotechnic weapons: pole arms like conti, hastarii, khetens, and lances; missile weapons like arbalests and slings. They represent the highest technology to be found on the planet, perhaps even in its solar system. Most of the pole arms in the Urth Cycle are pyrotechnic, but it is difficult to be certain in some cases whether a given pole arm is of smith level (as the pilete is) or Urth level (the kheten, for instance). The legal ownership of such powerful weapons seems to vary from place to place within the Commonwealth.

Stellar technology is the highest level and includes energy weapons like arquebuses, fusils, jezails, and pistols. These devices cannot be produced on Urth, and are, no doubt, obtained from the Hierodules at great cost.

**teratoid** "We had descended perhaps a hundred steps when we reached a door painted with a crimson teratoid sign that appeared to me to be a glyph from some tongue beyond the shores of Urth" (II, chap. 18, 166).
*History:* having the appearance or character of a monster or monstrous formation.

**teratornis** a prehistoric bird similar to a condor, but larger (I, chap. 35, 298).

**Terminus Est** the carnificial sword that Master Palaemon gives Severian. It seems to be Palaemon's, since he says, "I used her for many years before you came to the guild" (IV, chap. 34, 270). That period would seem to be Palaemon's time of exile. The sword's name is translated by Severian as "This Is the Line of Division" (I, chap. 14, 129), and by Typhon as "This is the place of parting" (III, chap. 25, 202). It could also be read "This Is the End" (either a message to the condemned or a name denoting the final work of the weaponsmith), or perhaps most intriguingly, "This Is Terminus, God of Boundaries."

Meteorites were worshiped in ancient times, and the sacred thunder-stone of Terminus at Rome stood under a hole in the roof of Jupiter's temple, as if it had landed there. That Severian's sword could have been forged from the Terminus meteorite is made all the more interesting by this passage from *Castleview,* regarding *Excalibur,* the Sword in the Stone:

> the stone had fallen from Heaven, so it had pretty obviously been a meteorite. In fact, the whole legend was clearly the gussied-up history of a king in the Dark Ages who had gotten his throne by learning to extract meteoritic iron, from which weapons could be forged. Thus Arthur had in a very real sense drawn a sword from a stone that had fallen from the heavens. And furthermore, he'd drawn it through an anvil (113).

Both *Terminus Est* and *Excalibur* are linked by a possibly meteoritic origin, and the name "Jovinian" (craftsman of *Terminus Est)* suggests the Roman thunder god Jove. There are also scenes in *The Book of the New Sun* that echo events surrounding *Excalibur:* when Severian recovers his sword from the Lake of Endless Sleep, he touches Dorcas and notes "it seemed the hand's owner was returning my property to me" (I, chap. 21, 178), as when the Lady of the Lake gives the sword to King Arthur; and when *Terminus Est* is destroyed, Severian returns its fragments to another body of water, Lake Diuturna (III, chap. 38, 272), just as *Excalibur* is returned to the Lady of the Lake after Arthur's death.

**tessellated** composed of small blocks of variously colored material arranged to form a pattern; formed of or ornamented with mosaic work; of a pattern resembling a chessboard (I, chap. 4, 43).

**tetrarch** a minor king under Roman protection, originally a ruler of any of the four provinces together making up a larger kingdom (III, Appendix, 296). The same would seem to hold true for the Commonwealth. It is probably an exultant title.

**Thadelaeus the Great** a typo for "Thalelaeus" in the early paperback edition (I, chap. 10, 78).

**Thalelaeus the Great** "It was the thought of Thalelaeus the Great that the democracy desired to be ruled by some power superior to itself" (I, chap. 10, 97). A Perfect Master of philosophy mentioned in the brown book, he is contrasted with Yrierix the Sage.

*History:* there are two Saints Thalelaeus. The first (died 284?), believed to have come from Lebanon, practiced medicine in Anazarbus and was beheaded during the persecution of Numerian; the second (died 450?), born in Cilicia, became a recluse near a pagan shrine at Gabala, later living in an outdoor cage.

**Thais** a former courtesan of the House Absolute who is a survivor of the deluge and is venerated by later generations on Ushas as the goddess of night (v, chap. 51, 367).
*Onomastics:* "the bond" (Greek).
*History:* Saint Thais is penitent, saint, patron of fallen women or courtesans in 4th-century Christian legend. An earlier Thais was a celebrated Athenian hetaera who was loved by Alexander the Great. She came up with the idea of burning the palace of Persepolis, and Alexander did it, so Thais has a "destruction of the palace" element that finds an echo in Thais of Urth.

**thalamegus** a large, richly decorated barge used for luxurious water travel, ceremonies, floating parties, and the like; a ship fitted with cabins (ES, 23). The plural is thalamegii (I, chap. 14, 131).

**thalassic** connected with the sea; marine (v, chap. 42, 301).

**thaumaturge** "I am a thaumaturge, and these optimates are actors" (I, chap. 16, 148). A worker of marvels or miracles; a wonder-worker.

**Thea** exultant leman of Vodalus, and half-sister of Thecla (I, chap. 1, 14). She is with Vodalus and Hildegrin in the necropolis when Severian first sees her. She is compared to a dove (I, chap. 1, 14) and has a heart-shaped face (I, chap. 1, 13). The sisters seem close in age.

*Onomastics:* [THEE-ah] "goddess" (Greek).
*History:* Saints Meuris and Thea (died 307) were two maidens martyred at Gaza in Palestine.

**Thea's khaibit** when Severian sees her on the stairs at the House Azure, and she says "My dear sister" to Thecla's khaibit (I, chap. 9, 91), it is a strange moment. After all, it was Thea whom he had seen first, and he might have chosen her khaibit if given the chance. This Proustian moment of mixing sexual tension with regret might also relate in a punning way to "esprit d'escalier," a French phrase (literally "spirit of the staircase") referring to a clever remark or reply that is not thought of at the appropriate moment; an afterthought. Thea's khaibit is certainly a "spirit of the staircase."

**Thecla** a chatelaine of a powerful exultant clan of the North, she is Thea's half-sister, and a member of the inner circle of concubines that surrounds the autarch. Her face is triangular and her eyes are violet (I, chap. 7, 69). Her perfume is the scent of a rose burning (I, chap. 9, 90), which seems like a potent symbol of Catherine. See FAMILY TREES.

Thecla is taken secretly by the autarch's supporters (IV, chap. 25, 204) and imprisoned in the Matachin Tower in an attempt to influence Vodalus through her sister Thea, but then Thecla is put to torture. She takes her own life to avoid further torment by the in-dwelling demon awakened inside of her by the device called "the revolutionary." Her body is recovered and feasted upon by the Vodalarii when Severian joins them. As a result of this, Thecla lives on within Severian, and on occasion takes over his body.
*Onomastics:* "fame of God" (Greek).

*History:* there are eight Saints Thecla, but the most pertinent is the 1st-century follower of Saint Paul who became the first female Christian martyr. In "The Acts of Paul and Thecla," a book of the Apocrypha, she is said to have miraculously survived torture (trials by beast and fire) and then escaped her tormenters to live in a cave for several decades. When a second group came to kill her, Saint Thecla was saved from their designs by the timely collapse of her cave.
*Commentary:* according to other sources, Thecla, or "famous one," is a title of Ephesian Diana, whose shrine in Seleucia was a popular pilgrimage center in pagan times, and remained so even after the goddess was Christianized as a saint. Tertullian denied the legend connecting Thecla with Saint Paul, calling it a lie invented by a misguided church elder, and hinting that Paul might have been honored by the connection.

**Thecla's books** see BROWN BOOK, GREEN BOOK, SAFFIAN BOOK, and FOURTH BOOK.

**Thecla's father** gives a ball for her each year on her birthday under the zodiac sign of the Swan, but he dies some years before she meets Severian (IV, chap. 23, 190).

**Thecla's khaibit** the prostitute whom Severian chooses at the House Azure (I, chap. 9, 90). She is somewhat shorter than Thecla and wears the same perfume but more strongly (I, chap. 9, 90). It is unknown what becomes of her after Thecla's death.

**Thecla's uncle** had a huntsman named Midan.

**Theoanthropos** a variant of "Theanthropos," a title given to Jesus Christ as being both God and man (I, chap. 21, 189).

**theocenter** "We all seek to discover what is real. . . . Perhaps we are drawn to the theocenter" (I, chap. 9, 94).

**theogony** the origin and genealogy of the gods, especially as recounted in ancient epic poetry (III, chap. 38, 295).

**Theologoumenon** a theological statement or utterance on theology as distinguished from an inspired doctrine or revelation (II, chap. 10, 85).

**Theophany** a manifestation or appearance of God or a god to man (III, chap. 27, 221).

**thiasus** a company assembled to celebrate the festival of one of the gods (especially Bacchus) with dancing and singing (II, chap. 11, 97).

**Thiasus Marshal** "The Thiasus Marshal has promised to bring something for all of us" (II, chap. 22, 194). The House Absolute official (or steward) in charge of festive activities.

**Third Battle of Orithyia** the battle Severian fought in (IV, chap. 22) as he later referred to it (V, chap. 7, 47; chap. 38, 270; chap. 49, 350). Father Inire in his letter writes that the three Commonwealth groups there who took the most casualties were the Tarentines, the Antrustiones, and the city legions (IV, chap. 35, 288). Severian saw two distinct and exotic groups on his side, and if one assumes that the city legions would look "normal" to him, then it is possible that the Tarentines were the riders with their shaggy squires, while the Antrustiones were the Persian cherkajis and the Daughters of War. It is also possible that the two groups were simply legions from different cities and the text shows nothing of the Tarentines or the Antrustiones.

**thodicy** a misspelling of "theodicy," a vindication of divine justice in the face of the paradox that God is both omnipotent and benevolent and yet permits evil to exist among men (III, chap. 38, 295).

**tholus** a circular domed building or structure; a dome, cupola; a lantern (I, chap. 19, 175).

**Thrax** the city in Acis Valley, located at the foot of the first cataract, ninety percent of the way up the length of the Gyoll. The seat of provincial government, Thrax is also known as the City of Windowless Rooms, and the City of Crooked Knives. Public buildings include a harena, a pantheon, and a bath house. The archon, who lives in a palace by the river, has seven squadrons of dimarchi, each with its own commander. Acies Castle is on the cataract, overlooking the city. The vincula has 1,600 prisoners. The building-to-population ratio is 1:5, the inverse of the ratio in Nessus.
*History:* Thrace was the mountainous northern frontier of ancient Greece.
*Latin:* [tracks] "Thrace," and "Thraxacis" (Thrax + Acis) means "Thracian," or "a Thracian."

*Myth:* (Greek) Thrax was a child of Ares by an unknown mother. When he attacked the shrine of Apollo on Delos, the god afflicted him with leprosy. The region of Thrace is named after him.

**threnodic** of or related to a "threnody," a song of lamentation; specifically a lament for the dead, a dirge (II, chap. 4, 35).

**thurible** a burner for incense; a censer (I, chap. 9, 91).

**thyacine** a wild animal that apparently roams the streets of Nessus (I, chap. 18, 162).
*History:* a misspelling of "thylacine," the native Tasmanian "wolf" or "zebra-wolf." *Thylacinus cynocephalus* was about the size of a collie and had a long tail and a wolflike head with short ears and strong jaws. Its coat was brownish with black stripes across the back. A nocturnal hunter, the thylacine preyed on animals up to the size of small kangaroos. It was marsupial.

**thylacodon** a primitive opossum (I, chap. 4, 38). This prehistoric creature is a familiar garbage scavenger in Nessus.

**thylacosmil** another great cat of the Commonwealth (V, chap. 13, 96).
*History:* a marsupial saber-tooth, very similar to the saber-toothed cats except that it had no incisors at all. A flange covered the sabers when the mouth was closed. Stalked about in South America during the Pliocene.

**Thyme** a god-like being in EFF (SS, 246). He would be recognized on Earth as Father Time. "The Increate is father to all. I

take them from him — that is my function. And then I return them again." When he walks west, he and those with him age; when he walks east, they grow younger; and when he stops, Thyme stands still. It is quite likely that Thyme is the husband of Fauna, alluded to in "The Old Woman Whose Rolling Pin Is the Sun" but never named.
*Myth:* Father Time is related to Saturn, the Roman god of time, who in turn is related to Chronos (Greek for "time"), the titan who castrated his father Ouranos (Sky god) with a sickle and married his sister Rhea or GEA (Earth Mother goddess) to father the next generation of gods. The reign of Chronos was sometimes regarded as the Golden Age, but it ended when he was overpowered and dethroned by his son Zeus.
*Commentary:* Thyme and Fauna quietly stand near the apex of the Increate pyramid, he reaping and she sowing, not unlike Chronos and Rhea.

**Timon** an apprentice torturer. When Eata became captain of apprentices he beat Timon at once (V, chap. 46, 324), just as Severian had beaten Eata (I, chap. 5, 48).
*Onomastics:* [tee-MOHN] "respect" (Greek).
*History:* Saint Timon (1st century), one of the first deacons to be appointed by the apostles themselves, is recorded only in Acts 6:5.

**tincture** a medicinal substance dissolved in alcohol (I, chap. 3, 29).

**tokoloshe** "Bad spirits . . . When man think bad thought or woman do bad thing, there is another tokoloshe" (I, chap. 21, 191).

*Mythology:* in African folklore a mischievous and lascivious hairy dwarf, according to the OED. Fear of these monsters is apparently widespread in Africa, suggesting that the missionaries Robert and Marie of the Jungle Garden are in equatorial Africa.

**torture chamber tools** the kite, the apparatus (it letters a slogan into client's flesh: a direct homage to Kafka's "In the Penal Colony," which describes the machine in gruesome detail), the post (removed from the Old Yard at the complaint of the witches), Allowin's necklace (it tightens with each breath), and the revolutionary (a form of electroshock torture that induces suicidal behavior) (I, chap. 12, 115–16).

**Trason** a ship-owning friend of Maxellindus's uncle (IV, chap. 37, 301). On the mysterious night on the river, Maxellindus's uncle saw a galleass going up the river, in the center, contrary to custom. Then he saw Trason carrying a boatload of soldiers who were unusually tall and pale-faced.
*History:* Saint Trason (died 302?) was slain with others at Rome for aiding Christians awaiting death during the Diocletian persecution.

**travail** a rough framework to which a load can be tied to facilitate carrying or dragging it (I, chap. 12, 117).

**tribade** lesbian (II, chap. 11, 93).

**trilhoen** (German) a swivel gun mounted on a saddle or howdah (IV, chap. 23, 186).

**trilophodon** a genus of mastodons having molar teeth with three transverse ridges (IV, chap. 1, 12).

**Triskele** the name of Severian's three-legged dog (I, chap. 4, 37).
*History:* a design consisting of three radiating legs.
*Commentary:* John Clute says that "in classical times the word triskele designated a three-legged icon used in the worship of the god Apollo" (*Strokes,* 151).

**trompe l'oeil** (French "deceive the eye") a technique of depicting objects so realistically that the viewer is tricked into believing that they really exist in three dimensions, or a trick painting in this style, such as a window frame on a sheer brick wall (II, chap. 17, 145).

**Trudo** the ostler at the Inn of Lost Loves (I, chap. 26, 229). He seems to come from the Algedonic Quarter (230).
*History:* Saint Trudo (died 690?) was of Frankish parentage.
*Commentary:* Robert Borski suspects that Trudo is the prisoner in Thecla's cell (*Solar Labyrinth,* 77). See PRISONERS.

**trumeau** "An oddly angled mirror set above a trumeau at one side of the strange, shallow room caught his profile" (II, chap. 20, 166).
*History:* a central pillar supporting the tympanum of a large doorway, especially in a medieval building.

**tushes** tusks (II, chap. 1, 7).

**Twisted Way** a street in Nessus, located between the rag shop (of Agia and Agilus) and the Adamnian Steps (I, chap. 18, 145).

**Two Sealers, The** Hallvard's story about his uncles Anskar and Gundulf (IV, chap. 7). It is about the intense passion the men of his people have for their women, a dedication that verges on madness.

**Typhon** a "two-headed" man, the last monarch of Urth. He dreamed of a Second Empire to rival or surpass the fallen First Empire. Despite his tyrannous efforts, including the longevity he gained by usurping Piaton's body, he failed in his ambitions and died, abandoned and forgotten more than a chiliad P.S. From clues in *Lake of the Long Sun* it seems that the rebels Typhon is fighting against in *Urth* are led by members of his own family. It also seems likely that some of these rebellious children grow up to become Other Lords, making Typhon a real "father of monsters." See HISTORY OF URTH.
*Greek:* stupefying smoke; hot wind; or hurricane.
*History:* in *Castle of Days,* Wolfe writes, "The typhoon has blown his name into the modern world" (254). Allusions to Greco-Roman-Egyptian mythology aside, the more common etymology of "typhoon" is from the Chinese "tai fung" (big wind), just as "tycoon" comes from "ta kiun" (great prince). John Brunner supposes "tai fung" to have been carried back from the China Sea by Arab sailors, leaving "tufan" in Hindi (16th century) and "tuffon" in India (17th century), before being confused with mythology in the Mediterranean and entering English as "typhoon." This cross-cultural echoing reinforces the terrible force implied in the word.

*Myth:* (Greek) a giant who breathed fire and was a rival of the gods. Typhon (son of Hera, or Zeus and Niobe) was killed by Zeus, imprisoned in a mountain where he smolders as a volcano. *Commentary:* the fact that Typhon's head is grafted onto Piaton's body is an apt expression of the amalgamation between the several different (yet similar) myths. Gregory Feeley points out the Satanic element by comparing the encounter between Ty-phon and Severian with Jesus' Temptation in the Wilderness.

**tyrannosaur** "like that of a tyrannosaur over the topmost leaves of a forest" (III, chap. 33, 262).
*History:* the largest meat-eating animal ever to have lived, it measured about forty-five feet from head to tail, stood about twenty feet tall, and had a four-foot head with six-inch teeth. From the Cretaceous.

**tyrian** from "Tyrian purple," a reddish dyestuff obtained from the bodies of certain mollusks of the genus *Murex* and highly prized in ancient times, from Tyre, source of the dye (I, chap. 16, 151; II, chap. 25, 239).

**Tzadkiel** the captain of the ship that takes Severian to Yesod (V, chap. 1, 1). Tzadkiel is a HIEROGRAMMATE of Yesod and proves to have a number of forms, some masculine and others feminine.

- Captain: a butterfly-winged giantess (V, chap. 24, 172) who can also assume human form.
- Exile: little Tzadkiel, a miniature female with wings (V, chap. 40, 283); a wild thing that was banished from Tzadkiel to live by Brook Madregot (285).
- Judge: a golden king (V, chap. 21, 150).

❧ Zak: an apport that grows up into the Judge (v, chap. 1, 7). See ZAK.

In addition, Tzadkiel has son named Venant.

*Myth:* (Hebrew) angel of justice. In the Kabbalistic book *The Zohar,* Tzadkiel is fourth of the ten archangels of the Briatic world. See SEFIROTH; YESOD.

**Tzadkiel's ship** the ship which sails between the stars has no name, but is usually called "ship of Tzadkiel." Sometimes it is called "The Ship" in the belief that there is only one starship (v, chap. 4, 26–27). The ship has seven sides, and three decks have deep bays.

After delivering Severian to Yesod, the ship's next mission is to both mete out justice to the jibers and deliver colonists to Urth in time for the Deluge. These colonists are memory-erased sailors who had fought against Severian at his trial and fled. This trip is presumably the one that links Hethor, Jonas, and the Kim Lee Soong Group (supposing that they are all jibers abandoned on low-tech Urth).

# *U*

**uakaris** short-tailed monkeys, *Cacajao* (I, chap. 21, 190).

**uhlan** a road patrol in the Commonwealth (I, chap. 13, 125). They have orders to kill anyone found on the road and permission to loot the bodies of those they slay, enforcing the law made by Autarch Maruthas. See IBAR and MINEAS.
*History:* (from Turkish "boy, servant") a special type of cavalryman or lancer in various European armies (originally in Slavonic countries, especially Poland; latterly specific to the German Empire). Of Tartarian origin, they were armed with lances, pistols, sabers, and later with carbines, and were employed mainly as skirmishers and scouts.

**uintather** [yew-in-ta-THEER] an Ascian beast of burden (IV, chap. 29, 231).
*History: uintatherium,* a grotesque rhinoceros-sized mammal, with three pairs of bony protuberances on its head: a front pair on the tip of the nose, a second on the forehead, and a third at the back of the head. The upper canines were enlarged, saber-like structures protected by a flange on the lower jaw. Lived in North America during the Eocene.

**Ultan** the blind librarian of Nessus (I, chap. 5, 51). When Master Ultan says, "It is unwise to know too much about these practices [involving the analeptic alzabo] . . . though when I think of sharing the mind of a historian like Loman, or Hermas" (I,

chap. 6, 52), he echoes Socrates: "What would not a man give if he might converse with Orpheus and Musaeus and Hesiod and Homer?" (Plato's *Apology,* 40B).
*Onomastics:* "ravine" (Celtic).
*History:* Saint Ultan was a 7th-century bishop of Ardbraccan, said to have collected the writings of Saint Brigid.
*Commentary:* according to C. N. Manlove, Ultan means "the last" (*Science Fiction: Ten Explorations,* 211). There are hints that Ultan is Borges himself (see BORGES, JORGE LUIS). Borges served as director of the National Library in Buenos Aires (leading some readers to see "Nessus" as a phonetic corruption of "Buenos Aires") and then lost his sight, as alluded to in his "Poem about Gifts" (collected in *Dream Tigers)*:

> Let none think I by tear or reproach make light
> Of this manifesting the mastery
> Of God, who with excelling irony
> Gives me at once both books and night.

This line is paraphrased by Ultan: "He who had given all books into my keeping made me blind so that I should know in whose keeping the keepers stand" (I, chap. 6, 61).

**Unicorn** a constellation of Urth, visible in spring and summer (III, chap. 18, 146).
*Astronomy:* our Unicorn or Monoceros, a summer constellation of the southern hemisphere (January, February, and March). Because the constellation is in the same season as on Earth, this suggests that Urth is in a Piscean Age at least 26,000 years in the future.

**upanga** the nose flute (II, chap. 11, 98).

**uranic** astronomical, celestial (V, chap. 27, 191).

**Urbis** another name for the town of "The Tale of the Town That Forgot Fauna" (V, chap. 33, 232). See also PESTIS.
*Latin:* walled town.

**Uroboros** in the Commonwealth, it seems to mean

1. The equator. "You have been in the jungle north of the mountains, where no battle has been since they turned our flank by crossing the Uroboros" (IV, chap. 33, 265).
2. A river or sea at the equator separating the Commonwealth from Ascia proper, hence Ocean. "The sea — the World-River Uroboros — cradling Urth" (I, chap. 15, 140), and "the great river there [to the north] that flows to its own source, or the sea itself, that devours its own beginnings" (II, chap. 27, 255).
3. An equatorial monster. "I've heard that in the hot forests of the north, the Autarch of All Serpents is Uroboros, the brother of Abaia, and that hunters who discover his burrow believe they have found a tunnel under the sea, and descending it enter his mouth and all unknowing climb down his throat, so that they are dead while they still believe themselves living" (II, chap. 27, 255).

*History:* (also Ouroboros) in world folk belief, a serpent or dragon devouring its own tail; often a symbol of eternity. A Gnostic symbol. See also AMPHISBAENA.

**ursine man** an unnamed character who is one of Guasacht's men (IV, chap. 19, 151). He is almost Severian's height and twice his weight (thus 350 pounds). He is a destrier trainer and whistles to make the piebald attack Severian. Severian associates such fighting destriers with the Bear Tower of the Citadel (152), further emphasizing the bearish aspect of this man.

**Urth** the name of the world where the events of *The Book of the New Sun* take place, the planet of the past (II, chap. 23, 209). See SOLAR SYSTEM TABLE.
*Myth:* (Norse) Urth is the eldest of the Norns and represents the Past.

**urticate** [ER-tick-ATE] to sting, as or like a nettle; to affect with a tingling pain or stinging sensation; or to flog with fresh stinging-nettles; also to flagellate, whip (I, chap. 7, 78).

**Urvasi and Pururavas** "Urvasi loved Pururavas, you know, before she saw him in a bright light" (I, chap. 19, 172).
*Myth:* when the Hindu gods churned the ocean, among the beings that emerged were the Apsaras ("daughters of pleasure"), multiple spirits of all possibility, dancers and singers of the heavens, renowned for wantonness. Urvasi (a name sometimes used of Ushas) was the most famous, born when a sage surrounded by tempting Apsaras slapped his thigh.

Urvasi once consented to live with a human king, but she told him that human nakedness disgusted her. He promised she would never have to see him unclothed, but then he forgot one day, and she fled. (In some versions, a flash of lightning exposes him.)

Only when he promised to leave his throne and become an erotic singer-dancer did she agree to return.

**Ushas** the name of the new Urth, after the arrival of the New Sun, as given in Dr. Talos's play (II, chap. 24, 223). The "Adam and Eve" of this new world are sailors who, having fought against Severian and fled (V, chap. 21, 155), then had their memories wiped before being landed as new colonists (V, chap. 51, 369). They are taught everything by the four survivors of Urth: Odilo, Pega, Thais, and the Sleeper.
*Myth:* the Hindu dawn goddess who is reborn every morning and rides in a chariot pulled by cows or red horses. She is a wanton goddess, and she is said to be the mother or lover of the sun.

**uturuncu** a shaman of the Quechua (Peru and Bolivia), capable of assuming the form of a tiger (IV, chap. 28, 228).

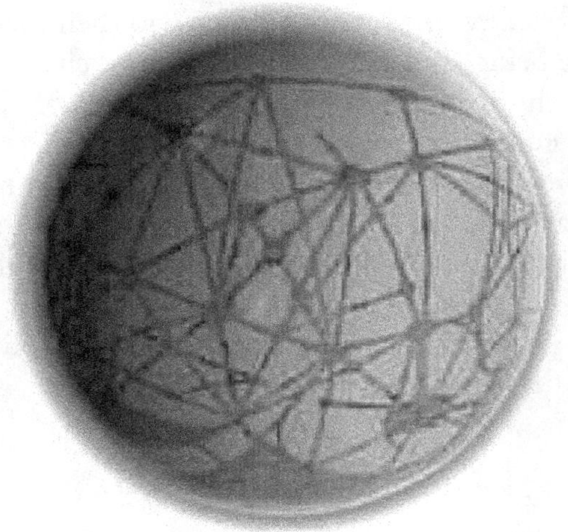

*Verthandi*

# V

**Valeria** an armigette of the Citadel, first met by the apprentice Severian near the Atrium of Time (I, chap. 4, 44). Her family had first occupied their towers in some dimly remembered period: "They had waited, at first, to leave Urth with the autarch of their era," and since no autarch between Ymar and the old autarch took the trip, this suggests that the family has been on standby for up to one thousand years. After ascending the Phoenix Throne, Severian marries Valeria. When Severian prepared for his journey to Yesod, he seems to have assumed that it would take less than a year and he left Father Inire in control as wazir (V, chap. 34, 239). Severian's unexpected absence over years must create a crisis, a crisis that drives Valeria to become "autarch" (really a pseudo-autarch), ending Inire's stewardship. Eventually she marries Dux Caesidius, under the assumption that Severian has died. Valeria's reign lasts for decades: though the beginning year is uncertain, being sometime after 11 S.R., it ends in 50 S.R. when she is killed by an assassin immediately prior to the deluge.
*History:* there are three Saints Valeria: the 1st-century alleged mother of Saints Gervase and Protase, and wife of Saint Vitalis (she seems to be fictitious); a virgin martyr who probably never existed; and one of a group believed to be contemporaries of Jesus Christ, and among the early martyrs.
*Literature:* when Valeria says "I am all the sisters we breed . . . And all the sons" (I, chap. 4, 34), she echoes Viola (a twin disguised as a man) in Shakespeare's *Twelfth Night*: "I am all the

daughters of my father's house, And all the brothers too" (act II, scene 4, line 123).
*Onomastics:* "strong, valiant" (Latin).
*Commentary:* John Clute points out that Valeria "bears the name of a Roman family famous for having served Emperors over the span of a millennium" (*Strokes,* 166). In some way she stands for the Moon as Severian stands for the Sun: "It did not seem to me that I slept, but Valeria sat beside me weeping for drowned Urth . . . I woke and found . . . that Lune was concealed behind clouds from which fell a gentle rain" (V, chap. 48, 340). In light of this, Valeria's assassination seems related to a solar eclipse.

**vasculum** a special kind of case used by botanists for carrying newly collected specimens (II, chap. 13, 108). Usually made of tin in the form of a flattened cylinder, with a lid on one side opening along the length.

**vates** "You should know, vates" (V, chap. 35, 249). A poet or bard, especially one who is divinely inspired; a prophet-poet.

**Vatic Fountain** an oracular device in the House Absolute, which is activated by the tossing of a coin into its waters (I, chap. 10, 97).

**Veil of Maya** "I had rent the Veil of Maya" (V, chap. 47, 332).
*History:* the Indian word "maya" is complex in meaning. It can mean an illusion created by a supernatural agency, but it can also mean the generative force within the primeval substance. Buddha is said to have awakened from the dream-like process of maya and escaped the web of illusory experience.

**Velleity** from Hildegrin's business card: "Or inquire at the Alticamelus around the corner on Velleity" (I, chap. 23, 205). A street in Nessus that crosses Argosy Street.
*History:* the fact or quality of merely willing, wishing, or desiring, without any effort or advance toward action or realization.

**Venant** seemingly a middle-aged man, he is actually a Hierarch, a son of Tzadkiel who is killed in the melee at Severian's trial (V, chap. 21, 153–54). He is first seen in the company of two middle-aged women following Zak-as-autarch in the procession to the trial (V, chap. 16, 111).
*Astronomy:* an obscure name for Regulus, one of the Four Royal Stars of ancient Persia (Allen, *Star Names,* 256). The full set is Hastorang (Fomalhaut) to the North; Venant to the South; Tascheter (Aldebaran) to the East; and Satevis (presumably Antares) to the West.

**vermilion** Severian's manuscript is written in vermilion ink (I, chap. 35, 294; III, chap. 30, 240). A color, vivid red to reddish orange.

**Vert** the capital of the Green Empire of the East in EFF, Vert has a stable dynasty. Green is their currency (emeralds) as well as their nature-symbol (laurel trees). After more than a chiliad of battle against the Yellow Empire, the national color changes to argent (French "silver"), because of either the installation of a new regime by the Yellow Empire (silver is akin to gold), or the successful invasion by a third party (perhaps the creatures of SPECULA, who would certainly use silver, the color of mirrors, as their standard).

*French:* green.
*Commentary:* the mutually fatal battle between the trees and the vines finds an interesting parallel with the love between ASH and his wife Vine, the first man and woman.

**Verthandi** as a planet of Urth's solar system, this corresponds to our planet Mars (I, chap. 35, 292). Terraformed in the First Empire period of the Age of the Monarch. See HISTORY OF URTH; SOLAR SYSTEM TABLE.
*Myth:* (Norse) one of the three Norns (along with Urth and Skuld), Verthandi represents the Present.

**vespers** see WATCHES OF THE DAY (IV, chap. 36, 290).

**Vici** [VIKY] a village in the Commonwealth (V, chap. 29, 203).
*Latin:* "vicis" meaning change, interchange.

**vicuna** "Soft, wool-like, yet softer, much softer. A blend of linen and vicuna?" (I, chap. 17, 154).
*History:* a South American animal closely related to the llama and alpaca, inhabiting the higher portions of the northern Andes and yielding a fine silky wool used for textile fabrics; also, cloth made of this wool. In pre-Columbian Peru, cloth made of vicuna was reserved for the use of the Inca himself, thus becoming a symbol of his semidivine status as a descendant of the Sun God.

**vincula** "the house of chains," the prison of Thrax (III, chap. I, 10). The vincula employs a lictor, a sergeant, and several clavigers.
*Latin:* "vinculum," a band, cord, chain, fetter, or tie.

**vingtner** "the thwacks of the vingtners' rods and the howls of the unfortunates who had been hit" (II, chap. I, II). See MILITARY ORGANIZATION.
*History:* a sergeant commanding twenty infantrymen, from the Renaissance British Army.

**virescence** "The curve of Lune lay just visible in the east, sending streamers of virescence" (ES, 26). The state or condition of becoming green.

**viridian** a durable bluish-green pigment; a shade of bluish-green (III, chap. 28, 232).

**vivarium** a place of enclosure especially adapted or prepared for the keeping of living animals under their normal conditions (V, chap. 4, 24).

**Vodalarius** a follower of Vodalus; the plural form is "Vodalarii" (I, chap. I, 16). Following is a list, in order of appearance.

- Thea.
- Hildegrin.
- Black-bearded volunteer at Saltus, the fifth man on the battering ram at Barnoch's house (II, chap. 2, 19). He later takes Severian hostage (II, chap. 8, 72). He takes *Terminus Est.* He is decapitated.
- Barnoch.
- Man with scarred face and dirk (II, chap. 8, 72) who is pushed off the baluchither.
- Baluchither trainer (II, chap. 8, 72), decapitated.
- Innkeeper at Saltus, probably (II, chap. I, 12; II, chap. 18, 163).

- Five guards, including one armiger referred to as "Waldgrave" (II, chap. II, 92).
- Alcmund.
- Old leech.
- Female guards on the jungle march.

**Vodalus** a revolutionary, resurrectionist, king of the forest, yet ultimately a pawn of the autarch (I, chap. I, 13). An exultant, he openly defies the autarch and hopes to usurp him. He calls Abaia and Erebus his masters. His Vodalarii serve the Ascian army in limited scouting capacities, including the hit-and-run harassment mentioned in the letter of the DEAD SOLDIER. Agia eventually kills him with the worm of white fire, another one of Hethor's pets, and then she replaces him as adversary to the autarch. See LIEGE OF LEAVES.

*Onomastics:* the word "vod" is an obsolete Scottish form of "wood" (OED).

*History:* Saint Vodalus (died 725) was an Irish or Scottish monk who crossed over to Gaul as a missionary and died a recluse near Soissons.

**volunteers** the following is a brief list.

- Twelve men to guard the dead in the necropolis (I, chap. I, II). The leader plus two others sprint after Eata, two grab Drotte. Once inside gate, the groups scatter on left, right, and center paths. The leader (with a knife) and two others (one with an ax, one with a pike) meet the robbers (Vodalus, Hildegrin, Thea). The leader's knife goes into the ground, then he wrestles Vodalus. Vodalus gets the knife, and stabs the leader. The Axman raises his ax, Severian stops it at the top and kills him. The pikeman flees.

❧ Four men to break Barnoch's door. (A fifth man joins; he is a Vodalarius.)

**voulge** a kind of halberd (IV, chap. 1, 12). A long-bladed axe with two loops at the rear, secured to a haft that was usually about the height of the user. Stone says that historically the halberd was evolved from the voulge, but that this form was a later peasant weapon.

*Waterbuck*

**wain** a large, open farm wagon (I, chap. 18, 161).

**waitress** the cafe waitress met by Severian, Baldanders, and Dr. Talos, a thin young woman with straggling hair who has worked there for about a month (I, chap. 16, 147–48). She is transformed into Jolenta. Maybe her name really was Jolenta, but it seems more likely that Jolenta was her stage name; a parallel to Jonas, who got that name after his own transformation.

**Waldgrave** a title (II, chap. II, 93), same as WILDGRAVE. This character is an armiger who captains the guards escorting Severian and Jonas to the feast. He hopes the meal will not be another tribade, which may be an allusion to the DEAD WOMAN IN THE NECROPOLIS.

**Wall of Nessus** the wall that encloses Nessus is circular according to the map in *Plan[e]t Engineering* and has a radius of 10 leagues (30 miles), which would give a circumference of around 63 leagues (189 miles). (Note that the radius is the distance that Severian travels from tower to Wall in 3.5 days of interrupted walking.) Honeycombed with passages and chambers, this ancient and mysterious structure is perhaps more than one league tall (III, chap. 13, 104).
*Commentary:* such a monumental barrier recalls the Great Wall of China, a defense against the northern horse barbarians which was begun in 214 B.C. and stone clad in the 1370s. The Great Wall is

twenty-five feet high at its tallest point. In comparison, the Grand Canyon averages one mile in depth.

The true height of the Wall of Nessus is difficult to gauge, but the more concrete details suggest it is considerably shorter than one league. Clouds move across it and Severian wonders if it would be difficult for waterfowl to fly over it (1, chap. 35, 298), but technically low clouds are below 6,500 feet, and the flight ceiling of waterfowl is around 4,000 feet. So a height of perhaps 3,000 feet is implied.

Direct observation in the text is in two sections: first when Severian is on the ground level at the Sanguinary Field (1, chap. 25, 218–19; chap. 27, 234), and second when Severian describes the view from the top of the Matachin Tower, located "near the center of the city" (1, chap. 35, 296). The tower seems to have ten stories of varying height, but if they average eight feet each then the top is eighty feet above ground.

The view from the tower shows the Wall as a black line on the horizon to the north, that is, it is barely visible at that elevation. If one assumes that the elevation of the tower plus the Citadel Hill is 200 feet, then at the top the horizon is 19 miles away. If one sets the Wall height to 3,000 feet, it has a horizon of 74 miles. Adding these horizons makes the distance from tower to Wall equal to 93 miles, a number that is three times larger than the distance suggested by the map in PE. Lowering the Wall to 2,000 feet and the tower to 200 feet makes the distance 80 miles. Scaling down to the 30 mile distance of PE gives a tower/hill height of 120 feet and a Wall height of 300 feet.

| Distance | Height of Tower + Hill | Wall Height |
|---|---|---|
| 30 miles | 120 feet | 300 feet |
| 50 miles | 200 feet | 500 feet |
| 93 miles | 200 feet | 3,000 feet |
| 97 miles | 300 feet | 3,000 feet |

In the area of the Sanguinary Field the Wall is "a line of bitter black" that "goes halfway to the sky" and looks like an approaching storm. At that point Severian seems to be around twelve miles from the Wall. If the Wall is .57 miles tall (3,000 feet) and the distance is twelve miles, then the viewing angle is 2.7° from the horizontal. In other words, from base to top the Wall blocks out 2.7° of sky, which is equivalent to a stack of five Moons (each .52° seen from Earth).

The old sun appears to have an angular diameter of 15°, and the western horizon lifts 15° per hour. The trumpet is blown when the disc appears to touch the upper edge of the Wall (1, chap. 26, 228), and Severian hears it as he leaves the Inn of Lost Loves (233). When Severian is 100 strides away from the Sanguinary Field, the solar disc is "a quarter concealed" behind the Wall (1, chap. 27, 235). The horizon moves this distance in fifteen minutes.

Tattoo is blown at sunset (1, chap. 26, 229). If the Wall is 3,000 feet tall, tattoo would come one hour and eleven minutes (or about one watch) after the first signal.

Comparative heights from contemporary Earth: the Sears Tower in Chicago is 1,451 feet tall. The tallest inhabited building in the world is Taipei 101, at 1,667 feet.

**watch** a period of time based on the length of a sentry's duty (III, appendix, 301), one twentieth of a twenty-four hour day (CD, 228), being equal to an hour and twelve minutes. At the equinox there are ten watches of daylight and ten watches of night. See MEASUREMENT TABLES; WATCHES OF THE DAY.

## Watches of the Day

| Watch | Name | Time of Day |
|---|---|---|
| 1 | Prime | 6:00 A.M. |
| 2 | | 7:13 |
| 3 | Tierce* | 8:26 |
| 4 | | 9:39 |
| 5 | | 10:52 |
| 6 | Nones | 12:05 P.M. |
| 7 | | 1:18 |
| 8 | | 2:31 |
| 9 | | 3:44 |
| 10 | | 4:57 |
| 1 | Vespers | 6:10, sunset |

* Not mentioned in the Urth Cycle, but it fits the pattern of canonical hours.

**Water Way** a road that borders Gyoll in Nessus (I, chap. 14, 130).

**waterbuck** a species of antelope found in watered districts in central South Africa; an animal of this species, which is marked with a characteristic white ring around the buttocks (I, chap. 25, 221).

**Well of Green Chimes** the spiral ramp near the antechamber, which connects the garden surface with the subterranean House Absolute, has some green gongs hanging in the center near the bottom (II, chap. 16, 138). Whenever the door at the bottom is opened, air passes through and rings the gongs (II, chap. 14, 121–22).

**Well of Orchids** the autarch's harem of 500 exultant women and their khaibits (I, chap. 7, 75). See HOUSE ABSOLUTE.

**wend** "Where wend you, little one . . . ?" (I, chap. 18, 162). *History:* to proceed on or along (one's way); go.

**Werenfrid** a torturer of olden times. Master Werenfrid has a special place in the lore of the guild. He is the protagonist of Palaemon's joke (CD, 269–70), as well as the following passage:

> being in grave need, [he] accepted remuneration from the enemies of the condemned and from his friends as well; and who by stationing one party on the right of the block and the other on the left, by his great skill made it appear to each that the result was entirely satisfactory (I, chap. 33, 281).

*History:* Saint Werenfrid (died 780) was an Englishman who worked with Saint Willibrord among the Frisians, and he died at Arnheim.

**White Fountain** a white hole, the boon promised to the autarch who can pass the test at Yesod. The Old Sun becomes the

New Sun when the White Fountain is placed into it. The White Fountain seems to be moving across the galaxy at sub-light speeds, since its starlight can be seen long before it arrives.
*Commentary:* Peter Nicholls, in his insightful review of *The Urth of the New Sun* (in *Foundation no. 41,* winter 1987) points out a certain "male principle" involved here, and notes that the romantic interlude between Apheta and Severian may signal the birth of a universe.

**white wolf** just as rats might infest a house, so do the terrible white wolves live in the hollow walls of the House Absolute (II, chap. 19, 158). Probably introduced as a kind of accident (a few wild animals wandering into the Secret House), the white wolf apparently found an untapped niche and has thrived within it.

**wildgrave** "some tyrannical wildgrave or veneal burgess had been delivered to the mercy of the guild" (I, chap. 2, 24). A title for "the chief of a band of foresters" in the Commonwealth (CD, 236). It seems to be an armiger title: see WALDGRAVE.
*History:* formerly the chief magistrate of an uncultivated or forest region in Germany; specifically the title of a hereditary race of rulers in parts of the Rhineland.

**wingward** the farm worker who cares for the doves (CD, 276).

**Winnoc** a slave of the Pelerines (IV, chap. 12, 91). Nearly fifty years of age, he was whipped by Journeyman Palaemon in decades past, before he was twenty (IV, chap. 12, 92). Winnoc says,

> In the olden times . . . slavery was by skin color. The darker a man was, the more a slave they made him. That's hard to believe, I know. But we used to have a chatelaine in the order who knew a lot about history and she told me. She was a truthful woman (IV, chap. 12, 93).

It is just possible that this historian among the Pelerines was the mysterious monial Catherine. The timeline does not exclude it, since Palaemon was exiled thirty years ago and Catherine left the order around twenty years ago. More alarming is the link to our own history. Whoever the historian was, she was very wise indeed: perhaps even a time-traveler.
*History:* Saint Winnoc (died 717?), probably of royal blood, was raised in Brittany and became a monk at Saint Sithiu.

**witches** "It is said that in ancient times there were both men and women in the guild. . . . But Ymar the Almost Just, observing how cruel the women were and how often they exceeded the punishments he had decreed, ordered that there should be women among the torturers no more" (I, chap. 2, 20). A guild that accepts only women, the witches have (or claim to have) supernatural knowledge and premonitions, and they take part in orgiastic rites, sometimes dancing wildly in the Old Court on nights of rain, other times screaming with abandon from the upper levels of their Witches' Keep. They use kettles for their visions and count the Cumaean as one of their own. Presumably, Ymar (or a later autarch) reformed the jailers of his time (who were living in the abandoned hulks of the spaceport Nessus) into two distinct and separate groups, the torturers and the witches, and assigned them quarters in the hulks later known as the Matachin Tower and the Witches' Keep. This reform movement probably began with the sudden death of Prefect Prisca.

**Wolf** the foster parents of Frog are he-wolf and she-wolf in "The Tale of the Boy Called Frog" (III, chap. 19, 150).
*Literature:* Mowgli is raised by wolves in the Jungle books by Kipling.
*Myth:* (Roman) Romulus and Remus were suckled by a she-wolf, which some say was sent by Mars, but Wolfe seems to favor Fauna, and he should know.

**Wolf** a constellation of Urth, located near the Unicorn (III, chap. 18, 146).
*Astronomy:* probably our Canis Major, or Large Dog, which is found near the Unicorn. (Our Wolf, Lupis, is near Scorpius.) The constellation Little Wolf is probably our Canis Minor, located on the other side of the Unicorn.

**worm of white fire** no longer than one's hand, a worm that glows with white fire (IV, chap. 30, 240). One has only to fling it, and it kills its target, then crawls back. It was brought to Urth via Hethor's mirrors.
*Commentary:* an elemental of the grave, perhaps a hybrid of fire and earth.

**Xanthic Lands** a group of about 200 islands in a sea located to the west of the Commonwealth (V, chap. 46, 327). Probably the mountaintops of submerged Indonesia/Australia ("Kim Lee Soong . . . a common name in places now sunk beneath the sea" [II, chap. 15, 130].) It seems likely the term is a back-formation from *Xanthoderms,* just as *Ascia* is from *Ascians.*
*History:* of or relating to "Xanthus," an ancient town in Asia Minor, or more likely from "xantho," yellow.
*Commentary:* the submerged continent could be Clark Ashton Smith's "Zothique." The name is similar, and Wolfe has acknowledged his debt to Smith in interviews. The mytho-scientific continent Lemuria or Mu also bears mentioning as the Pacific version of Atlantis.

**Xanthoderms** a race of people on Urth, presumably living in the Xanthic Lands (IV, chap. 35, 288). Meaning "yellow-skinned."

**xebec** "In form it might have been a xebec, sharp fore and aft, wide amidships, with a long, overhanging stern and an even longer prow" (III, chap. 29, 237).
*History:* a small three-masted (originally two-masted) vessel, commonly lateen-rigged but with some square sails, used in the Mediterranean, formerly as a ship of war, now as a merchant ship.

**xenagie** a cavalry unit of about 500 men (I, chap. 28, 243), or a dimarchi unit of 1,000 men (CD, 246).

*Ylespil*

# Y

**yellowbeard** a South American pit viper, the fer-de-lance or *Barba amarilla,* which has a yellow spot below the chin (I, chap. 21, 192). Also the jararaca *(Bothrops atrox).*

**Yellow Emperor** the ruler of the Yellow Empire in EFF. His capital is Zant. By holding Barrus (bastard son of Prince Patizithes) as a hostage, the Yellow Emperor hopes to gain victory in the long running war against the Green Empire.
*Myth:* the Yellow Emperor is a figure from Chinese prehistory. Huangti, the third of the Three Kings, invented pottery and houses. Around 2600 B.C., his people settled the land of fertile ground around the Yellow River, but before long, encroaching neighbors (led by Ch'ih Yu, who called himself the Red Emperor and worshipped the gods of fire) caused Huangti to fight the first war. He crushed Ch'ih Yu and took the entire area of fertile river land, then all the other tribes hailed him as lord. He moved his capital to Pingyang, central to the tribal lands, and ruled as the Yellow Emperor. (See SPECULA.)

**Yesod** the higher universe, home to the HIERARCHS and HIEROGRAMMATES (IV, chap. 34, 279), Yesod is also the name of the world-ship in orbit around a star in that hyperspace (V, chap. 15). The surface of this "heavenly" world is mostly covered by water, and on each of the countless islands a different galaxy is judged. The interior of Yesod is where most of the inhabitants live and work (journeys to the surface are rewards), and there is a passing

hint that it is somehow "hellish": at the threshold, an apprehensive Gunnie gives a quote, "No hope for those who enter here" (v, chap. 23, 165), a direct allusion to the famous line "Abandon all hope, you who enter here" of Dante's *Inferno*.
*Myth:* (Hebrew) the angel invoked by Moses to bring death to the firstborn males in Egypt, the name means "foundation." Yesod is also one of the SEFIROTH, the one that links Malkuth (Earth and the physical universe) to all the other sefiroth.
*Commentary:* there is some ambiguity about this topic. First of all, Yesod is properly a sefira, and in some of the more famous illustrations, it is depicted as being within the world (or universe) of Yetsirah (in the abdominal area of "Adam Kadamon"). Yetsirah is certainly a higher plane than Earth, stuck as we are on Malkuth in Asiyah (the legs of "Adam Kadamon"), so the idea of Yesod being a higher universe from Urth seems at first glance to fit in nicely, with the "Brook Madregot" as the line running from Yesod to Malkuth.

In the second glance, however, there is Briah. Briah would appear to be a different spelling of Beri'ah, the second of the created worlds. The idea that Urth resides in a universe governed by the three sefiroth of Strength, Beauty, and Mercy is undercut by the nagging fact that Yesod is not in a higher universe from Beri'ah, but a lower one! (An argument could be made that Briah equals Binah, another sefira, but as Binah is located in the first world, the head and shoulders of "Adam Kadamon," this only causes more confusion.)

**Yesod: the mechanics of hyperspace** it seems likely that time in Yesod travels in a direction opposite that of Briah. This is the case in the two-universe model of Wolfe's non-Urth story "Procreation" (collected in *Endangered Species)*, and it is supported by details from *The Urth of the New Sun.*

For example, in its voyage to Yesod, Tzadkiel's ship travels into the future, taking millennia or billions of years to get there. Severian's visit on the worldship of Yesod lasts a day, and then, rather than returning to Tzadkiel's ship by tender, Severian and Gunnie are teleported from inside the worldship to a deepspace point in Briah where they are picked up by Tzadkiel's ship in transit to Urth. The ship slows and they are dropped off at Urth, where eventually Severian finds he is a thousand years in the past from when he had left. Since teleportation (from inside worldship Yesod to deepspace Briah) implies simultaneity, then it implies that a day on worldship Yesod equals at least a thousand retrograde years in Briah. That is, supposedly if Severian had taken the tender back up to the Ship, as his predecessor had, he, too, would have come back to Urth at a time only a few months after he had left. Severian is given a short cut by way of teleportation, but it puts him into the past.

Based on Baldanders's physics lesson (v, chap. 42), there are three universes: a hyperspace called Yesod, a normal space called Briah, and an unnamed subspace which might be termed "Abaddon." In this model, a black hole consumes matter and energy in one universe to expel it as a white hole in the universe above it, so black holes in Briah (including the one eating at the heart of the old sun) lead to white holes in Yesod, and the white fountain in Briah is therefore the exit point of a black hole in subspace Abaddon.

(In addition there are some other mini-universes: the corridors of Time, which has a time travel aspect bound to Briah, as well as a "dream space" aspect; the Brook Madregot, which links the corridors of Time, Yesod, and Briah.)

Near the threshold of hyperspace Yesod, the ship of Tzadkiel passes through a "ghost region" that would seem to be the destination of imploded beings like Master Ash (whose memory is invoked by Severian during the transit of this region (v, chap. 14, 98–99), and by extension probably also Hildegrin. It is also the likely destination for creatures who have stepped into Briatic magic mirrors (Jonas and Sancha's cat): "That marvelous circle of specula by whose power a living being may be coalesced from the ethereal waves, or, should such a being boldly enter them, circumfused to the borders of Briah" (ES, 213).

If mirror travel is interdimensional travel that is as one-way as blackhole to whitehole travel is; and if the Briah ghost region is where all who enter mirrors in Briah go; then the creatures that emerge from mirrors in Briah (slug, notule, peryton, salamander, etc.) must come from a second ghost region, one that separates normal space Briah from subspace Abaddon.

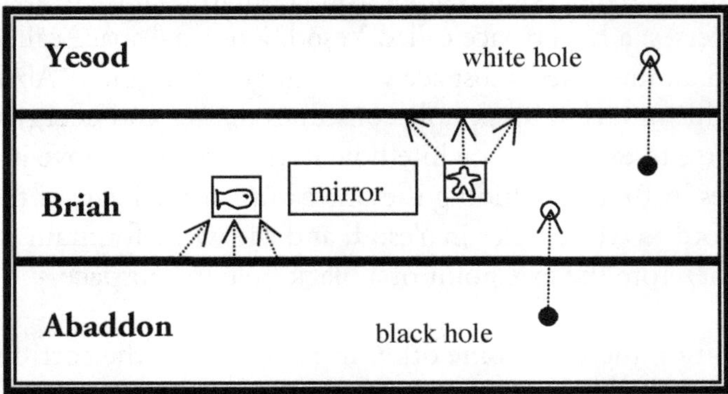

**Ylem** "Thus by the paradoxical nature of knowledge, it is seen that though the existence of the Ylem, the primordial source of all things, may be doubted, yet the existence of his servants may not be doubted" (III, chap. 27, 220). Here used as an aspect of the Increate.
*History:* (probably from Greek "hyle") the primordial first substance from which, according to some theories, the elements are formed.

**ylespil** the hedgehog (III, chap. 37, 291).

**Ymar the Almost Just** a nearly legendary autarch of Urth, living a chiliad before the birth of Severian (I, chap. 2, 21). Despite his humble origins as a torturer's apprentice (see REECHY), Ymar's reign marked the end of the Age of the Monarch and the beginning of the Age of the Autarch. An anecdote regarding Autarch Ymar:

> Disguising himself, he ventured into the countryside, where he spied a muni meditating beneath a plane tree. The Autarch joined him and sat with his back to the trunk until Urth had begun to spurn the sun. Troopers bearing an oriflamme galloped past, a merchant drove a mule staggering under gold, a beautiful woman rode the shoulders of eunuchs, and at last a dog trotted through the dust. Ymar rose and followed the dog, laughing (I, chap. 17, 158).

*History:* Saint Ymar (died 830) was a monk of Reculver in Kent, martyred by the Danes.

**Yrierix the Sage** a Perfect Master of philosophy mentioned in the brown book, where he is contrasted with Thalelaeus the Great: "[It was thought by] Yrierix the Sage that the commonality would never permit one differing from themselves to hold high office" (I, chap. 10, 97).
*History:* Yrieix (without the second R) is another name for Saint Aredius (died 591). Born in Limoges, France, he served at court, then became abbot-founder of the monastery of Atane, in the Limousin, where the village of Saint Yrieix was named for him.

**yurt** a circular domed hut consisting of skins or felt stretched over a collapsible lattice framework (III, chap. 2, 20). Used by the Kirghiz and other Mongol nomads of Siberia.

**Zak** a being that seems to rapidly evolve on Tzadkiel's ship. He arrives as an apport, a creature spontaneously generated by the ship's sails, possibly a reflection of Severian himself (v, chap. 1, 7). First he is a blind, shaggy animal (v, chap. 3, 16), something like a pika (v, chap. 4, 25), that bites Purn's hand (v, chap. 6, 45). Then he is Zak the hairy dwarf who helps Severian (v, chap. 9, 66), followed by Zak the sailor (v, chap. 13, 92), and the false autarch with long blond hair and heroic physique of a twenty-five year old (v, chap. 15, 110). Finally he becomes the golden judge at Severian's trial.
*Onomastics:* a sailor's nickname form of Tzadkiel.

**Zama** a sailor of Os who drowned off Baiulo Island, he is reanimated as a zombie by Ceryx, but resurrected by the Conciliator (v, chap. 31–32). The only time he spoke after being resurrected was to say, "Don't cry, Mafalda" (v, chap. 32, 228). In the end, Zama kills Ceryx and the townspeople kill Zama.
*History:* Saint Zama (died 268?) is listed as first known bishop of Bologna, Italy. Zama is also a town in Numidia adopted by King Juba as his capital, and it is the traditional site of Scipio's defeat of Hannibal in 202 B.C.

**Zambdas** hetman of the village Murene on the shore of Lake Diuturna (III, chap. 28, 229). He owns the slave Pia and his wife beats her whenever he is away.

*History:* Saint Zambdas (died 304) is said to have been the thirty-seventh bishop of Jerusalem, and he was connected with the legend of the Theban legion.

**Zant** capital of the Yellow Empire of the West, Zant has chronic usurpation of the throne. Yellow is their currency (gold) as well as their plant symbol (vine). At war with the Green Empire to the East for a chiliad.

**Zed** a world in the story "The God and His Man."

**Zelezo** an android sailor on Tzadkiel's ship.
*Onomastics:* not a name, it is the word "iron" (Czech).

**ziggurat** "What the ziggurat had once been, I never guessed. Perhaps a prison indeed; perhaps a temple, or the atelier of some forgotten art" (IV, chap. 26, 212). The jungle prison where Severian was held by Vodalus before being taken to the Ascians. It seems to be mentioned in the play *Eschatology and Genesis.*

> [Second Demon]: Our travels but lately took us to the northern jungles, and there, in a temple older than man, a shrine overgrown with rank vegetation until it seemed hardly more than a leafy mound, we spoke to an ancient shaman who foretold great peril to your realm (II, chap. 24, 225).

*History:* a form of temple common to the Sumerians, Babylonians, and Assyrians, it was a pyramidal structure, built in receding tiers upon a rectangular, oval, or square platform, with a shrine at the summit. Access to the shrine was provided by a series of ramps on one side or a continuous spiral ramp from base to summit. Similar structures were built by the Mayan cultures of Central America.

**zoanthrop** in the Commonwealth one who elects to become a type of beast-man by having his or her forebrain surgically removed (III, chap. 1, 11). Primitive in the extreme, they are capable of carrying and using ironwood bludgeons.
*History:* one afflicted with "zoanthropy," a form of insanity in which a man imagines himself to be a beast.

**zodiac** Urth's zodiac remains sketchy. The GREAT BULL is probably our Taurus; the SWAN may be our Sagittarius; and Stonebuck (IA, 45) is our Capricorn.

**zoetic** of or relating to life; living, vital (V, chap. 36, 258). Thus, the "zoetic transport" referred to (probably an old name for the Bear Tower) is a live-cargo ship.

# SYNOPSIS OF SEVERIAN'S NARRATIVE

*The Shadow of the Torturer*

Severian, an apprentice torturer, has a chance encounter with the exultant rebel Vodalus and his henchmen robbing a grave. He spontaneously aids the outlaw by killing a volunteer guard (1). Earlier in that same day, Severian had nearly drowned while swimming in the River Gyoll, but after a near-death dream-vision involving the ghost of Master Malrubius, he had been saved by an undine (2). Severian hides the coin Vodalus gave him and reflects on his guild (3). The next winter, Severian wanders into a lost part of the citadel searching for his dog and meets a young woman named Valeria near the Atrium of Time (4).

Severian becomes captain of the apprentices (5) and goes on an errand to the Library of Nessus where he gets four books (one of them is *The Book of Wonders of Urth and Sky,* henceforth known as "the brown book") for an exultant prisoner (6). He meets Thecla, the prisoner who requested the books, and learns from Master Gurloes that she is being held as a lever against Vodalus, since her half-sister Thea is Vodalus's lover (7). To guard against infatuation with a prisoner, Gurloes sends Severian to "The House Azure," a brothel in the Algedonic Quarter where he hires a woman who calls herself Thecla (9). Severian falls in love with Thecla anyway (10).

Severian is elevated to journeyman and has another dream-vision (11). Two days later the torture of Thecla begins, and Severian breaks the law by giving her a knife with which to kill herself (12). For this crime against the guild he is ordered to become the Lictor of Thrax, a distant provincial capital to which he must walk (13). As a parting gift Master Palaemon gives him the sword *Terminus Est* and he also takes the brown book (14).

After crossing the bridge into the living city, Severian meets Baldanders the giant and Doctor Talos, has a dream-vision of undines and puppets (15). At a breakfast café Talos tries to convince Severian to travel with them and act in their play (which is based upon Canog's long lost *The Book of the New Sun)*, but Severian decides to skip their planned meeting at Ctesiphon's Cross and goes to a rag shop to buy traveling clothes (16).

Agilus, the shopkeeper of the rag shop, tries hard to talk Severian into selling *Terminus Est* to him, but Severian refuses; suddenly, a soldier (Agia in disguise) enters the shop and wordlessly delivers a challenge to mortal combat with averns (17). Agia, twin sister of Agilus, agrees to help Severian prepare for the duel but involves them in a cab race that results in the destruction of the altar of the Pelerines and the loss of the Claw of the Conciliator, a holy gem (18).

Severian and Agia go to the Botanic Gardens to select an avern flower for the duel, but get sidetracked by visits to the Sand Garden (19) and then the Jungle Garden (20, 21). They enter the Garden of Endless Sleep, which is both park and aquatic cemetery. They meet an old boatman searching for his long dead wife "Cas." His boat is too small to ferry them. Severian loses *Terminus Est* in the Lake of Birds and dives after it (22). He is helped out of the water by Dorcas, a young woman with amnesia, and the three of them are ferried across the lake by Hildegrin the Badger, a man Severian recognizes as the grave-digging henchman of Vodalus (23). Severian picks the flower before leaving the garden with Dorcas and Agia (24).

They make reservations for dinner at the Inn of Lost Loves, staying for a snack and getting involved in a little intrigue with the staff (25). Then it is time for the duel: Severian goes and is treacherously struck dead, but he rises up and his opponent panics, killing spectators in his attempt to flee (27).

Severian wakes up the next morning in the lazaret of the Blue Dimarchi (28) and learns that he must execute his former opponent, who turns out to be Agilus (29). The night before the execution, Severian meets an old sailor named Hethor, who is Agia's secret lover (30). After the execution, while Severian and Dorcas are walking towards the gate of Nessus, Severian suddenly discovers he has been carrying the Claw of the Conciliator (planted on him by Agia after the crash) and they see the miracle of the flying cathedral (31). By accident they meet Doctor Talos's dramatic troupe just in time to act in the play (32), after which Severian has a dream-vision involving the ghosts of Master Malrubius and Severian's dog Triskele (33). He learns the stage name of Jolenta (34). The party meets a sailor named Jonas who falls in love at first sight of Jolenta, just before the party is separated by a commotion at the Piteous Gate (35).

*The Claw of the Conciliator*

Severian and Jonas are in the village Saltus, a few days after the disturbance at the gate. They both want to meet up again with Dr. Talos's troupe, but Severian has to practice his art to make money. Severian learns he must execute a spy of Vodalus (1). As the spy is removed from his long-sealed house, Severian glimpses Agia (2). Trying to find her, he wanders into Saltus fair and meets the enslaved Green Man, a plant/man from the future. He leaves the Green Man a tool for escape (3).

## Synopsis

Severian performs tortures and executions (4), after which he receives a secret note from Thecla, telling him that she is alive and waiting for him in a nearby mine (5). At this mine he encounters the man-apes, guardians of the Autarch's treasure (6) before falling into the ambush set by Agia, author of the secret note (7).

Severian and Jonas are taken by cut-throats (8) to meet their leader Vodalus, who gives them the option of joining his rebellion against the Autarch (9). They join (their first mission is to deliver a message to a spy in the House Absolute) and for their initiation they must drink analeptic alzabo and eat the flesh of a dead follower of Vodalus, thereby gaining the memories of the deceased: the corpse turns out to be Thecla's (11).

On the road again, Severian and Jonas are attacked by notules and are only able to escape by getting the notules to kill a patrolling soldier (12). Remorseful, Severian uses the Claw of the Conciliator to resurrect the soldier, then Hethor shows up (13). Too close to the House Absolute, they are all captured by Praetorian Guards and thrown into the antechamber (14). Talking with the prisoners there, Severian realizes that many of them have been imprisoned for generations, but Jonas becomes very upset, somehow recognizing them through their family histories. A group of demons raid the antechamber, lashing the prisoners with electrified whips (15). Jonas is wounded and becomes delirious (16). To pass the time, Severian reads "The Tale of the Student and His Son" from the brown book (17).

By sifting Thecla's memories, Severian learns that the "demons" were just mischievous young exultants having their cruel fun. He finds the secret door leading out of the antecham-ber, but in the next room they come to, the Presence Chamber, Jonas sees his opportunity to escape Urth and enters the mirror teleportation device (18).

Severian wanders alone through the subterranean House Absolute, encountering Odilo and finding *Terminus Est* (19). Rudesind the curator again gives him directions, and Severian meets up with the brothel manager from the Algedonic Quarter, learning that he is the spy Vodalus wanted him to contact (20). Through an accidental miscommunication, the spy opens *The Book of Mirrors* for Severian, but Severian balks at entering it, instead choosing to remain on Urth. Severian realizes that this "spy" is actually the Autarch himself (21).

Severian finds Doctor Talos's troupe (22) and has a romantic tryst with Jolenta (23). He takes his part in the play (24), which ends prematurely in a firefight with aliens in the audience (25). The troupe breaks up the next day, with Talos and Baldanders heading toward Lake Diuturna and Severian, Dorcas, and Jolenta walking toward Thrax (26). That night, Severian is awakened by the undine calling from the river (27). She tempts him, offering him the ability to breathe water, but he is reluctant. She unsuccessfully tries to seize him before swimming away. Meanwhile, Jolenta has attempted suicide (28).

The group stays in a peasant's sod house: the Claw performs a few minor miracles (29). They enter the stone town and encounter the Cumaean, her assistant Merryn the witch, and Hildegrin (30). Dorcas gives Hildegrin a secret message from the spy at the House Absolute. Hildegrin boasts that he had followed them to the Sanguinary Field, helped capture Agilus, watched the execution, saw the play at Ctesiphon's Cross, and did not lose them until the trouble at the Piteous Gate.

The six of them together participate in a group ritual summoning of Apu-Punchau, an avatar from the past, but when he appears, Hildegrin attacks him and Severian finds himself wrestling with Hildegrin. A crack of thunder brings him back to the stone town, where he finds himself alone with Dorcas: Hildegrin is destroyed, the Cumaean and Merryn have fled, and Jolenta has finally died (31).

*The Sword of the Lictor*

Severian and Dorcas are getting settled into life at Thrax, a few months after the incident at the stone town, but their relationship is being strained by both his profession and her unknown past which she is slowly remembering (1). After a long walk through Thrax (2), Severian finds Dorcas despondent by the waterside and arranges for separate lodgings for her at the Duck's Nest inn. Trying to find his way back to the Vincula, he meets a poor boy named Jader who has a deathly ill sister (3).

Back at the Vincula, the archon of Thrax invites Severian to come to a costume party at the palace and, furthermore, to perform a quiet execution there without using any tools (4). At this party Severian meets Cyriaca, an armigette wearing the costume of a Pelerine (5). He hears her "Tale of the Library" and has an amorous adventure with her (6) before learning that she is the one he has been ordered to execute (7).

Leaving the palace, Severian goes to Jader's hut and uses the Claw on his sister, miraculously healing her (8). Then he tries to make his way to the Duck's Nest inn, but encounters a fiery salamander which has been searching for him. The monster pursues him into a cliff house, where its own heat burns out the floor, causing the salamander to fall down the cliff to its death (9).

At the Duck's Nest, Dorcas admits her terrible secret: she was one of the dead in the Garden of Endless Sleep, a corpse accidentally brought to life by the Claw. She must seek her past back in Nessus, and Severian must flee to the north for refusing to kill Cyriaca (10, 11). Severian tells what Cyriaca told him, that the Autarch serves the cacogens, even as the cacogens aid the Autarch's enemies, the Ascians. Dorcas and Severian go their separate ways, she by boat and he by the prison sewage drain of the Vincula itself (12).

Alone in the mountains, Severian feels Hethor magically tracking him (13). After descending the perilous league-high cliff, he finds the house and family of pioneer Becan (wife Casdoe, son little Severian, daughter Severa, and Casdoe's father) and receives shelter (14). But it turns out that Agia is hiding upstairs and as she begins to attack an alzabo cries at the door in the voice of Severa (15). Using Becan's voice, the alzabo gets into the house. The others leave Severian downstairs like a sacrifice for it, but he makes a deal with the monster: he will leave the house in the morning and will not hunt it in the future (16).

The next day Casdoe, her father, and her son abandon their home. Severian follows far behind. The family is set upon by seven zoanthrops, but as Severian runs to help them, the alzabo charges into the fray, defending the family. Severian and little Severian are the only survivors. Severian adopts the orphan (17). They hike for the rest of the day (18) and then Severian reads him "The Tale of the Boy Called Frog" from the brown book (19).

Heading into the mountains, Severian and son stumble into an arboreal village of sorcerers who deftly kidnap the boy (20). In order to get him back, Severian has to fight a magical duel with one of the sorcerers (21), a duel interrupted by the arrival of the blob-like slug, another one of Hethor's pets (22).

They escape the village and climb further up Mount Typhon. In the lap of this carved idol they find the cursed town, where buildings left over from the construction period stand waist-high to the giant carving automatons still milling about (23). Investigating the central building, they find the desiccated corpse of a two-headed man, but the boy is more curious about the gold ring on Mount Typhon's finger, so they hike up there. Little Severian is killed by hidden energy weapons as he touches the gold. Suicidally depressed, Severian sleeps in the cursed town (24).

When he wakes up he meets a living two-headed man, the corpse having been revived by the Claw. It is Monarch Typhon, a tyrant whose name has been forgotten for a thousand years (25). Typhon uses a boat-like elevator to transport them to the head-chamber of the mountain and tries to tempt Severian with the throne of Urth, but Severian manages to kill Typhon (26).

Descending the mountain, he comes to Lake Diuturna (27). His attempts to intimidate the villagers into giving him free room and board backfire: he is drugged, and the Claw is taken away from him (28). The villagers try to transport him as a bound prisoner to the same dreaded tower across the lake that they had sent the Claw to (29), but as floating islands close in on them, Severian seizes the opportunity to escape by splashing water onto the natrium slug thrower, destroying the hetman's boat in an explosion (30). Rescued by the islanders and determined to retrieve the Claw, Severian plans an assault on the strange tower which happens to look like a toadstool since a flying saucer is hovering over it (31). When he knocks at the gate in an attempt to bluff his authority as lictor of Thrax, he is surprised to see Dr. Talos open the door and welcome him in (32).

Inside, Baldanders and Talos are involved in delicate negotiations with three aliens or "hierodules" (Ossipago, Barbatus, and Famulimus) over high tech knowledge and/or artifacts. Severian is at first baffled by the hierodules because they seem to know him, then shocked to learn that Talos is a homunculus created by Baldanders (33). Severian asks for the return of the Claw, and the hierodules ask to see it. They are not impressed. They leave without giving Balanders any gifts (34).

In fury that Severian's superstition has cost him new knowledge, Balanders throws the Claw from the top of the tower. The islanders, having been waiting for a sign from Severian, launch their attack on the tower (35, 36). *Terminus Est* is destroyed in the fighting, and Baldanders escapes by diving into the lake, where he uses his self-made powers to breathe water (37).

The next day Severian searches for the Claw, and finds amid the broken glass of its outer case the heart of the Claw: a rose thorn. The Claw of the Conciliator was never really a gem at all; it was a thorn encased in pretty blue glass. He leaves the lake, heading north (38).

*The Citadel of the Autarch*

A few days later Severian stumbles upon the body of a soldier who died of disease while deployed against Vodalus's rebels (1). Severian uses the Claw on the corpse and it revives. Together they walk out of the forest (2), following the road and looking for the army (3). They find a lazaret (in this case the hospital is a medical tent) maintained near the front lines by the Pelerines and Severian succumbs to fever-driven vision dreams (4).

## Synopsis

After the fever breaks, Severian meets fellow patients Foila (an armigette), Melito (a farmboy soldier), Hallvard (a seal hunter turned soldier), and Loyal to the Group of Seventeen (an Ascian prisoner). Severian learns about Correct Thought and Approved Texts (5). The resurrected soldier, named Miles by Severian, is somehow also Jonas returned from Yesod, two souls in one body searching for Jolenta, Jonas's true love. But when Severian tells him that Jolenta has died, Miles/Jonas wanders off in a daze.

Since Melito and Hallvard both want to marry Foila, she decides that they will have a story-telling contest for which Severian, as an outsider, shall be judge (6). Hallvard tells his story about sealers (7). In the evening, Severian meets a Pelerine nurse who has been in the order for thirty years and he tries to return the Claw to her, but she is skeptical of his claims to have resurrected the dead with it and refuses to believe that the thorn he shows her is somehow the heart of the gem she remembers (8).

The next day, Melito tells his farm animal fable (9). In the evening, Severian meets Ava, a postulant (an apprentice of the Pelerines) originally from an optimate family living in the Sanguinary Field area of Nessus. She had witnessed his duel with Agilus but does not recognize him as the "exultant in masquerade" she remembers fighting Agilus. Having heard about Severian's "delusions" from the Pelerine, Ava is also skeptical at first, but gradually she comes to quietly believe (10).

The next day, Loyal to the Group of Seventeen enters the contest with a story of his own, told with lines of Authorized Text, translated by Foila (11). In the evening Severian hides the Claw in the altar of the Pelerines. He is approached by Chatelaine Mannea, the highest ranking Pelerine currently at the lazaret, who asks him to undertake an urgent mission to retrieve an anchorite (holy hermit) from a hermitage that is about to be overrun by Ascians. He agrees to go (14).

With safe-conduct in hand, he walks the twenty leagues to the Last House. Despite his shortcuts, it takes exactly as long as she told him it would take: two days (15). He meets the anchorite Master Ash, and sleeps upstairs at the hermitage, know as the Last House (16). In the morning he looks out the window onto a world covered in ice: the Ragnarock future. Severian figures out the time-bending architecture of the Last House, where each floor exists in a different age. Following Mannea's instructions, he drags Master Ash out of the Last House. Ash discorporates and the Ragnarock timeline implodes (17).

Upon his return to the lazaret, Severian finds that the whole area has been razed in an Ascian attack. After following the trail of survivors he manages to find Foila who tells him the others are probably dead. Her dying wish is that he remember the stories, so he writes them down onto the blank pages of the brown book (18).

He spends two days wandering, then joins Guasacht's troops, the Eighteenth Bacele of the Irregular Contarii (19). Some time later they find an armored coach of the Autarch, bearing gold and mastiff-man guards, bogged down in the mud and harassed by Ascian soldiers. Guasacht's forces pin down the Ascians, but a new mob of treasure-seeking camp followers threatens to overwhelm them all, so a desperate alliance is formed between the mastiff-men, the irregulars, and the Ascians. Once they break out, the irregulars blast the Ascians, but before they can loot the coach themselves a squadron of anpiels arrives to preserve the gold for the Autarch (20).

## Synopsis

The Eighteenth Bacele is deployed at the frontlines (21) and takes part in the Third Battle of Orithyia, where Severian is wounded (22). He is found by the Autarch (23), who takes him aloft in a flier (24). The flier is shot down and the Autarch is wounded. Severian and the Autarch are captured by Ascians, but then the Ascians are wiped out by Vodalarii mounted on airborne monsters drawn by Hethor's mirrors and commanded by Agia (25).

They are taken to Vodalus's base, an ancient ziggurat in the jungle. For payment, Agia wants to be allowed to kill Severian but Vodalus refuses (26). Vodalus had been expecting to capture the Autarch but doesn't recognize his old House Absolute spy as the autarch, suspecting instead that Severian might be the one. Severian tells him the Autarch escaped (27).

They are marched toward an Ascian camp (28). At the camp they are questioned by Ascian commanders. The Autarch, near death from his wounds, convinces Severian to become the new autarch by taking a powerful dose of the analeptic alzabo, then killing the Autarch and eating his brain. Severian obeys (29).

He is rescued by Agia and the Green Man. Agia has killed Vodalus and now leads the rebellion herself. Before leaving him, the Green Man summons a small flying saucer for Severian. On this ship the ghost or aquastor Malrubius answers many questions as they fly south (30). Severian is dropped off on the beach where Gyoll meets the sea, and there he brushes a rose bush. A thorn breaks off in his skin. He recognizes it as the Claw (31).

Severian gets a ride on the Samru, a ship heading up river. At his request they drop him off for a short visit in the dead part of Nessus, where he finds Dorcas sitting before the dead body of her husband, the old ferryman of the Garden of Endless Sleep who had been looking for "Cas." She had managed to return to him, but tragically too late: he has died. Severian slips away unseen (32).

At the Citadel he proves he is the new Autarch (33), talks with Master Palaemon (34), and receives a report from Father Inire (35). He retrieves the hidden coin that Vodalus had given him that night in the graveyard: it turns out to have been counterfeit all along (36).

Severian returns to the Inn of Lost Loves, interrogates Ouen the waiter as to the intrigue with the staff on his last visit, and determines not only that Ouen is the middle-aged son of Dorcas, but that Ouen is also Severian's father. Severian takes Ouen to the dead city and commands him as Autarch to tell his life story to Dorcas, and to protect her with a laser pistol Severian gives him (37).

Severian returns to the Citadel and retraces his steps through the deep tunnels until he finds the Atrium of Time and calls for Valeria to make her his wife (38).

*The Urth of the New Sun*

Ten years later, Severian boards Tzadkiel's ship for the voyage to Yesod, the higher universe where he will plead for a new sun on behalf of Urth. He goes onto the deck to throw his manuscript overboard but ends up falling into space (1). He manages to get back to the deck, but in a different section of the ship. He meets middle-aged Burgundofara (she prefers "Gunnie"), Purn, and albino Idas, led by Sidero, an iron-class mechanical officer. They are hunting for "apports," escaped or newly arrived creatures running loose on the ship, and press Severian into service: Sidero actually pushes him off a ledge (2). After falling in low gravity,

Severian finds the shaggy apport and helps capture it, then he finds a new cabin for himself next to Gunnie's in the crew section (3).

After wandering around the surreal landscape of the ship Severian finds his old stateroom again (4). The hierodules Ossipago, Barbutus, and Famulimus visit him, meeting him for their "first time," and since they are moving backwards through time, he knows that this will be the last time he sees them. He visits their strange quarters (5).

Outside their room he finds a murdered crewman. He tries to use the Claw to resurrect him but it does not work. Instead the gangway is plunged into darkness and Severian feels very sick. He shoots his laser pistol on low setting and clips a would-be assailant. Severian searches through the dark ship for the killers and is jumped by one in the hold but the shaggy apport bites the attacker (6).

The attacker escapes and the lights come back on. Back in his crew cabin Severian finds Idas, the tall albino sailor. They end up fighting: it turns out Idas is actually an undine child sent to assassinate him, but she commits suicide before he can question her much further (7). Severian wants to report her death to the mysterious captain whom he has never met, so he wanders through the ship again. He finds Sidero with one arm torn off and learns that there is a mutiny in progress (8).

He climbs inside of Sidero, using him as a suit of armor, and fights a strange pale monster with large wings. He is thrown down an airshaft and has a vision of his own death. When he wakes up at the bottom of the airshaft he is being helped by a hairy dwarf called Zak and later tended by Gunnie. There is no sign of Sidero (9). After a few sleep cycles and a romantic interlude, Severian tells Gunnie he knows that she was the assailant he clipped with the laser (10).

Later Severian and Zak fall in with some loyal sailors hunting "jibers" (mutineers). Purn is with them. Severian figures out that Purn was the assailant bitten by the apport: and that the apport had subsequently metamorphosed into Zak (11). Purn admits to being a sailor-assassin from the Commonwealth of Severian's era, sent to kill Severian to save Urth from the destruction that will happen if the New Sun comes. Purn escapes. Severian asks Zak if he is the apport and Zak runs away.

Severian is captured and bound by jibers (12). There is a brief fight and he is rescued by Sidero. Among Sidero's band of loyalist sailors is a man who introduces himself as Zak, metamorphosed again. Sidero refuses to believe Severian is Autarch of Urth and assigns him to the rearguard. There is a big battle with jibers and the hull is breached (13).

The battle takes to the forest of the masts, where jibers struggle to cut down sails. Severian fights with a humanoid who has the hands of an arctother. Severian wins and the ship leaves Briah (normal space), entering the hyperspace of Yesod (14).

The sails are immediately reefed. Severian looks for the flier that will take him to the surface of planet Yesod, but he falls in with a royal procession of sailors and officers following a tall naked man whose hands are tied behind him (15). This prisoner is as tall as an exultant, at least, and has golden hair. The crowd believes him to be the Autarch of Urth: Gunnie and Purn stop Severian from trying to convince them otherwise, telling him he is a trickster or delusional. On the flier Gunnie points out that since Tzadkiel's ship sails back and forth through Time, the golden one could possibly be one of Severian's successors to the throne (16).

The party is dropped off on an isle. Severian meets Alpheta, an exultant lady. From her he learns that the golden one will be judged by the Hierogrammate Tzadkiel the next day, and that Severian will now lead him into the courtroom. As he does so, he calls the golden one "Zak," recognizing that the apport has metamorphosed again. Zak flees down the corridor (17).

The portico of the Hall of Justice is crowded with people from Severian's past: they help him catch Zak. At the boulder, Severian chains himself rather than Zak. He waits for the trial to begin, surrounded by the crowd of sailors and those from his past, including the alzabo that ate Severa. Night falls. The crowd becomes agitated and begins fighting (18). Unseen people free Severian and lead him behind the Seat of Justice to a narrow stair that exits the building. Apheta meets him and they walk through the quiet town of white marble. She convinces him that she is not human, rather she is a hierogrammate larva (19). He follows her into a room coiled like a nautilus shell. Apheta is glowing and they share a romantic interlude that results in the creation of the white fountain (20).

The next day Severian goes to face the Hierogrammate Tzadkiel and finds Zak on the Seat of Justice, now metamorphosed into his hierogrammate form, like an angel with butterfly wings. Severian realizes that this "masculine" being is an aspect of the larger being "Tzadkiel" which is also "feminine" and "ship." Tzadkiel tells Severian that he has been tricked: there was no test. The Hierogrammates wanted to see the timeline Severian would forge, and having seen it, they know he is the New Sun. They will return Severian to Urth and the old planet will be destroyed at his command to make way for the new world.

The Urthman sailors in the audience draw their knives at this news. They attack and kill the Hierarch Venant, identified as Tzadkiel's son. Again the aquastors (based upon people from Severian's past) fight against the sailors. Gunnie helps Severian (atonement for her betrayal of the Conciliator [ch. 34]) and the sailors are defeated. The aquastors dissolve (21).

After answering questions, Apheta leads Severian and Gunnie beneath the surface of the world Yesod (22). Gunnie is hurt to learn about the carnal relations between Severian and Apheta. Severian learns that the world is also a ship, and that most of the work happens inside. Gunnie becomes frightened, recognizing a form of Hell in Yesod. The two of them are teleported back into Briah space (normal space) near Tzadkiel's ship, where they are spotted by sailors and hauled aboard. Severian discovers he is no longer lame (23).

A group of Hierogrammates, wearing their customary human masks, escorts the pair to meet the captain, the giantess Hierogrammate Tzadkiel. Severian is surprised that she does not recognize him, but then he realizes that they were thrust into the past when they were teleported. The others are dismissed. Severian alone remains to tell his story. Tzadkiel forms a human-sized version of herself to guide Severian to his stateroom using secret passages that turn out to be links to and from the grassy fields around Brook Madregot, a pocket universe "between" Briah and Yesod (24).

While he sleeps, Thecla visits him in physical form. Later on he is walking through the ship and realizes that what he sees around him is being manufactured for him and his passage. He tries to outrun the process and succeeds, entering an alien landscape before losing consciousness (25). He wakes up and sees two versions of Gunnie: the middle-aged one he remembers and a younger one who still uses her full name Burgundofara. In examining this paradox, Severian admits that his newly repaired face is that of Apu-Punchau, and he explains the mysterious wrestling between Hildegrin, Apu-Punchau, and himself at the stone town. Gunnie tells Severian to take Burgundofara with him to Urth (Severian sees Barbatus and Famulimus another last/first time). Severian and Burgundofara leave Tzadkiel's ship and board a tender outside of the orbit of Dis (Pluto), bound for Urth (26).

The tender is captained by a Hierodule and crewed by human sailors. Severian is aware of a connection between him and the White Fountain, a white hole still many light years away and moving at relativistic (sub-light) speed. The time dilation onboard the tender is very strong and they arrive at Urth in less than one day (27).

The pair is let off at a village called Vici. Severian meets Herena, a girl with a withered arm, and he is able to heal her (28). He has become like the Conciliator himself. The next day the three of them go to Gurgustii, another village, where Severian heals Declan, a sick man on his deathbed (29). The day after that finds them in Os, where Ceryx the Necromancer challenges Severian to a duel. Severian refuses and arranges passage to Nessus on a ship. Ceryx sends a zombie after him (30). Rather than destroying the zombie, Severian resurrects it into the man it once was. He makes friends with the young man, whose name is Zama (31).

Burgundofara spends the night with Hadelin the ship captain. In the morning they all go to the ship and Ceryx appears again.

Zama attacks and kills Ceryx, then the townsmen kill Zama. Severian feels sickened (32). On the ship, Severian finds that Declan and Harena have come aboard to follow him against his orders (33).

The ship is caught in a sudden storm that threatens to capsize it. The first mate begs Severian to make it stop, even offering to kill the captain for sleeping with Burgundofara. Declan and Harena plead also. Severian comes to realize they are all correct: he had unconsciously called up the storm. He quiets it with a word, drawing back into himself the emotions he had denied.

The ship arrives at Saltus, but Severian cannot quite recognize the village. He has two new followers, and he asks one if there were no mines in the area. The sailor tells him one has just been started about a year ago. Suddenly soldiers enter the inn and demand to be shown the Conciliator. Burgundofara points out Severian (34).

Severian kills three of them before they take him down. Another has a broken neck. Severian tries to heal himself using the White Fountain, but cannot, so he channels Urth's energies instead.

The soldiers take him by powerboat to Nessus. On the way he repairs the broken neck of the wounded soldier (35). At Nessus they take him to a prison: suddenly he recognizes the Citadel of the Autarch and realizes that he must be in the time about a thousand years before his own birth. He kills the sadistic leader of the jailers and tries to flee but is struck down by spaceship weaponry fired from the Matachin Tower. Miraculously, he survives: the physician says that an earthquake hit at just the same moment, saving Severian's life by spoiling the gunner's aim (36).

Severian meets Reechy, an apprentice jailer who brings him his food and gives him some coins. The next morning Burgundofara and Captain Hadelin visit. Burgundofara begs forgiveness and Severian forgives her. In the evening his four followers visit and he tells them a long story so they will not despair when he is gone. Canog, a prisoner in the next cell, writes it down as *The Book of the New Sun,* which will become the holy text of the Church of the Conciliator (37).

The next morning he learns that "Reechy" is just a nickname; the boy's real name is Ymar. Severian realizes he is the boy who will become the first autarch. Severian is taken by flier to meet the monarch of the world at a mountain that is being carved into his likeness to serve as his tomb: the monarch is none other than Typhon (38).

Severian is detained on an isolated part of the mountain. He frees and befriends a chiliarch who had treated him badly. When this chiliarch's troopers arrive they decide to desert the army with their commander. As a parting gift, Severian gives them the rose thorn he has kept since his encounter with Master Malrubius on the beach, i.e., he gives them the Claw of the Conciliator. Then he steps off a cliff and into another world (39).

He finds himself in the grass beside the Brook Madregot. He talks with a tiny version of Tzadkiel, who has been banished from the main body and will not tell Severian her name or why she was banished. He asks her how to get back to his proper time and place. She tells him and he goes (40).

Severian winds up on the grounds of the House Absolute near a cenotaph erected in his memory. He enters the Second House and accidentally resurrects a long-dead assassin (41). He goes to the throne room and sees a crisis unfolding (42). Revealing himself, Severian learns he has returned to Urth forty years after he had left on the trip to Yesod, arriving at the moment of the Commonwealth's destruction. The city of Nessus has drowned two days before. In the chaos of these revelations, the assassin enters and kills Autarchia Valeria. Severian is wounded and loses his healing powers (43).

Urth is destroyed and reborn as Ushas, the world of the New Sun. Severian falls in with some survivors of the deluge (Odilo, Thais, Pega) floating on debris (44). They are rescued by a boat piloted by an old sailor (45) who turns out to be Eata, Severian's boyhood friend (46).

While the others sleep, Severian leaves the boat to swim in the water, no longer needing to breathe. He explores sunken Nessus (47). When he returns to the surface, Eata's boat is gone. He finds a more ancient sunken city that remains nameless. He meets Juturna again and she points the way to the corridors of Time (48).

Severian responds by jumping into the corridor and running as far into the past as he can. He ends up with a tribe of primitive people and tries to help them. They become suspicious and try to test him, but when sunrise is delayed for him in the Miracle of Apu-Punchau (sunlight actually occluded by the sails of Tzadkiel's ship) they accept him as divine king (49).

Decades go by. Severian finds he cannot enter the corridors of Time anymore. As Apu-Punchau he teaches the tribe many things. When he finally tries to leave them, they panic and kill him.

He wakes up inside his tomb. The hierodules Ossipago, Barbatus, and Famulimus are there. So is the corpse of Apu-Punchau. Severian realizes that he himself is an eidolon, a ghost generated by someone else, yet once generated, capable of gaining substance to become a material being. As if that were not enough, he discovers that he had actually died in that fall with Sidero on Tzadkiel's ship (chapter 9). He is only stranded in the Age of Myth until the first light from the White Fountain reaches Urth.

Meanwhile, the corpse begins to breathe (50).

The danger to Severian is enormous, for a similar situation obliterated Hildegrin. Severian should not destroy the corpse, but he also does not want to be too close to it. Luckily enough, he receives help from the Green Man and escapes into the corridors of Time at the first possible moment. He runs up to Ushas. There he finds an island of people who worship four gods named Odilo, Pega, Thais, and the Sleeper.

They recognize Severian as the Sleeper (51). The End.

# OLD MAPS

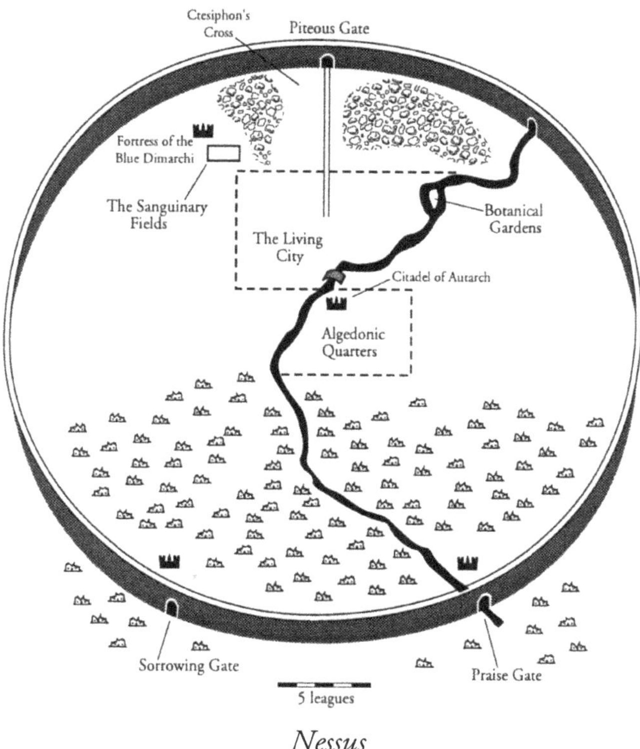


*Nessus*

The first edition versions of maps for Nessus, the northwest area of the Commonwealth, and the Commonwealth/Ascian hemisphere. Also a new version of Alice K. Turner's thematic map (the earlier version appeared in AE&2).

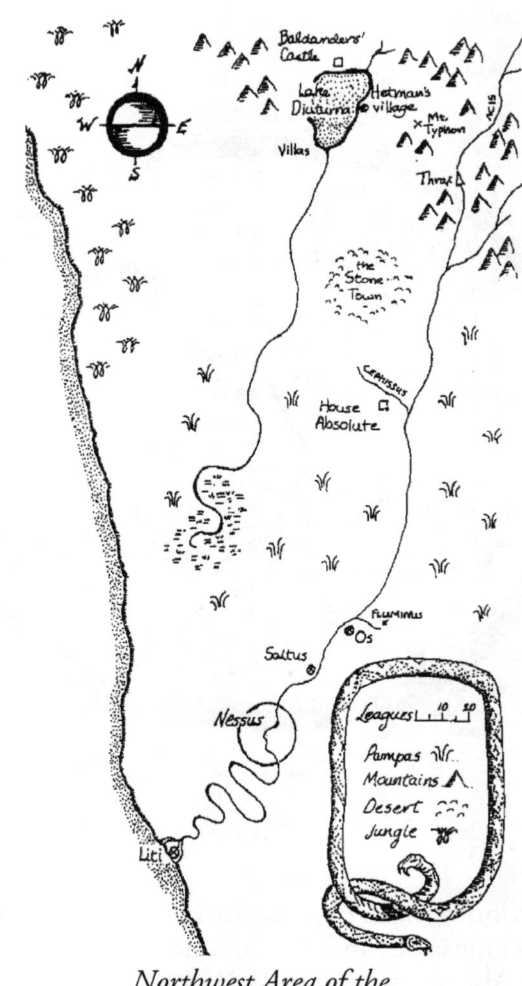


*Northwest Area of the Commonwealth*

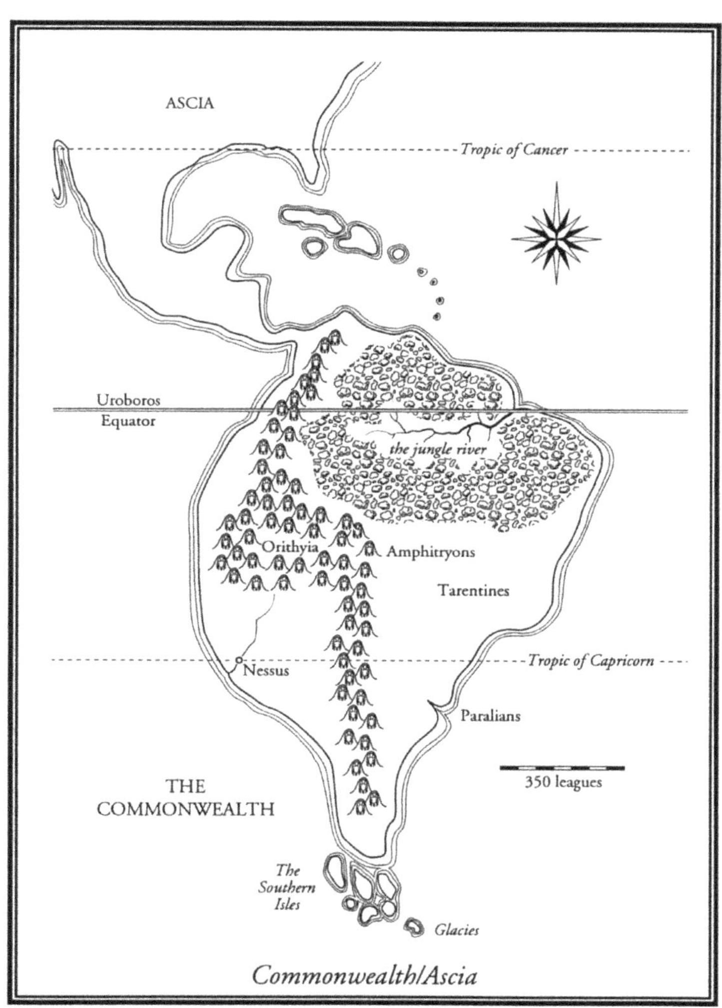
ASCIA
Tropic of Cancer
Uroboros
Equator
the jungle river
Orithyia
Amphitryons
Tarentines
Tropic of Capricorn
Nessus
Paralians
350 leagues
THE
COMMONWEALTH
The
Southern
Isles
Glacies
Commonwealth/Ascia

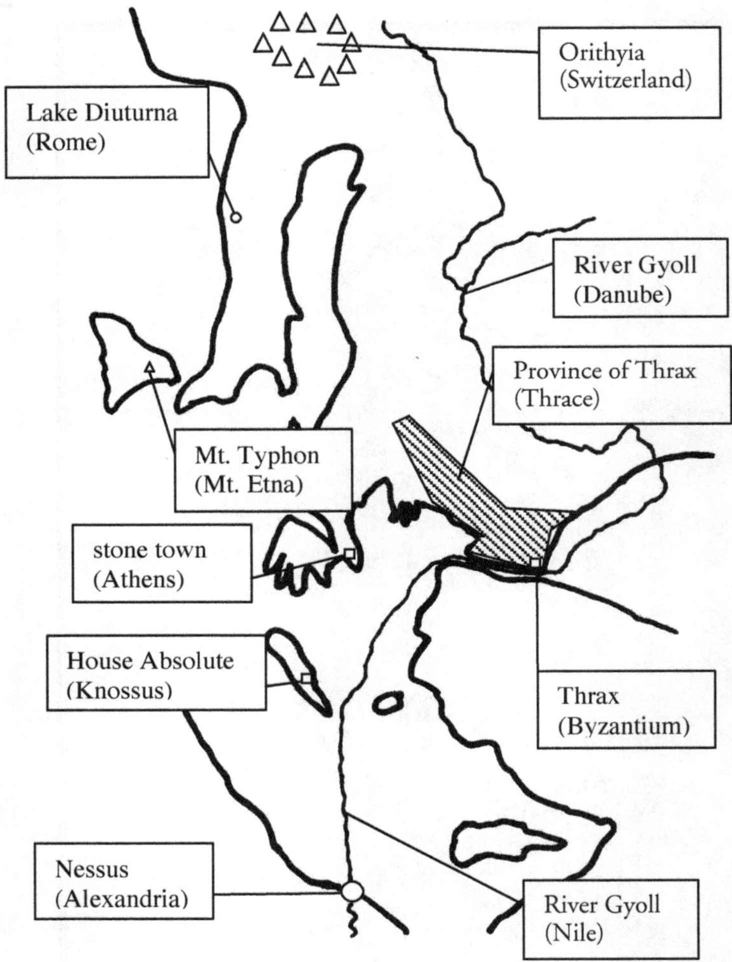


*Turner's Thematic Map of the Commonwealth*

**Animals (Extinct)**
alticamelus
arctother
arsinoither
baluchither
barylambda
basilosaur
coryphodon
diatrymae
glyptodon
hesperorn
kronosaur
mammoth
megathere
merychip
oreodont
pelycosaur
phenocod
phororhacos
platybelodon
smilodon
thylacosmil
trilophodon
tyrannosaur
uintather

**Armor**
barbute
burginot
cuir boli
cuirasses
haubergeon
jazerant

**Arms**
achico
alfange
arquebus
athame
badelaire
batardeau
berdiche
braquemar
caliver
carronade
cerbotana
clava
contus
coutel
craquemarte
culverin
curtelaxe
demilune
dream
estoc
falchion
glaive
hastarus
hydraknife
jezail
kheten
korsekes
misericorde
pacho
pilete
ransieur
sacar
scorpion
shotel
spadroon
spathae
trilhoen
voulge

**Gods & Goddesses**
Abaia
Abraxas
Adonai
Apeiron
Bona Dea
Caitanya
Demiurge
Destiny
Discontent
Early Summer
Erebus
Fiend
Fauna
Gea
Hypogeon
Increate
Jurupari
Juturna
Night
Oannes
Paraclete
Pega
Spring Wind
Thais
Theoanthropos
Thyme

## Subject Listing

Ushas
Ylem

**Hydrography**
Acis
Cephissus
Diuturna
Fluminus
Fons
Gyoll

**Peoples**
amphitryon
Ascian
autochthon
Antrustione
ecclectic
Paralian
perischii
Tarentine
Xanthoderm
zoanthrope

**Physicians**
old leech
p. at old hulk
Dr. Talos

**Poison**
Agia
avern
Ceryx
dead assassin
Decuman
Morwenna

**Settlements**
Famulorum
Gurgustii
Incusus
Liti
Murene
Nessus
Os
Quiesco
Saltus
Thrax
Vici

**Ships**
"Alcyone"
caique
carrack
dhow
felucca
galleass
"Samru"
shallop
thalamegus
Tzadkiel's
xebec

# SELECTED BIBLIOGRAPHY

Allen, Richard Hinckley. *Star Names: Their Lore and Meaning.* New York: Dover, 1963. [SWAN; VENANT]
Borges, Jorge Luis. *The Book of Imaginary Beings.* New York: Penguin, 1974. [BORGES; SPECULA; ULTAN]
Borski, Robert. *Solar Labyrinth.* Lincoln, Nebraska: iUniverse, 2004. [INIRE; PRISONERS; RACHO]
Byfield, Barbara Ninde. *The Book of Weird.* Garden City, NY: Doubleday, 1973. [MUTTON]
Cirlot, J. E. *A Dictionary of Symbols (Second Edition).* New York: Philosophical Library, 1971. [LAURENTIA OF THE HOUSE OF THE HARP]
Clute, John. *Strokes.* Seattle: Serconia Press, 1988. [AUTARCH; BORGES; MERRYN; OUEN; TRISKELE; VALERIA]
Clute, John, and Peter Nicholls. *The Science Fiction Encyclopedia.* Garden City, NY: Doubleday/Dolphin, 1979. [ANDROID; ROBOT]
Cotterell, Arthur. *A Dictionary of World Mythology.* Rev. ed. Oxford: Oxford University Press, 1986.
Davidson, Gustav. *A Dictionary of Angels.* New York: Free Press, 1971.
Edwards, Malcolm, and Robert Holdstock. *Realms of Fantasy.* Garden City, NY: Doubleday, 1983. [CLAW OF THE CONCILIATOR]
Epstein, Perle. *Kabbalah.* Garden City, NY: Doubleday, 1978. [BROOK MADREGOT]
Feeley, Gregory. "The Evidence of Things Not Shown." *New York Review of Science Fiction* 31 (1991): 1, 8–10; 32 (1991): 12–16. [LUNE; MANDRAGORA; MERRYN; NAVISCAPUT; ROOD; TYPHON]
Finney, Ben R., and Eric M. Jones. *Interstellar Migration and the Human Experience.* Berkeley: University of California Press, 1985. [ASTEREOENGINEERING]
Flaubert, Gustave. *Salambo.* New York: Berkley Pub. Corp, 1955. [MAYA]
Fogg, Martyn J. *Terraforming.* Warrendale, PA: Society of Automotive Engineers, 1995. [ASTEREOENGINEERING; LUNE]
Frazier, Robert. "The Legerdemain of the Wolfe." *Thrust* 19 (Winter/Spring 1983): 5–9. (Collected in Wright's *Shadows of the New Sun.*) [EXULTANT HEIGHT; SEVERIAN]
Gordon, Joan. *Gene Wolfe* (Starmont Reader's Guide 29). Mercer Island, Washington. Starmont House, 1986.

# Selected Bibliography

Grant, Michael. *Myths of the Greeks and Romans.* New York: New American Library (Mentor Books), 1962.

Graves, Robert. *The Greek Myths.* 2 vols. Rev. ed. New York: Penguin, 1960. [PALAEMON; SIDERO]

———. *I, Claudius.* New York: Vintage, 1934. [AVERN]

———. *King Jesus.* New York: Farrar Straus Giroux, 1964. [ETHNARCH]

———. *The White Goddess.* New York: Vintage, 1959. [ESCHATOLOGY AND GENESIS; ISID 1000 1000E]

Halevi, Z'ev ben Shimon. *Kabbalah.* New York: Thames and Hudson, Inc., 1979.

Heifetz, Josepha. *Mrs. Byrne's Dictionary.* Seacaucus, NJ. Citadel Press and University Books, 1974. [AUTARCHIA; PINAKOTHEKEN; SCOPOLAGNA]

Horace. *Satires and Epistles.* Chicago: University of Chicago Press, 2002. [BARRUS]

Jobes, Gertrude. *Dictionary of Mythology, Folklore and Symbols.* New York: Scarecrow Press, 1961.

Kafka, Franz. "In the Penal Colony." (Collected in *The Complete Stories.* New York: Schocken Books, 1995.) [TORTURE CHAMBER TOOLS]

Kurtén, Bjorn. *Age of Mammals.* New York: Columbia University Press, 1972.

Lurker, Manfred. *Dictionary of Gods and Goddesses, Devils and Demons.* Trans. from the German by G.L. Campbell. New York: Routledge & Kegan Paul, 1987.

Manguel, Alberto, and Gianni Guadalupi. *The Dictionary of Imaginary Places.* Expanded ed. San Diego: Harcourt Brace Jovanovich, 1987. [BALDANDERS]

Manlove, C. N. "Gene Wolfe, *The Book of the New Sun* (1980–83)." In *Science Fiction: Ten Explorations,* pp. 198–216. Hampshire: Macmillan, 1986. [AVERN, ULTAN]

Monaghan, Patricia. *Book of Goddesses and Heroines.* St. Paul, Minnesota: Llewellyn Publications, 1990. [DIUTURNA]

Pournelle, Jerry. *A Step Farther Out.* New York: Ace, 1979. [ASTEREOENGINEERING]

Scheele, William E. *The First Mammals.* Cleveland: World Publishing Co., 1955.

Schweitzer, Darrell. "*Weird Tales* Talks with Gene Wolfe." *Weird Tales* 290 (Spring 1988): 23–29.

Shelley, Mary Wollstonecraft. *Frankenstein.* New York: Grosset & Dunlap, 1970. [BALDANDERS]

Smith, Clark Ashton. *Zothique.* New York: Ballantine Books, 1970. [XANTHIC LANDS]

Stephensen-Payne, Phil, and Gordon Benson, Jr. *Gene Wolfe, Urth-Man Extraordinary.* Bibliographies for the Avid Reader, vol. 19. Albuquerque: Galactic Central, 1992.
Stone, George Cameron. *A Glossary of the Construction, Decoration and Use of Arms and Armor in All Countries and in All Times.* New York: Jack Brussel, 1961. [FALCHION; KHETEN; PILETE; SCORPION; SHOTEL; VOULGE]
Vance, Jack. *The Dying Earth.* New York: Lancer Books, 1969. [DEODAND]
Walker, Barbara G. *The Woman's Encyclopedia of Myths and Secrets.* San Francisco: Harper & Row, 1983.
Wells, H. G. *The Island of Doctor Moreau.* London: Heinemann, 1896. [MAN BEASTS]
———. *The Time Machine.* London: Heinemann, 1895. [MAN-APES, OLD SUN]
Wolfe, Gene. "The Boy Who Hooked the Sun." *Weird Tales* 290 (Spring 1988): 21–22. (Collected in *Starwater Strains.*)
———. *Castle of Days.* (omnibus of *The Castle of the Otter* and *Gene Wolfe's Book of Days).* New York: Tor Books, 1992.
———. *Castleview.* New York: Tor Books, 1990.
———. "The Cat." (Collected in *Endangered Species.*)
———. *The Citadel of the Autarch.* New York: Simon & Schuster, 1982.
———. *The Claw of the Conciliator.* New York: Simon & Schuster, 1981.
———. *Empires of Foliage and Flower.* Cheap Street, 1987. (Collected in *Starwater Strains.*)
———. *Endangered Species.* New York: Tor Books, 1989.
———. *The Fifth Head of Cerberus.* Scribners, 1972.
———. "The God and His Man." (Collected in *Endangered Species.*)
———. "The Map." (Collected in *Endangered Species.*)
———. *Nightside the Long Sun.* New York: Tor Books, 1993.
———. *The Old Woman Whose Rolling Pin Is The Sun.* Cheap Street, 1991. (Collected in *Innocents Aboard.*)
———. *Plan[e]t Engineering.* Cambridge, Massachusetts: NESFA, 1984.
———. *The Shadow of the Torturer.* New York: Simon & Schuster, 1980.
———. *Soldier of Arete.* New York: Tor Books, 1989.
———. *Soldier of the Mist.* New York: Tor Books, 1986.
———. *The Sword of the Lictor.* New York: Simon & Schuster, 1981.
———. *There Are Doors.* New York: Tor Books, 1988.
———. *The Urth of the New Sun.* New York: Tor Books, 1987.
Wright, Peter. *Attending Daedalus.* Liverpool: Liverpool University Press, 2003. [INCREATE]
———. *Shadows of the New Sun.* Liverpool: Liverpool University Press, 2007.

www.ingramcontent.com/pod-product-compliance
Lightning Source LLC
Chambersburg PA
CBHW031514270326
41920CB00035B/16/J

* 9 7 8 0 9 6 4 2 7 9 5 0 6 *